Mything in Action

Also by Don Lago:

On the Viking Trail: Travels in Scandinavian America

Mything in Action

✦

American Identity Lost and Searched for in the 2004 Election

Don Lago

iUniverse, Inc.
New York Lincoln Shanghai

Mything in Action
American Identity Lost and Searched for in the 2004 Election

iUniverse books may be ordered through booksellers or by contacting:

iUniverse
2021 Pine Lake Road, Suite 100
Lincoln, NE 68512
www.iuniverse.com
1-800-Authors (1-800-288-4677)

ISBN-13: 978-0-595-40181-9 (pbk)
ISBN-13: 978-0-595-84558-3 (ebk)
ISBN-10: 0-595-40181-3 (pbk)
ISBN-10: 0-595-84558-4 (ebk)

Printed in the United States of America

Mything in Action: American Identity Lost and Searched for in the 2004 Election

—Don Lago

Contents

Acknowledgments

My first thanks are for the hospitality given me by Pat and Ken Gray in the Rocky Mountains and by Dan and Sarah Bates in Des Moines.

It was good to see and campaign with some old friends again, including Cam Kerry (thanks for listening), Tom and Tori Vallely, David Thorne, and Jim and Hope Winship; and to make new friends like John Hurley, Landon Thorne IV, and Lars Erickson. A special thanks goes to John Norris and Jonathan Epstein for giving me the free run of the Iowa campaign. Among the Iowa staffers I enjoyed knowing are Maclyn Humphrey, Charles Richardson and Stephanie, Ari Melber, Casey Slaughter, Matt Deferranti, CM Hall, Karla Hardy, Marygrace Galston, Jack Ryan, Laura Capps, Michael and Anna Teeter, Beth Leonard, Chris Hayler, Matt Slutsky, Julie Andreeff, Stevie Stephenson, and Angela de Prairie. Among the Iowa super-volunteers are Carl Zeh, Elizabeth Hendrix, Amanda Kuhlman, Brooke Borkenhagen, Kate Gronstal, and Carol Wolchok. An Arizona thanks goes to Jim Babbitt, Karan English, Summer Oesch, Gary Rose, Mike Rossi, Mike Moffo, and Greg Buczek and the whole Flagstaff DFA.

Introduction

There are times when nations are no longer sure of what they are and what their purpose is, and for America 2004 was such a time. There was a widespread feeling that America's basic sense of itself had been thrown open to question and renegotiation.

The one thing about the 2004 presidential election that Americans seemed to agree on was that this was the most important election in a generation. You heard this opinion from media commentators, respected historians, and average voters; you heard it from Iowa cafes and Berkeley coffee houses and Alabama pulpits; you heard it from environmentalists and fundamentalists, from labor unions and corporate CEOs, from soldiers and antiwar activists. Even hyperbole-prone presidential campaigns could say this and be taken seriously. In many respects this was an unlikely statement, for America had seen far worse times of economic, social, and overseas troubles. Yet there was a widespread perception that America's basic sense of identity was facing unusually serious trouble.

The genius of democracy is that it offers a people a regular opportunity for reexamining their national identity. Actually it doesn't happen very often that America addresses the core elements of national identity, the national stories or myths that define who we are, our reasons for existing as a nation, the nature and lessons of our national experience, our values and ideals and heroes, our goals and expectations and dreams, our norms of behavior both within our society and towards outsiders. As long as national stories or myths go on functioning smoothly they are usually left unexamined. If presidential campaigns touch upon these myths it's usually to celebrate them, or to discuss tiny adjustments to meet new circumstances. It usually requires a crisis to force a reexamination of national identity, a crisis involving a serious discrepancy opening up between old myths and new realities. Such crises can happen abruptly, as with the Great Depression, or accumulate gradually over decades, as with the Gilded Age polarization of wealth that increasingly contradicted the American Dream, both the Jeffersonian dream of agrarian democracy and the immigrant's dream of a land of opportunity.

Even when the nation knows that it's facing an identity crisis and that a presidential campaign is the main outlet for addressing that crisis, candidates may not be speaking in such terms. In 1932 Americans understood that American capitalism had suffered a catastrophic breakdown and that the American social contract, the basic relationship between democracy and capitalism, was wide open to renegotiation, yet the campaign rhetoric of Franklin Roosevelt was pretty mild and vague. In 1860 America was painfully aware that decades of evasion and compromise over slavery and federalism was failing, yet Lincoln's campaign rhetoric was full of evasions. Nevertheless, FDR and Lincoln were fully aware of the historical imperative and finally faced it forthrightly, resulting in major revisions of American identity.

While the election of 2004 might not be as pivotal as the elections of 1860 or 1932, the widespread perception that this election was dealing with some basic matters of national identity was, I believe, quite correct. Indeed, the identity questions at stake in 2004 were nothing new, although they'd been given new urgency by September 11 and the Iraq war. The identity questions of 2004 were part of a slow-motion identity crisis that has been going on for quite some time. Americans had already engaged these questions passionately in the election of 1968 when they debated the meaning of Vietnam and the duties or non-duties of a diverse people to care about one another. The identity questions of 2004 went deep into the most basic stories or myths that have guided us as a nation right from the beginning, and the reason why those guiding myths are now in question is because they are failing us, and they have been failing us for quite some time.

Even as Lincoln and FDR were making substantial revisions of national identity, neither of them questioned the belief that America was founded with a great historical mission, frequently conceived as a God-given mission, to redeem a dark tyrannical world with the gift of democracy. Indeed, both Lincoln and FDR powerfully invoked America's world mission as the justification for their initiatives. For a long time after 1776 America's world mission seemed self-evident, for we were the world's only role model for democratic reformers, and an even more admirable role model after the disaster of the French Revolution. Even when Europe began to grow democracies they were usually stunted by centuries of feudalism. America's relative lack of class boundaries was very impressive to Europe, especially to the tens of millions of peasants who fled Europe and found greater opportunities in America. After 140 years of looking to America as a role model, European democracies welcomed American armies to save them from tyranny. Why, then, should Americans doubt their long-proven mission of saving the world?

Yet somewhere along the way, while Americans were hardly watching, Europeans and much of the rest of the democratic world were deciding that America was not, after all, the best role model for democracy. In fact, America was a long way down the list of good role models for democracy. Europeans might still envy America's economic success but they did not admire the social values and costs that went with it, the role of economic competition as the highest and decisive social value, to which everything and everyone could be sacrificed. Europeans saw in America one of the most extreme cases of individualism in the democratic world, individualism that might have served America well in the taming of a vast and hard frontier but which now left Americans unable to care about one another, the last holdouts against national health insurance and other forms of social support, and indeed which left Americans happily preying upon one another with guns and ruthless business practices. True, America's individualism had even served it well in the turmoil of early twentieth-century social change, when much of Europe plunged into Marxism or into the nationalization of industry; American reformers were more constrained and focused on how to inject democratic values and safeguards into capitalism. It would turn out that this was what Europe would want for itself, and after World War Two Europe pursued many variations of social democracy. It might be a trick to balance capitalist prosperity with social needs, and some nations did better than others, but even the lamest social democracies didn't admire an America that produced the wealth to take care of its people but simply refused to try to do so. It was the social democracies of western Europe, and not Ronald Reagan's America, that eastern Europeans were watching and admiring when they rebelled against communism. Ironically, by the end of the twentieth century a nation whose great-grandfathers had fled the economic stratification of Europe had become more economically polarized than Europe. The American social fabric was under serious relentless tension and fraying ever inward. After nearly two centuries of being the role model of the democratic world, America was now being widely ignored and often emphatically rejected.

The weird part of it was that Americans hardly noticed. Indeed, after the fall of communism America went into a frenzy of self-congratulations. Conservatives celebrated America's version of capitalism as the ultimate winner of all human history, the only conceivable model for the world. They celebrated Ronald Reagan for single-handedly defeating communism by talking and acting tough like John Wayne. As if America wasn't already seriously out of step with the rest of the democratic world, conservatives gleefully pushed America even further to the extreme, attacking even basic social safeguards like Social Security. They drew the lesson that the world was just waiting for us to help them become like us.

It wasn't just as a role model that America was increasingly facing a serious discrepancy between its self-image and its image for the rest of the world. It was one thing to project your self-image overseas, and a much more serious thing to send your military overseas to serve that self-image. Firmly encased in a carnival-mirror bubble of national self-confidence, America sent armies to Vietnam and Iraq and elsewhere expecting them to be enthusiastically welcomed. It hardly registered on Americans that Asians had been fighting off western armies for a very long time and might not welcome another one. Even after years of military deadlock in Vietnam a large portion of the American public adamantly refused to consider the possibility that something might be wrong with America's self-image; the fault must be with political leaders or war protestors for failing to live up to our self-image. Vietnam should have served as a warning that something was wrong with America's sense of reality, and for awhile it did, but self-doubt isn't much fun, especially when you are accustomed to a heroic and confident self-image, and it was easy for Ronald Reagan to summon Americans to the restoration of the old self-image and self-confidence. When Reagan's confident asserting of America's old self-image was followed by the fall of communism, America's self-image and self-confidence seemed more validated than ever. If the whole world was yearning to be like us, then surely the Iraqi people too would be thrilled to see American tanks coming. It hardly registered on Americans that the Muslim world had been bitterly fighting off western armies, from crusaders to colonialists, for a thousand years.

National self-images or myths are a powerful thing, even more so when they have brought enormous success. America is one of the most successful nations in the history of the world, and this success strongly validates American national myths and self-confidence and leaves little motivation or support for questioning them. America's faith in itself was greatly magnified because America was a nation of immigrants who had to believe strongly in America to begin with or they would have stayed home, and who then as outsiders often felt obligated to prove they were loyal to America. To people proudly inhabiting a proven national identity, it is baffling and infuriating to hear people questioning that identity. Sometimes this deep faith has served America well. In the Great Depression many Europeans were declaring that democracy was dead, but Americans kept the faith. But this deep faith has also made it very difficult for Americans to even recognize that our self-image is now seriously detached from reality, that our long world mission is now leading us astray in the world, and that the myths and social values that have made us great are also extracting serious penalties within American society.

It's an old story in human history, nations becoming prisoners of their own success. It has a lot to do with why nations rise and fall and why world leadership seems continually to change hands. A nation comes up with something that makes it a huge success, perhaps a new technology, a social system, an economic practice, a trade strategy, or a military tactic, and it organizes itself around that success and goes on practicing it even as circumstances change and other nations are coming up with new ideas. The most dramatic and disastrous examples of nations becoming prisoners of their own success come from military history, where strategies that prove successful become obsessions. The infantry tactics that worked brilliantly for the Roman legions were passed down for centuries, and even when generals saw the insanity of sending infantry charging into walls of modern rifles and machine guns and cannons, they couldn't believe their eyes, and thus Lee wasted his army at Gettysburg and World War One generals sent millions to futile deaths between the trenches. In much less dramatic ways Americans watch a constant stream of lessons in what happens to companies that become prisoners of their own success. For example, Woolworth had a famous New York skyscraper to prove the success of building retail stores in every downtown in America, and any board member who suggested they should worry about some guy in Nowheresville, Arkansas, who was starting to build bigger stores on the edge of towns would have been dismissed as crazy.

It wasn't just as a democratic role model and as a military power that America was a prisoner of its own success. America's enormous economic success left it with a deep faith that economic growth and the American Dream were guaranteed. Since tomorrow would always be better than today, Americans stopped worrying about piling up debt, either national or personal debt, and didn't worry much when the factory doors that had once been the doors to the American Dream began to close. After centuries of having an endless frontier supply us with endless natural resources and endlessly absorb pollutants, Americans were living in a mythic bubble that was seriously dissociated from environmental realities. To the rest of the democratic world the spectacle of America refusing to acknowledge realities like limited oil supplies or global warming, refusing to join global environmental efforts, refusing to even discuss its own extravagant waste of resources, and then expecting Europe to send troops to help America perpetuate its extravagant waste of oil, made for a severe disqualification of America as the leader of the free world. America's economic success was also accompanied by serious social costs. Merely as a nation of immigrants, of diverse races and ethnic groups spread across a vast continent, Americans had a harder time identifying with and caring about one another than did the more homogenous populations of Europe. To this weakness was added a frontier experience that strongly emphasized rugged individualism, an 'every-man-for-himself' ethos that may have been unavoidable and even adaptive on the frontier but which left modern, urban, industrial American society seriously un-cohesive, unwilling to pay for the health care of total strangers, and conversely quite willing to rob and murder total strangers. Even as American national experience and social values left a weak social bond, they gave a high sanction to greed as a leading social value, sanctioning corporate robbery or simply consumers robbing themselves of sanity and healthy human relationships in order to pursue status symbols. Finally, America's enormous success validated the founder's sense that America was God's chosen nation, and encouraged the rise of a strong religious right and its claims that America's further success was wholly dependant upon America serving God's plans, a situation very unique in the democratic world and very troubling to our allies.

It was an old story in human history, nations becoming prisoners of their own myths, reliable old myths tricking nations into failure, and now it was happening to America, and by 2004 it had been happening for quite some time. America's long leadership of the democratic world could earn only so much momentum and good will, and by 2004 that momentum and good will was being squandered at a very serious rate.

It wasn't new for Americans to wrestle with the adequacy of our founding myths. We argued over democracy being contradicted by slavery and then by Gilded Age capitalism and then by discriminatory barriers. To an extent that is not always fully recognized, American political ideologies are defined first of all by the degree to which people have accepted or questioned the adequacy of our founding myths, with conservatives finding them adequate and liberals finding them inadequate and pushing for a better definition or translation of democracy. If the founding fathers hadn't included blacks in the American community or had left poor immigrants to fend for themselves, then that was adequate for conservatives, more than adequate considering America's economic success, even more adequate for those directly profiting from cheap labor. Even when liberalism was motivated not by philosophical discomfort or vision but by the raw survival needs of the underclass, liberalism usually found itself pushing against the boundaries of America's founding myths.

Yet even as Teddy Roosevelt was declaring the inadequacy of frontier individualism in an industrial world he was still robustly celebrating frontier myths and virtues. Even in the middle of America's worst economic collapse Franklin Roosevelt wasn't questioning America's self-confidence or the American Dream; his popularity was due to his embodying America's self-confidence and promising to restore the American Dream. John F. Kennedy eagerly invoked frontier symbolism and was brimming with confidence in America's ability to lead the democratic world.

And then, something changed. After World War Two America was thrust into world leadership, and before long there were warning signs that America's self-image and founding myths were an inadequate guide to this challenge. The strongest warning sign, of course, was Vietnam. Yet even Vietnam could not prompt most conservatives to question the adequacy of America's myths, and indeed their response was to celebrate those myths more fervently than ever. The task fell upon American liberalism to question and challenge those myths, and to challenge them in ways that FDR and JFK never had. Challenging two centuries of success-validated national self-confidence is not an easy assignment. American liberalism has aroused much wrath for pointing out the drawbacks of trying to steer either a tank or a society by gazing into a carnival mirror. After dominating the middle third of the twentieth century, liberalism was so badly routed in the final third that 'liberal' became a dirty word and leading Democrats were afraid to say it.

Much more than ever before, American political ideology in the final third of the twentieth century was defined first of all by the spectrum of belief or doubt in America's founding myths, with 'conservative' signifying belief and 'liberal' signifying doubt. What was now seriously different was that liberals were not just pushing on the boundaries of American myths but had pushed right through those boundaries and were left standing on the outside of some of the most elemental myths of American history. For the first time ever, conservatives were left in sole possession of the enormous power of elemental national myths. They no longer had to compete against the absolute confidence of FDR and JFK. This came as a big surprise to conservatives, who after the 1964 election wondered if they were dead for good, and after rubbing their eyes in amazement they proceeded to make the most of this bonanza. Perhaps curiously, conservatives often had a clearer grasp of the historical situation than did liberals. Conservatives defined the fundamental political choice as 'We believe in America and liberals don't believe in America.' When the historical moment was dominated by a crisis of faith in America, millions of voters stood ready to ignore smaller issues in order to affirm their faith in America, though many of those smaller issues became symbols of belief or disbelief in America. And the conservatives were quite correct: they did believe in America and liberals didn't. Or to put it more accurately, conservatives went right on believing in national myths that were now failing badly, while liberals recognized that something was going wrong.

The response of American liberalism to this situation has been filled with confusion and timidity and failure. At a time when America urgently needed to come to grips with the failure of its guiding myths and to fire up the national unconscious to generate better visions and values, both the political leadership and the intellectual leadership of liberalism have faltered.

Perhaps it wasn't so surprising that the political leadership came up short. Politicians spend most of their time immersed in the technical details of specific policy proposals. They receive very little schooling in the dynamics of national myths and would consider it quite weird to come out and say: "Our myths are malfunctioning and we need to change them." And yet, this is what it all comes down to. It's very difficult for liberal legislators to push international caution and cooperation or to push national health insurance or to push environmental restrictions when they are pushing against the most powerful currents in American history. When post-election polls showed that the first thing on voters minds in 2004 wasn't any specific policy proposal but values, many liberal commentators reacted as if this was a new and mysterious discovery, but values are one of the central elements of national myth, and moral values take on a special significance and anxiety when national myth holds that national success depends heavily on America being aligned with God's purposes. The liberal political leadership also faltered because it was always preoccupied with winning elections, and every time voters punished liberals for doubting America the survivors ran for cover and got out their American flags and waved them frantically.

It was more disappointing that the intellectual leadership of liberalism had trouble coming to terms with the historical moment. Every time a Democratic presidential candidate lost there was a sprawling argument over why, when all that liberals needed to do was to tune in to the conservative's take on it: 'We're winning elections because we believe in America and you don't.' Like America, the Democrats had become prisoners of their own success, reluctant to acknowledge faltering habits. The primary mission of the Democratic Party had always been to serve economic outsiders, and this mission had made the Democrats enormously successful for the middle third of the twentieth century, so it was hard not to go on repeating the old formulas, even when millions of working-class Democrats were voting on identity issues and not economic issues, voting against national self-doubt and for America's old identity—especially for the American Dream.

The liberal intellectual leadership wasted a huge amount of energy personalizing the problem, demonizing Ronald Reagan and George W. Bush when Reagan and Bush owed their popularity to being effective channelers of American myth, just like FDR and JFK, and after Reagan and Bush were gone the real problem would remain. Increasingly, liberal intellectuals dwelled within an academic ghetto where they had virtually no contact with real blue-collar workers or real fundamentalists, and increasingly they dealt in caricatures of dim-witted, easily-fooled, hate-filled, inbred yokels, which not only left the real problem unaddressed but which was very annoying to the "yokels." The most serious intellectual failure was that the left side of liberalism absolutely refused to engage in any discussion of malfunctioning American myths. To the left there were no malfunctions, only diabolical economic plots inside every American thought, feeling, deed, and institution. The result was a strange alliance of the right and the left to ignore any possibility that American myths were going wrong. Yet while the right ransacked the raw materials of American history to build a lattice to support its agenda, the left was burning its bridges with American history, not only rejecting the rich raw materials that could have supported a liberal vision and agenda, but turning Jefferson and Lincoln and FDR into demons or at best frauds, all of which only reinforced the conservative case that they were the true believers in America.

Merely being on the outside of 200 years of successful national myth was enough to doom liberalism to a long defeat, and openly challenging those myths was certain to turn 'liberal' into a dirty word, even if that challenge was conducted with the greatest coherence and vision. But it wasn't. Faced with one of its greatest challenges, American liberalism wasted enormous energies in confused, useless, self-defeating ways. The tragedy of it was that even though America might not know it, it needed liberal leadership and vision and values more than ever.

This book is an old story, the story of a nation trapped by its past, grappling with the failure of its guiding myths, or much more often, failing to grapple with it. This book tells this story as it played itself out through the events of the 2004 presidential campaign. But unlike most books about campaigns, this book focuses much less on what the candidates were saying and doing and more on the national unconscious at work out in the country.

Much of the impetus for this book came from my continuing sense of déjà vu throughout the 2004 campaign. Back in 1972, when the nation was deeply polarized and frustrated over Vietnam and John Kerry was the most impressive anti-war spokesman, I spent five months working in Kerry's losing campaign for a seat in congress. Kerry was quite a lightning rod for the confused and angry energy loose in America then, and I got a very good look at this energy. Throughout the 2004 campaign I recognized this same energy over and over again. It was most obvious in the enduring resentments over Vietnam, but I also recognized it in the confusion over yet another war in which America was supposed to be playing the hero. I recognized the exact same angry phrases I'd heard hurled at John Kerry a third of a century before. It was like being in a twilight-zone time warp. This time warp included domestic issues too, for a third of a century ago I'd heard John Kerry advocating national health insurance and other initiatives, which had never happened even as the problems grew worse and conservatives tried to reconstruct the Gilded Age. It was a sad, dismaying time warp. In the end my sense of living in a time warp turned out to be instructive, for America itself was trapped in a time warp.

It isn't an easy task to map out the dynamics of national myth. You can't weigh myth with the quantitative tools of sociology or polls. Nor can the descriptive tools of history writing or the analytical tools of political commentary really do justice. A great deal of the power of national myth resides in symbols, symbols made out of places, heroes, events, and stories, and this is why many of the most magnetic and enduring national symbols come from novelists and artists and moviemakers. Thus much of the weight of this book is carried by symbols, beginning with the symbolism of places. Campaigning for John Kerry offered me a good framework for viewing American myths at work, for it took me to some of the most iconic American places, from Lexington and Concord on the 4th of July to John Wayne's hometown, from the natural realities of the Grand Canyon to the dream worlds of Las Vegas and Hollywood and Beverly Hills, from Iowa cornfields to a Mark Twain riverboat town to Old West towns full of real Native Americans and not-always-real frontier myths. Many of these places are almost definitive of some of the great themes of American life and readily invite contemplation. Lexington and Concord on the 4th of July invite thoughts about the birth of American identity; Hollywood and Beverly Hills invite thoughts about the realities and unrealities of the American Dream; and the Grand Canyon invites thoughts about the place of human society in nature. Even at normal times these invitations are strong, and a presidential campaign can cast these themes into even sharper focus. Many of these places are rich with the symbolisms of heroes and stories and great events, of iconic American literature and film.

This book isn't the usual 'Making of the President' play-by-play inside account of campaign events, personalities, and decision-making. There is very little of that here. Rather, this is an attempt, using the tools of personal, creative nonfiction, to observe a nation facing an identity crisis—and largely failing to face it successfully. America must now decide whether the purpose that has guided us from the beginning and which has made the world a much better place has now spent itself, leaving America degenerating into a sad spectacle; or whether America can, as it has before, draw upon its creative depths and renew its promise.

1

The 4th of July

And the rocket's red glare, the fireworks bursting in air, gave proof over the Lexington battlefield that nearly 200 years after the red glare of muskets had sparked the fire of national identity here, that fire was still burning strong.

At the start of that April morning America had not existed, but at sunset it did. At the start of that April day the people of Lexington had thought of themselves as British, but at sunset they knew they were no longer British and were required by history to become something new. Their old identity could be burned away by the fire of a few muskets because this fire meant that they and their purposes had become so different from the British that finally they were opposed, so opposed that the protection of British identity required the destruction of what opposed it. The musket's red glare made manifest and final a distance that had been growing in people's minds for decades.

It's a mysterious thing, the creation of national identity. National identity emerges from the poorly-mapped psychological terrain in which humans define who they are and what they value and why they bind together. One thing at the center of it is a story, a mythology. From the first languages around the first campfires humans told themselves stories to define patterns in the sky or in the behavior of bears, to define why humans are different from bears or why one group of humans is different from others. As the group gets larger the story becomes more important, for the ties of genetics or neighborly reciprocity grow thinner. The story defines what people have in common and why, and how people should behave inside the group and towards outsiders. A nation is first of all a common story that a lot of people have agreed upon. But things can get complicated when people who are supposed to agree upon a common story begin to disagree.

Why would the British colonists in America start to disagree about the British story? Plenty of colonists thought it was a great story. They were part of the world's greatest empire, protected and linked to the world by the world's greatest fleet, and allowed to revel in centuries of glory for king, church, and country. Breaking the gravity of this story required a powerful new story. To read American history textbooks for two centuries to come, the American breakaway was all about King George: King George was a very bad man who treated Americans very badly. To this day the British find this a very peculiar story, and they answer that as British tyrants went, King George wasn't so bad, and as his mistreatment of his subjects went, Americans got off very easy. King George had to be demonized to help break the spell of the British story.

The new American story arose when Americans no longer identified with Britain. A steadily larger portion of colonists had been born in America, had never been to Britain, and had lost touch with relatives and institutions there. The glories of the British story, which mainly glorified the lace-and-marble British aristocracy, were an emotionally shallow fit for the lives of independent log cabin farmers facing a huge wilderness. The local tavern tall-tales about self-sufficient frontiersmen were much more satisfying. For a significant portion of the American population, such as the Irish, the religious refugees, and the once-hopeless and landless peasants, the British story had been so unappealing even while they'd been in Britain that they'd left. Even Americans who remained loyal to the British story recognized that Americans were forging a unique identity, a new story.

Some of this new story was being written in Europe. Log cabin frontiersmen might be oblivious of what was going on in Paris salons and might happily accept George Washington as the American king, but the George Washingtons of America were quite aware of the Enlightenment currents flowing in Europe. The core Enlightenment ideas were an enticingly good fit for the American experience. While European churches and kings proclaimed themselves the only source of moral and political authority, the Enlightenment held that the ultimate source was Nature. If Americans were backwards in many ways, Nature was one thing at which we beat Europe by miles. While European churches and kings proclaimed that monarchy was sanctioned by God, the Enlightenment held that monarchy was fundamentally irrational and that human reason could be trusted to design and run more rational forms of society. Americans already felt that King George was mismanaging their affairs and that their own efforts at town-hall self-government were going well, and the Enlightenment gave these feelings a rather grand ratification. Most enticing of all, the Enlightenment promised that human society could be revolutionized if only someone had the boldness to start the world anew.

Even illiterate log cabin frontiersmen who thought that a Locke was something only for doors in fancy houses were hearing their preachers talk about the special destiny awaiting America, for American Protestantism had developed a strong sense that the settling of America was part of God's plan for redeeming the corrupt churches of Europe and unfolding God's will on earth. Even un-philosophical and unreligious frontiersmen could feel a sense of national destiny as they stood with European technology and faced a vast rich continent that had been touched only by stone tools. From several sources Americans developed a strong sense of a great destiny awaiting them, yet the British story showed no recognition of such a destiny, and British rulers were managing America for the sake of the British Empire. Americans were increasingly ready for any excuse, such as a tax on tea, to toss their British identity overboard.

It was the unlikely but lucky confluence of America's founding that two very dissimilar historical forces, the self-sufficiency of crude frontiersmen and the lofty ideals of the Enlightenment, met and mixed and merged in the lives and minds of the men who gathered at Independence Hall, who then mixed these forces into a new form of government. The founding of America was a very unusual event in the history of nations in that it owed so much to an intellectual act, to some bright men who sat down together and tried to reason out a better system of social relationships. Yet even for America the forging of a new identity required the usual crises and violence, for national identities are powerful gods, sometimes more enduring than religious gods, the old identities refusing to give way easily. Nor did a new American identity emerge easily or emerge complete. Because the mixing of pioneering realities and Enlightenment ideals was not easy or complete, because Thomas Jefferson wrote the words "All men are created equal" but could not write the Emancipation Proclamation, America was born with a split personality that could not go on forever. The forging together of American realities and American ideals would require the heat of Gettysburg cannons. American realities and ideals diverged again when the life of the Jeffersonian farmer was replaced by the life of a factory worker in a world of economic tyrannies still run on the frontier ethos of 'every man for himself,' the ethos of a sinking ship.

The fireworks bursting in air painted the walls behind me red, white, and blue, and they painted my mind red, white, and blue too. It was easy to be patriotic, and not just because I was only six years old and history was defined by simple images, but because America was younger too. It was 1962, and patriotism wasn't nearly as complicated as it was soon to become.

It was also an easy place to be patriotic. We lived just down the road from the Lexington green where the American Revolution began, the green with the famous statue of the minuteman. People came from all over the country to look at this statue. Thousands of town squares in America had statues of soldiers, but none of them had the power of the minuteman. Perhaps local kids took the statue for granted, but not me, for I was just visiting Lexington for two summers while my father had a fellowship at MIT. Back home in Missouri I'd learned about the battle of Lexington and Concord from books and TV. I even had a book called *We Were There at the Battle of Lexington and Concord*, one of a 'We Were There' series offering stories that placed kids at key events in American history to make history more personal. Now that I was personally here, history jumped off the page and became magically alive. Perhaps some of the magic derived from a kid's vague sense of reality. To my logic, since we were going to be living in Massachusetts and since President Kennedy was from Massachusetts, we had a plausible chance of running into President Kennedy. Likewise, it wasn't impossible that some of the old men sitting on benches on the green had been minutemen in the battle. I kept an eye out for musket balls scorched into the trees or buried in our yard. I could almost hear Paul Revere galloping off towards Concord.

It was symbolic of being in the center of American history that we didn't even need to leave our house to watch the 4th of July fireworks. Our house was perched high atop a hill right next to the public school grounds where the fireworks were shot off, offering a bird's eye view of the fireworks.

The fireworks flowered and boomed, rattling the windows, registering in my flesh, giving history a real, personal, exciting impact.

The national story America was celebrating on that 4th of July in 1962 was basically the same story Americans had been celebrating all along—not that I was thinking about such matters at age six. But the whole point of national myths is that no one needs to think about them, not even professional historians, not even presidents of the United States. National myths are the mental superstructure that organizes all the events of national experience and gives them meaning. It usually takes a serious failure of national myths to force people to doubt and reexamine and change them. America had known very little failure, and even our worst crises, the Civil War and the Great Depression, we'd ended up counting as successes, and a nation that can count such crises as successes is probably one very confident nation.

The main story Americans had been celebrating—even before 1776—was that of national expansion. Events were defined as important if they mattered to national expansion, and people became heroes for serving national expansion. Things or people that got in the way of national expansion were defined as bad. Daniel Boone and Lewis and Clark were heroes for leading the way west, but they couldn't compete with Davy Crockett for dying fighting the foes of national expansion. The primary foes, of course, were the Indians; in the words of John Wayne: "There were great numbers of people who needed new land, and the Indians were selfishly trying to keep it for themselves."[1] But there were a few good Indians, like Sacagawea, who weren't selfish. General Custer and other soldiers became heroes according to their sacrifices and successes for national success. In addition to heroes of exploration and war there were heroes of invention, like Thomas Edison, who served America's economic expansion. The admission test for American iconography had remained consistent for two centuries, the American story only updating its details along the way, advancing from Plymouth Rock to moon rocks, from Lexington to Normandy, from Ben Franklin's lightning kite to atomic power. If blacks and women were hardly mentioned in this story it was because picking cotton and sewing quilts weren't on the cutting edge of national destiny. If lumberjacks and 49ers and railroad barons were in the history books but there was no mention of Thoreau at Walden Pond or Muir in Yosemite, it was because Thoreau and Muir were weirdoes who questioned the frenzy of national expansion.

Integral to the story of national expansion was the theme of freedom, though there seemed to be some vagueness about how freedom and national expansion fit together. In some versions national expansion and personal success seemed to be the primary goals of the American story, and freedom was simply a means to an end, useful for setting loose human energies and opportunities. In other versions freedom was the whole point of the American story, and national expansion and prosperity simply illustrated the value of freedom and equipped freedom to compete on the world stage and complete its destiny of redeeming the world. Other versions placed religious goals first and credited freedom with making them possible. Even some of the central heroes in the American story owed their stature to hard-to-dissect multiple sources. How much of Thomas Jefferson's heroism was for serving freedom with the Declaration of Independence, and how much was for serving national expansion with the Louisiana Purchase? Was Lincoln a hero for the Emancipation Proclamation, or for stopping national disintegration? At least all Americans agreed that freedom was the key ingredient in the story and that America was the obvious model for the world.

While six-year-olds may not worry about such matters, they are definitely already absorbing the basic assumptions of national myth. These assumptions were clearly displayed in the titles of my 'We Were There' series, which were almost entirely about pioneer adventures, famous battles, and technological inventions. We were there on the Oregon Trail. We were there at the Alamo. We were there at the driving of the golden spike. Yet if this series had been produced two decades later it would be obvious that some kind of upheaval had occurred in American myth. The titles might include: We were there at Wounded Knee. We were there on a slave plantation. We were there when Teddy Roosevelt met John Muir at Yosemite.

There were few inklings of such a coming change on the 4th of July in 1962. Yet by age six I had already stumbled upon the possibility that patriotism might be more complicated than a 4th of July celebration. This story may seem trivial, but considering that I still remember it, it must have seriously offended my sense of innocence. Was this merely the innocence of a six-year-old, or was it the innocence of 1962?

In the back of a comic book I saw an advertisement for a set of toy Revolutionary War soldiers. The illustration showed a dramatic battle between redcoats and Americans. This was my chance to re-enact the battle of Lexington and Concord. The toy soldiers were an amazing bargain too, way more than you'd get in a toy store for that little money. Maybe the toy company was trying to promote patriotism. I sent in my dollars, and finally a small box showed up in the mail, an impossibly small box for a hundred soldiers. I opened it up and peered inside at some very thin wafers of plastic. These toy soldiers weren't anything like the illustration in the comic or like toy-store toy soldiers. The base on these soldiers was so thin that some soldiers were more inclined to fall over than to stand up. As every kid knew, a toy soldier lying down was a dead soldier. This toy company had sent me a bunch of dead American soldiers.

I tried to be historically accurate in setting up my toy soldiers. The British army was famous for lining up in tight rows, so I lined up my British soldiers side by side. But when one of the tipsy soldiers fell over it turned the British army into a game of dominoes, the entire row falling down. This was actually kind of a cool thing to see, and there was some justice in it too. The British were the bad guys because they had a king and they were too regimented, so it served them right that their too-regimented army all fell over. Yet sometimes I lined up the Americans in a row, and then they too all domino died. It took several minutes of careful work to set up my armies, so when they all collapsed it was frustrating and I got angry at the toy company again and my boundaries of good and evil shifted to include as evil a toy company that would send American soldiers out to die for a botched, dishonest, doomed mission.

Ten years later I was back in Lexington for another 4th of July. I was walking the public school grounds where the fireworks were shot off to celebrate America. But a great deal had happened in the last ten years, and celebrating America had become much more confusing. I was walking the grounds with John Kerry. John Kerry was an angry young man. John Kerry was an angry young man because someone had misled him and sent him a box full of dead American soldiers. It wasn't a toy company that had misled John Kerry but his own government, and it wasn't plastic soldiers that were dead but friends whose deaths were deep blows to him and in which he wanted to find redeeming purpose but finally could not.

We were walking through a fair that included carnival mirrors and carnival rides. We were looking for voters, but they were a bit scarce at midday on a week-day before the 4th. We were spending five days visiting 4th of July events all over the district where Kerry was running for congress. I was riding along with Kerry because I was in charge of recruiting volunteers for the campaign and this holiday offered our best-yet opportunity for Kerry to meet tons of voters and for the campaign to recruit volunteers. My job was to follow Kerry through a crowd, eaves-drop on his conversations, and when he hit it off with a voter, try to talk the voter into volunteering. I was also supposed to scout through the crowds to find appro-priate voters for Kerry to meet, saving him from wasting a great deal of time on nonvoters, Republicans, or unfriendly Democrats.

But the Lexington fair was very slow. We stopped at a carnival booth and John's wife Julia threw some balls at a target and hit it and won a prize. She cheered like a kid and took a brief look at her toy prize and then awarded it to me.

We turned a corner and headed for the carnival rides. Suddenly John Kerry froze. I looked at him and saw his face turn grim, truly pained, full of regret. He reached out his long arm and pointed down the row of rides. He looked at Julia, and Julia gave him an acknowledging look. He looked at me, silently. I looked down the row to where, amid the usual merry-go-rounds with fantasy horses, there was a merry-go-round that held only camouflaged army tanks, tanks going up and down, going around and around, going nowhere really, with a few chil-dren pretending to steer and smiling joyfully. Kerry just stood there pointing, reminding me of the stern Ghost of Christmas Future pointing Scrooge to his fate in the graveyard. Kerry was pointing to another generation that would grow up playing with toy soldiers and driving toy tanks and who would go on to com-mand real tanks churning dust clouds through the Persian Gulf desert. Going nowhere really.

We wandered on, and a young mother with a kid in tow spotted Kerry and eagerly came over to greet him. She said how much she had admired his testi-mony before congress, especially the part about 'how do you ask a man to be the last man to die for a mistake?' She was delighted that he was running for congress right here in Lexington. It was just so frustrating trying to do anything about the war and now his candidacy offered local activists a great outlet for their energies. She and Kerry talked awhile and then Kerry turned her over to me and I got her name and explained some of the opportunities for volunteers.

It wasn't always so easy. Soon afterwards I asked a man if he was a Democratic voter in the 5th district and he said yes, and then as I started to ask him if he would be interested in meeting John Kerry he spotted Kerry and glowered at him and then at me. He answered: "You go tell your John Kerry that inside his yellow belly he's got the guts of a chicken and he's the biggest traitor since Benedict Arnold."

"Yes sir, I'll be sure I tell him that." You got used to it.

Following John Kerry around for the 4th of July in the middle of the Vietnam War was a good way to map out the passions and pride and doubts of America. It was like walking through a thunderstorm carrying a lightning rod. The storm was a huge, dark, boiling, intensely charged confusion over America's national identity. Even on an ordinary weekend John Kerry was a symbol of the polarization in America, a symbol to which people reacted in very different ways. But this was the 4th of July weekend, meant to concentrate the mind on America, meant to spark mere textbook citizenship into a fireworks-burst of enthusiasm. All the long-proven symbols of patriotism were on full display in store windows and newspaper ads: the red, white, and blue, the images of George Washington and the Liberty Bell. Yet now these symbols had been cast into confusion. For people who were doubting America and feeling alienated from these symbols and who had heard John Kerry both validating their doubts and renewing their hope in America, to suddenly spot Kerry amid the 4th of July symbolism could be very gratifying. But for people who had come out to celebrate the same American identity their fathers and grandfathers had celebrated on the 4th of July, to suddenly spot amid the red, white, and blue ribbons a man who had doubted America and thrown his combat ribbons onto the ground was to feel a burst of anger. And it was my job to go up to preoccupied strangers and say: Look—there's John Kerry.

But I didn't need to be on the road with Kerry to see the angry lightning he attracted. I saw it almost every day in the headquarters. A steady stream of hate mail flowed in the door and I was the person it came to. Our large volunteer force periodically delivered brochures to every home in the district, and the brochures included mail-in volunteer cards. Some people felt violated to find a Kerry brochure tucked in their door and they retaliated by writing angry messages on the cards and mailing them in, draining our treasury of eight cents. For the campaign strategists the hostility to Kerry was experienced as clinical numbers in our polling, but for me this hostility showed itself in very personal—but almost always anonymous—expressions.

It was rare to receive a comment about domestic issues, and these were much less passionate, such as: "Where are you going to get the money to pay for your health insurance plan? Did you ever look at corporation financial statements and see the millions of dollars paid in real estate and income taxes? Do you want to kill the goose that lays eggs?"

Most cards were about Vietnam, or more generally about offended patriotism. The most popular response was to fill in the blanks with phony and sarcastic names and addresses. One very popular name was Benedict Arnold, but mounting a strong challenge to him was Jane Fonda. There were lots of 'Ho Chi Minh, Red Square, Hanoi, North Vietnam,' and sometimes Ho added a message in support of Kerry, such as: "You must know it—you support me. Killing South Vietnamese, Laos, Cambodians, and their American defenders." Some people skipped the name and got right to the address: 'USSR,' 'Siberia,' 'Traitor Street,' 'Bastard Street,' and the rather crowded 'Fuck You Street.' Some people simply altered our address from 'Kerry for Congress' to 'Commie for Congress'. Many people simply wrote messages:

"I vow to move out of the district if this pinko makes it!!!"

"Drop Dead. I'd rather work for the Vietcong. At least they admit you're for them or you're dead! [signed] a true veteran, not a turncoat."

"There aren't enough Benedict Arnolds in this district to send you to Washington. Why not campaign among the draft dodgers in Canada?"

"No!!! Ask the North Vietnamese. You support their invasions (4 countries), mass murders, and the result is World War III. You can never represent me!! Traitor and supporter of massacres by North Vietnam."

"There are planes leaving for Hanoi every day via Moscow or Peking. I am sure you will be able to obtain an all expenses paid, life-time vacation, and one-way ticket to North Vietnam. Eat your rice quickly or a bomb may fall in the bowl."

"He is a first-class ass hole. How stupit [sic] do you thing[sic] the American public are [crossed out] is. I will do all in my power to keep him out of officee [sic]. Vote for a [sic] American".

You got used to it. Still, it was interesting to hit the road with John Kerry and see such phrases emerging from the mouths of real people whose faces and clothes and factory hands suggested an entire life story. I quickly learned that nothing I could say would penetrate such phrases and the thoughts behind them.

Occasionally the cards brought expressions of support, but these often reflected an exhausting decade of chaos and confusion. Chaos had launched a surprise attack against American self-confidence by turning a Norman Rockwell Dallas street into a Jackson Pollock painted with a president's blood. Chaos claimed Martin Luther King and Robert Kennedy and left liberals despairing that the most humane idealism counted for nothing. Chaos burned the ghettos summer after summer. Chaos reigned in Vietnam. By now Americans agreed that something had gone badly wrong in Vietnam, but they angrily disagreed over what had gone wrong. The chaos in the jungles was echoed by a cultural chaos at home. Antiwar protests went from scholarly teach-ins to bombings, from posters of Gandhi to posters of Che Guevera. Chaos invaded millions of Norman Rockwell homes in the form of the counterculture.

The polarization of America in 1972 could be mapped out in many ways, and it showed up strongly in the political geography of the 5th district. John Kerry held enormous appeal in Lexington and Concord, which were now basically affluent suburbs of Boston, loaded with advanced college degrees, with Harvard professors and with engineers in the blossoming high-tech industries along Rt. 128. In a Democratic primary that included ten candidates, Kerry would receive 72% of the Lexington vote, leaving many of his opponents near zero. In Concord Kerry would receive 77%. Yet in the district's main city, Lowell, Kerry would get only 11%. In the district's other city, Lawrence, Kerry would receive 19%.

Like Lexington and Concord, Lowell and Lawrence were famous for launching an American revolution, the industrial revolution. Both cities were founded by wealthy Yankee families to be factory towns, using the water power of the Merrimack River to run textile mills. By the 1840s Lowell had become a national marvel, the Silicon Valley of its time, presaging a new technological and economic order. But by 1972 Lowell was a pioneer of rust-belt decay. Unemployment was 12% and would have been much higher if 30,000 people, one-quarter of the population, hadn't despaired and moved away in the five decades before 1972, leaving behind abandoned factories and ghost mansions and rotting tenements. Lowell and Lawrence had also pioneered the new realities of late nineteenth-century ethnic immigration to industrial America, and early twentieth-century labor organizing and strife. One immigrant group after another arrived in Lowell and Lawrence only to find itself trapped in a relentless downward economic spiral. Ethnic groups ended up competing fiercely for jobs and political power, and politicians gave up hoping for solutions and settled for fighting over spoils. You might think that the long-suffering blue-collar workers of Lowell and

Lawrence had a right to feel discouraged about America. But no, it was they who loathed John Kerry for doubting America.

I studied this political geography every day when the hate mail arrived, as the postmarks were never from Lexington or Concord, mainly from Lowell and Lawrence. I also studied this pattern every week when I prepared a progress report on volunteer recruitment; Lexington and Concord were consistently our best towns. It was the taken-for-granted reality of the campaign: Harvard-educated suburbanites who had benefited the most from the American system loved John Kerry for being ready to question America, while slum-and-trailer-park, blue-collar, economically-trapped Democrats loathed John Kerry for questioning America. Yet when seen in the history of American liberalism, this pattern was a dramatic and consequential development.

For a century, since the boom of the industrial revolution and the arrival of large immigrant populations in Northeastern industrial cities, the identity of the Democratic Party had been defined mainly by economic class, by the mission of protecting poor workers from the entrenched and often unkind power of Yankee capitalists. As the Gilded Age gathered the speed of a runaway train, prairie farmers also found themselves seriously outmatched by the power of railroads and banks, and they rallied behind the indignation of William Jennings Bryan. Southerners had their own motives for wanting to check the power of Yankee capitalists. It was an odd coalition, unlikely to last. After Teddy Roosevelt and Woodrow Wilson had built an institutional counterbalance to Gilded Age capitalism, the prairie farmers, who as landowners had a much more secure stake in American society than did peasants just stepping onto Ellis Island, began to fade out of the coalition, though prairie populism sank more lasting roots in Wisconsin and Minnesota. Even the immigrants working in factories would have preferred to rely less on the Democratic Party and more on the American Dream. The American Dream with its lack of class barriers was the whole reason they'd come to America. They found that class barriers in America were much looser than in Europe, but not nearly as free and easy as promised by the American Dream. When the capitalists got the economic train up to runaway speed again, the Wall Street crash and the Great Depression finally created an enduring consensus that runaway capitalism was not just unkind but irrational and downright suicidal, and the New Deal was able to rewrite the rules of the game to include significantly more social responsibility. The immigrant's need for the Democratic Party had been reinforced by a compelling socio-historical logic.

Yet all along liberals had been giving themselves a warning, if one unheard and unnecessary at the time. If the liberal diagnosis was all about economics, the liberal prescription said that there was far more to life than economics. Humans are social animals who derive much of their sense of value from groups, including nations. For liberals this meant building a society with values that honored the basic value of human beings. Yet value-hungry humans seek their value in many ways, including in God and ethnicity and national pride. There is abundant evidence from many realms of human behavior that humans often value other things more than money, even more than life itself. The young men who march eagerly off to war in every generation seem to value nation or at least heroism more than life itself. To take one example, at the outbreak of World War One socialists all over Europe, with impeccable credentials for possessing class consciousness, discovered that they cared more about nation or religion than about economic class.

For America World War One was a heady experience, for the national myth of America redeeming the world had finally taken the form of American armies marching into the old world. World War Two only confirmed America's sense of destiny. Americans had little doubt that our world mission also required us to save the world from communism. But in Vietnam something was going badly wrong.

The Vietnamese were supposed to welcome us with waving America flags, just as Europe had. It was weird just how hard the Viet Cong were fighting us. It was weird that all our superior technology, which was one of the foremost proofs of our national superiority, couldn't prevail. It was worse than weird, it was outrageous that many young Americans were questioning the war, even questioning America's fundamental sense of itself.

Over the months that I listened to the voices of Lowell and Lawrence it was clear enough what the hostility to John Kerry was all about. It came from people deeply loyal to America's long-standing sense of itself, whose never-questioned patriotism was now being questioned.

Unlike the population of Lexington and Concord, who were primarily old Yankee stock that had been in America for centuries, the population of Lowell and Lawrence represented the Ellis Island flood of immigrants. There were still plenty of accents on the streets. Almost by definition, Ellis Island immigrants had a deep faith in America. Europeans who didn't believe in America didn't move there. When immigrants arrived in America they were eager and often pressured to prove their faith in America. Establishing an American identity was a trickier business than was identity in Europe, where national identity was primarily a matter of ethnicity. If you were born a Greek, you had nothing to prove about being Greek. But a Greek arriving in Lowell had to transcend ethnicity, language, and religion. There were only a few patriotic symbols that every immigrant group could share, most visibly the flag, making Americans the most flag-crazed people on Earth. More importantly, immigrants needed to embrace American mythology with its pantheon of heroes and its sense of national heroism. Americans had to invent their own scale for measuring a good or bad fit into American society, making people "all-American" or "un-American." At the core of immigrant faith in America was the American Dream. Immigrants were willing to hear liberals outlining the barriers in the way of the American Dream, which only confirmed their own experience, but there was no provision for anyone to deny the basic reality or desirability of the American Dream. If immigrants weren't achieving the American Dream in Lowell, they did find an important success in the military in the world wars, perhaps not financial success but certainly success in winning respect. Men who were failures by the standards of the American Dream were heroes by the standards of patriotism, a heroism they clung to even more urgently with more years of economic failure; to them it was inconceivable and obscene that American soldiers might throw away the medals that proved their worth as Americans. Raised by the standards of patriotism, many sons of Lowell and Lawrence were now fighting in Vietnam. For many families religion was also an important part of their dislike of communism. Most of the leading ethnic groups in Lowell and Lawrence were Catholics, and the Catholic Church had long involved itself in fighting communism.

As the Democratic Party increasingly challenged the war, the Ellis Island blue-collar Democrats of Lowell and Lawrence and elsewhere increasingly realized that both patriotism and religion were more important than the economic needs that had made them Democrats. It wasn't just about Vietnam policy; the Democrat's challenge felt like a challenge to the basic heroic identity of America, and when you've fully internalized that identity, this feels like a denial of your own identity, something people take very personally. People felt compelled to defend the heroic identity of America and themselves, even if it required them to leave the Democratic Party and abandon its economic agenda and wreck its longtime winning coalition. The political geography of the 5th district offered liberals a clearer warning for the future than did other places, for in other places the defection of blue-collar Democrats was compounded by issues of race, and the fog of race made it harder to discern the shapes and importance of basic questions of patriotism and identity. But there had never been many blacks in Lowell and Lawrence, and I never received any hate mail accusing John Kerry of being a traitor to his race. What was unclear in 1972 was that this Vietnam-propelled polarization wouldn't end with Vietnam but would become an enduring and powerful structure in American cultural and political life for a long time to come.

Conservatives could never figure out why this was so. They did their best to dismiss Vietnam as an aberration and went back to celebrating America's old self-image. To them liberals seemed to be wallowing in an absurdly long hangover of national self-doubt: snap out of it! But if liberals were going to wallow in self-doubt and hand conservatives the role of a lifetime, a role as charged with power as defending belief in America, conservatives would gleefully take it. Liberals went right on speaking the language of economic class and couldn't understand why Ellis Island blue-collar Democrats seemed to have gone deaf and were listening instead to conservatives talk about patriotism and religion, about flag burning, the Pledge of Allegiance, and school prayer. Liberals frequently refused to consider the possibility that people might genuinely care about patriotism and religion more than economics, and they treated the whole thing as a clever trick to get workers to vote against their own interests. The corollary is that if workers can't recognize they are being tricked, they must be really stupid. It shouldn't have surprised anyone that when Lowell donut-shop Democrats listened for years to Harvard coffee-house liberals doubting America and calling them stupid, they might start resenting "the liberal elite." But many liberals did manage to be surprised by this term and this resentment, and they protested: hey, wait a minute, *they're* the elite; we're the champions of the people.

The Ellis Island Democrats of Lowell and Lawrence were quite right about one thing: America's identity was indeed being challenged. It was being challenged for the exact same reason that British identity had been challenged exactly 200 years before, and in the same places. Back in 1772 Lexington had gathered at Buckman Tavern on the green and Concord had gathered at Wright Tavern. Over coffee and ale men read newspapers and shared the word from Boston and beyond and discussed the meaning of it, and every week there were fresh discrepancies between the news and the beliefs that ruled America, between Americans and the identity we had inherited from the British Empire. Over the years these discrepancies accumulated into the conviction that the old identity was failing. Not everyone saw it this way of course, and thus uncomprehending eyes stared scornfully at the traitors mumbling at their table, traitors with names like Hancock and Adams.

Two centuries later Lexington was still meeting at cafes on the green and reading the news, now news from Vietnam and Selma, mixed with advertisements of a society with a runaway craving for status symbols. Perhaps better than anyplace, Lexington and Concord could feel the discrepancy between the ideals born here and the ongoing realities of American society and America's role in the world. They had seen the history textbooks that glorified riflemen like the minutemen and Davy Crockett become the boxes in the Texas School Book Depository behind which Lee Harvey Oswald had hidden and upon with he had steadied his rifle. They had seen the minuteman statue step down off his pedestal and aim his rifle at the civilians at My Lai and open fire. Over the years these discrepancies accumulated into the conviction that America's identity was faltering.

On Memorial Day weekend in 1971 the people of Lexington watched their archetypal sense of history spring into life on the Lexington green in a new battle of Lexington. The minutemen were played by Vietnam veterans, who were following the route of the battle, starting in Concord and retracing Paul Revere's ride and the British retreat back to Boston. This wasn't the first time that Vietnam Veterans Against the War (VVAW) had shown a keen eye for the symbolism of the American Revolution. It was on an eighty-mile march to Valley Forge that John Kerry first emerged as VVAW's most compelling spokesman. The Concord march began with the veterans camping beside Concord's Old North Bridge, made famous in Emerson's poem about "the shot heard round the world." As they marched to Lexington they recited Longfellow's poem about the midnight ride of Paul Revere. The veterans wanted to camp on the Lexington green but the city selectmen refused permission and suggested that the veterans camp in the city dump. The veterans went ahead and camped on the green anyway. They read aloud "On Civil Disobedience" by Thoreau, who had spent a night in the Concord jail for refusing to pay taxes for the Mexican war. At two o'clock in the morning, the veterans sound asleep, state police in riot gear moved in and arrested the veterans and marched and wheelchaired them away. A photographer captured John Kerry at this moment, his hands behind his head, his hair ruffled, looking sleepy and annoyed, surrounded by police in riot helmets. A year later this photo would be used in the 5ᵗʰ district race to prove that Kerry was a traitor to his country. A third of a century later this photo would be used nationwide by the Swift Boat Veterans for Truth to prove that Kerry was a traitor to his country, accompanied by angry assertions that nothing was wrong with the Vietnam war and nothing was wrong with traditional patriotism.

The veterans were hauled off to a makeshift jail in a city garage, and in the end they were fined five dollars and released. Many Lexington residents were very upset by these arrests done in their name. Now that the most prominent of those veterans was running for congress right here in Lexington they felt a very personal obligation to help him out. More than that, many residents felt a sense of history circling round, a sense that once again Lexington and Concord had a chance to address a faltering American identity.

I felt my own sense of history circling. I hadn't been back to Lexington in ten years, and I'm not sure I would have come back now for the Kerry campaign if not for the coincidence that his district included Lexington. For me Lexington was still mythic ground, still bearing a child's magical sense that history was still alive there. Back in 1962 I never did meet any minutemen, but here was a second chance to be There at the battle of Lexington and Concord and help make some important history. I was there for the fall campaign because my high school principle, a conservative Mormon who expected his students to stand every morning and face the flag and say the Pledge of Allegiance, believed in teaching citizenship and thought that my taking part in John Kerry's campaign would be a fine lesson in American civics.

We wandered around the school grounds awhile longer. When it was time for us to leave Lexington I glanced back towards the high hill from where a decade before I had looked this way at the 4th of July fireworks. In the geography of history too I realized that I was looking at the 4th of July from a very different angle. This year as for some years now the fireworks would streak upwards less like exclamation marks and more like question marks. Americans were questioning the basic sense of reality and confidence and mission that had long been celebrated here. This questioning might be essential, but still, it left me sad to feel the distance from the heroism with which my toy revolutionary soldiers had fought. But I had only been playing with toys. Some men had become real soldiers to serve that heroism and had ended up feeling like cheap toys serving only confusion.

We got in the car and headed for Concord. The road to Concord was full of ghosts, the ghosts of Paul Revere, British soldiers, minutemen behind trees, and Vietnam veterans.

Concord too was full of ghosts, the spirits of Emerson and Thoreau and Hawthorne and the Alcotts, all buried in Sleepy Hollow Cemetery. (And this year, at least, Concord also held the ghost of John F. Kennedy, for Caroline Kennedy was attending a private school in Concord and started coming into the Kerry headquarters in Lexington to help out). Concord was one of those rare places in human history overflowing with genius, or perhaps you could say that some places and times mandated the creation of genius. Because of the revolution Concord was already deeply engaged with the American story, and as America grew in the early 1800s, grew robustly but in vague directions, someone needed to fill out the American story in terms of philosophy and theology and literature, in the meanings and manners of society and in the symbols that inspired the human heart. Ralph Waldo Emerson, whose grandfather was the Concord parson on the day of the battle, concerned himself with Nature, Jefferson's Nature that is, a nature that powerfully mandated democratic values. Hawthorne wasn't so sure that Nature could be contained by Puritan values. Thoreau feared that the American juggernaut was racing away from Nature.

The questioning of America on this 4ᵗʰ of July in 1972 was not just about the present and the future, but also about the past; not just about Selma or My Lai, but about the basic American story. If it takes a trauma to force a people to reexamine their guiding myths, a trauma had finally occurred, a contradiction of our self-image sufficiently long and painful to require us to actually stare into the mirror. This Lexington café questioning was going on among engineers and housewives, who spoke about it in the vaguest terms, but it was also going on among Harvard historians and sociologists, who had a sharper focus for the internal edifice of the American story. The main edifice was still the story of national expansion. Now people were questioning if this story did justice to the past or offered a healthy value system for the future. At the least, it left out some perfectly good stuff; but more seriously, it left out some perfectly bad stuff; and worst of all, it celebrated some bad stuff. This questioning unleashed a Concord-like project of national definition, but instead of being conducted by a few geniuses it was a sprawling and confused energy. Much of this questioning wasn't anything new, and occasionally these questions had made inroads into American history texts, but never before had it been so widespread and made such fundamental changes in those texts. This project would play a large role in making the polarization of 1972 into a lasting and powerful reality in American culture and politics.

It was long overdue, and it was a healthy thing. It was time to talk about race in America, about what had happened to—no, what we'd done to Native Americans and blacks. It was time to talk about economic greed in America, about men driving themselves mad chasing status symbols while the Joads were driving themselves down Rt. 66, about Walden Ponds being ruined for profit, about chronic U.S. interventions in Latin America. It was time to talk about the times that democratic values didn't fit into the story of national expansion, to hear about the Mexican war from Thoreau's viewpoint or to hear about the Philippines from Mark Twain's viewpoint—or just to hear about them at all.

It might be time to talk, but defining a national story isn't easy even when you've got a bunch of geniuses in one Independence Hall or one Concord. A chaos of revisions competed for attention and loyalty.

The simplest scheme for revising the story was to plug a new set of heroes into the old story of national expansion. Thus instead of Buffalo Bill riding the plains there were buffalo soldiers proudly riding the plains; instead of John Wayne driving the covered wagon there were strong, smart women driving the covered wagon; instead of visionary industrialists building American prosperity there were heroic factory workers building prosperity. This wasn't the first time that the deck of heroes had been reshuffled, for earlier in the twentieth century Ellis Island immigrants got tired of reading about the progress of the WASPs and demanded that Italians or Catholics be admitted to the story. But such reshufflings didn't address the deeper moral questions, for after all the buffalo soldiers were still shooting Indians; the strong, smart women were still driving the covered wagons over the bones of the Indians; and the heroic factory workers were still proud of the pollution pouring into the air.

A deeper scheme was to maintain the theme of expansion but to redefine it not as territorial or economic expansion but the expansion of democratic values. This allowed honest attention to the status of Native Americans, blacks, women, or factory workers, and their poor initial status even turned the expansion of their status into a triumphant story of national progress. This edifice redefined national heroism so that George Washington Carver, whose economic heroism had made him almost the only black welcome in the national pantheon, was just peanuts compared to Martin Luther King. This edifice redefined some old heroes, emphasizing Teddy Roosevelt the conservationist and not Teddy the hunter, Teddy the progressive monopoly buster and not Teddy the Philippines buster. The main drawback of this edifice was that the stories of democratic expansion and of territorial and economic expansion didn't cohere smoothly, with territorial and economic expansion often running well ahead of democratic expansion, and often blocking it. The result was quite a patchwork of pluses and minuses, of starts and stops and reversals, and in general such patchworks are not what nations look for in national myths. Nations want heroic stories with clear contrasts between good and evil.

The revisionist project did indeed produce a story with strong good and evil. This story was largely the product of middle-class children of the American Dream, who should have been champions of the American Dream for all it had given them but who instead found themselves very alienated from the American Dream and the American story. They were the first generation to grow up with the American Dream a reality, and when they saw their fathers driving themselves to heart attacks to buy a newer Cadillac and a bigger house than the neighbors, the insufficiency of the American Dream as an ultimate social value stood nakedly exposed. When you added the daily TV coverage of blacks being treated very undemocratically in the South and of the war in Vietnam, the aura of intense national self-congratulations started to feel hollow. The glaring discrepancies between American myths and American realities started growing into a compulsion to discredit the self-congratulatory myths. This compulsion often started out as dorm room contests in de-congratulations: "America isn't so great: we sent the Japanese off to concentration camps just like the Nazis did to the Jews."

Vietnam produced a hyperinflation of alienation and doubt and discrediting, producing a lasting subculture with an adversarial relationship with the American story. This subculture produced historians who systematically worked their way through the American story to discredit it, turning every positive into some sort of negative. Needing a new edifice for organizing American history, they did what American intellectuals have always done: they turned to Europe. But Europe didn't have much history with democracy, so not surprisingly its templates for viewing history and society were heavily about economic class and empire. If the American left had started out by examining its own middle-class experience—a big contrast with previous generations of radicals with mainly working-class roots—they might have deduced that economic class didn't determine loyalties to the American story. Instead, at the very same time that millions of blue-collar workers were piling out of the Democratic Party because it was disloyal to the American story, thousands of young intellectuals were piling into universities and activism determined to view everything as a function of economic class and empire. In truth, America had left a ton of unfinished homework about the bad realities of economic self-interest in American history and foreign policy. Yet when even important truths were dressed up in the latest Parisian postmodernist fashions and paraded with relentless negativity about America, even mainstream liberals were reluctant to pay attention. More serious was the inability to even comprehend the dynamics of American history if you insisted on deleting democracy and Ellis Island and the American Dream. The left decided that its sole job consisted of finding malicious economic motives behind every event in American history. On the day that John Kerry and I were wandering around the Lexington school grounds, Noam Chomsky was probably at his Lexington home nearby writing another relentlessly negative version of America's motivations. While John Kerry was saying that Vietnam was a mistake, Chomsky was saying that it wasn't a mistake at all; it was all a diabolical plot, and the more diabolical, the better. The result was that the left "conspired" with the right to refuse to even consider the problem of American myth leading us astray in Vietnam or in larger ways.

The turmoil over the national story would have serious consequences for American liberalism. When the left demonized everything including Lincoln and FDR, it cut itself off from the persuasive power of American history, and when it refused to even speak the language of the American Dream, it cut itself off from effective communication with the American public. Yet Lowell blue-collar Democrats were very aware that something un-American was going on in Harvard and Hollywood. Every week on TV they saw Archie Bunker and his Ellis Island patriotism being ridiculed, and it hurt, it enraged. To those yearning for the American Dream it was incomprehensible why college kids who were enjoying the American Dream would turn against it. Precisely because Lowell Democrats were failing at the American Dream they needed to believe in it. If the liberal elite was doubting the reality and worth of the American Dream and wallowing in how the American Dream had never done anything for blacks, at least the Republicans were still giddy with confidence in the American Dream. If the liberal elite was ridiculing Ellis Island patriotism, at least the Republicans were still parading in red, white, and blue. The basic American myths and symbols still held a powerful appeal, and if liberals were going to shy away from those myths and symbols then three hundred years of national momentum and symbolic power would belong to conservatives. This national identity crisis played a large role in taking Republicans from their own funeral in 1964 to a third of a century of domination starting in 1968. What mattered most wasn't that liberals were right about Vietnam but that Americans hated to admit they were right because this meant that American myth was wrong. What mattered most wasn't that liberals might have useful ideas for addressing economic barriers but that Americans hated to admit that these barriers were real and that the American Dream wasn't so real. For American liberalism this was a terrible impasse and dilemma. Liberals had correctly recognized that American myth was failing, but when they tried to talk with the voters about it, the voters didn't want to hear it. This would have been a losing situation for liberals even if they had handled it perfectly, but they didn't. Between intellectual leaders refusing to speak in any language but class and empire, and political leaders unable to speak in any language but the formulas that had worked for FDR, the liberal response was hugely confused and ineffective. In a culture where the ongoing central political question was about national identity, conservatives understood that the Pledge of Allegiance connected with powerful currents, but to liberals this was merely a "wedge issue" distracting voters from the real (economic) issues. It's not about ideology, Democrats would say, but it was about ideology, and not just the ideology of taxes but the core ideas of American identity, just as the American Revolution was not about tea taxes but about identity.

We sped down the road to Concord, down the route of Paul Revere who called out history's summons: "The Americans are coming!" But I'll come back to Concord on the 4th.

I hardly thought about it at the time, but every time I hit the road with John Kerry I was carefully studying the ongoing separation of liberalism from symbols loaded with 200 years of power. To effectively scout through crowds for appropriate voters I had to develop a quick, intuitive eye for what a prospective Kerry voter looked like. The politicization of hair styles and clothing styles proved very useful. By 1972 another thing that had become very politicized was the American flag. Many conservatives wore it not just as a flag but as a political statement, and liberals were surrendering the flag. Through trial and error it became one of my search rules that if someone was wearing an American flag, I wouldn't ask them if they wanted to meet Kerry. But for the 4ᵗʰ of July there were far more American flags being worn than usual, and they were playing tricks with my search rules, forcing me to think more about the meaning of American flags. I skipped people who, I soon observed, were quite happy to meet Kerry, liberals whose 4ᵗʰ of July patriotism ran much deeper than the troubles and symbols of the moment. In working a Lowell crowd I suspended my flag rule, but it turned out there was still a high correlation between the flag and hostility to Kerry. There were definitely more American flags being worn in Lowell than in Lexington and Concord. I wasn't contemplating the implications of all this, but there was a clear danger in liberals surrendering symbols bearing 200 years of power even in the towns where that power was born, for those symbols and myths were connected with political power too, which liberals also risked losing. The losers would include the flag wearers of Lowell, for the revolution they were hailing was the Jeffersonian Revolution, the dream of agrarian democracy, a dream that had had a textile spindle driven into its heart by Lowell itself, by the industrial revolution, a dream that liberals had tried to restore on new terms.

The 4ᵗʰ of July blared forth gloriously from a marching band playing patriotic marches. The American flags paraded down the street. Around here 4ᵗʰ of July parades included a fife-and-drum corps and a platoon of revolutionary war soldiers. The crowd was enormous. Lots of people were applauding and waving at John and Julia, but some were booing and thumbs-downing. Some people were offended that John Kerry had the gall to march in a 4ᵗʰ of July parade.

In October Kerry would march in the Veteran's Day parade in Lowell, and the Lowell newspaper, in the midst of a barrage of articles attacking Kerry as a traitor, made the most of Kerry's participation, running an article about it with a huge photo showing Kerry looking uncomfortable, the veteran behind him giving him the evil eye. An editorial pointed out that in his famous speech before congress Kerry said that VVAWs would not soon be marching in Veteran's Day parades. But only a year later Kerry was indeed marching in a Veteran's Day parade. This proved that, while Kerry remained a traitor and a fanatical and dangerous leftwing anti-American ideologue, he was also a shameless opportunist who'd never meant anything he'd said and would do anything for votes.

It was a very busy 4th, with Kerry going to nine events all over the district: breakfasts, picnics, band concerts, and two fireworks events. In the car between events all weekend John and Julia would talk, things very personal and candid—there was only the driver and me—things about America on it's birthday, with no thought of hiding who John Kerry really was and where he was coming from. I came to understand, for example, how someone could feel such a deep sense of betrayal at the discrepancy between myth and reality in Vietnam and such urgency about telling the reality that he would commit political suicide, wrecking a promising career before it began by running in a district where too much reality was not welcome.

We sped down the road to Concord, and today the flags were out, flags on porches and street lights and stores, flags saluting the wind. In Concord we went to a neighborhood picnic. The campaign had decided that this would make a good photo opportunity and had dispatched a photographer to record John Kerry in Concord on the 4th of July with happy kids in Uncle Sam hats, with happy families picnicking before American flags. We were also surrounded by the ghosts of Emerson and American history.

Even before the Civil War, with slavery crippling America's moral claims and threatening the union, with Emerson a lonely champion of abolition and women's rights, Emerson had remained a strong believer in America's destiny of remaking the world. After the Civil War, even in the thick of Gilded Age greed and Wild West individualism, his faith continued. Emerson was still hearing the cannons of the Civil War when he wrote *The Fortune of the Republic* in 1878, one of his final public lectures:

> There have been revolutions which are not in the interests of feudalism and barbarism, but in that of society. And these are distinguished not by the number of combatants nor the numbers of the slain, but by the motive. No interest now attaches to the wars of York and Lancaster, to the wars of German, French and Spanish emperors, which were only dynastic wars, but to those in which a principle was involved. These are read with passionate interest and

never lose their pathos by time. When the cannon is aimed by ideas, when men with religious convictions are behind it, when men die for what they live for, and the mainspring that works daily urges them to hazard all, then the cannon articulates its explosions with the voice of a man, then the rifle seconds the cannon and the fowling-piece the rifle…then the gods join in the combat; then poets are born, and the better code of laws at last records the victory.

Now the culmination of these triumphs of humanity—and which did virtually include the extinction of slavery—is the planting of America.

At every moment some one country more than any other represents the sentiment and the future of mankind. None will doubt that America occupies this place in the opinion of nations, as is proved by the fact of the vast immigration into this country from all the nations of western and central Europe.[2]

It was all here: the sense of American destiny, the call of Ellis Island, the conviction that America was the vanguard of human progress, even the conviction that the gods themselves stood ready to man America's cannons. No listener would question Emerson's famously liberal values and goals:

Humanity asks that government shall not be ashamed to be tender and paternal, but that democratic institutions shall be more thoughtful for the interests of women, for the training of children, and for the welfare of sick and unable persons…than was ever any the best government of the Old World.[3]

Yet in hands less sophisticated and less humane than Emerson's, America's sense of destiny and America's cannons could easily lose their aim, could end up serving only greed and individualism. Emerson understood that it would be an ongoing struggle to shape America in a wise and humane direction. He had tried to do this by being an outspoken abolitionist. Concord had been a major center of abolitionism; Emerson and Thoreau had been among the Concord crowd warmly welcoming John Brown. When John Brown became a spark for the Civil War, Concord answered the fire. On the anniversary day of the battle of Concord, sixty-four Concord men, some of them descendants of the minutemen, gathered to join Lincoln's army. On the town green where Concord had celebrated the 4th of July for nearly a century, they ran up a flag and saluted it with a cannon boom. A crowd marched the soldiers to the train station and watched them disappear into Walden Woods and into the fire and charge and retreat and screams and doubt and hope of America's unending struggle for identity.

It wasn't sunshine patriotism but the crisis of the Civil War that prompted Longfellow to write "Paul Revere's Ride." The "midnight" in "Listen, my children, and you shall hear/of the midnight ride of Paul Revere" was suggestive of the dark doubt that America faced about its future and its promise. Longfellow wanted to summon the spirit and resilience of the minutemen.

> It was one by the village clock,
> When he galloped into Lexington…
> It was two by the village clock,
> When he came to the bridge in Concord town.

Okay, okay, so Paul Revere was really captured on the road between Lexington and Concord and never made it to Concord. Longfellow knew that. Concord knew that. But we're talking myth here. Emerson and friends understood that myths are what empower nations and that if liberals wanted to guide America to a wise and humane destiny, they needed to summon from the raw materials of American history, however imperfect, the words and symbols that could compete with the myths of plantation gentility and Wild West rugged individualism and Gilded Age corporate empires and the U. S. Cavalry charging to the rescue. So Longfellow sent Paul Revere onward not just into the night but into the future to spread democratic hope:

> For, borne on the night-wind of the Past,
> Through all our history, to the last,
> In the hour of darkness and peril and need,
> The people will waken and listen to hear
> The hurrying hoof-beats of that steed,
> And the midnight ride of Paul Revere.

We sped down the highway, the flags everywhere, the flags borne on the night-wind of the Past.

As the day wore on Kerry seemed to be wearing out, but at the two fireworks events he was fired up again, shaking hands at a vigorous pace. Finally it was dark and time for the fireworks. BOOM! And the rocket's red glare, the fireworks bursting in air. BOOM! Gave proof through the night that our flag was still there. BOOM! Red, white, and blue flowers were blooming all over America. BOOM! They say that many Vietnam veterans, suffering from post-traumatic stress disorder, couldn't hear a loud noise without flinching just as they had flinched in a jungle full of ambushes. BOOM! Now that would be a sad symbol, wouldn't it? Because of Vietnam, John Kerry flinching from the celebration of America. BOOM! I really wasn't paying much attention; it was dark and I was watching the fireworks. BOOM! As far as I noticed, John Kerry wasn't flinching. BOOM! Maybe American liberalism was flinching from even an Emersonian celebration of America. BOOM! But that wasn't the problem. BOOM! The problem was that America was flinching from facing the explosion of its myths. BOOM! And those who refuse to learn from history—BOOM! BOOM! BOOM! BOOM! BOOM!

2

The War of the Worlds

There was one thing about the 4th of July parade in Flagstaff, Arizona, that you could always count on, one thing that was always guaranteed to elicit the greatest applause from the crowd, and not just applause but a standing ovation that rolled loudly down the street like a wave. It wasn't the usual Americana of 4th of July parades everywhere—the flags, the patriotic floats, the antique cars. It wasn't the cowboys on horses. It wasn't the Native Americans in fancy pow wow costumes. It wasn't the old World War Two veterans carrying the Marine flag. It wasn't even the Iraq war veterans just off the plane.

The loudest applause was always for the Native American veterans, for marine and army uniforms just as proudly cleaned and creased yet worn by Navajo faces bearing the fingerprint of the hard red rock creases and master dust of the desert. The crowd sees them coming and begins to rise even before they get here, or if people are already standing they begin to applaud, or if they are already applauding they begin to applaud louder, their hands raised higher. Then come the Navajo veterans of World War Two, and they get nearly the loudest applause of all, for they are so old and bent that they are mostly riding and not walking and they have little time remaining in which to be applauded. But the loudest applause of all comes for the Navajo code talkers, who placed at the service of America not just their bodies but their culture, a language that planted upon the beaches of the South Pacific the flag of sunburned words for southwestern desert sand. Everyone here knows about the code talkers, for many code talkers came from around here and many are still here, and the most distinguished statue in town is R. C. Gorman's tribute to his code talker father who had lived here. Now everyone in America knows about the code talkers, for recently Hollywood made a movie about them. Yet the local Navajo veterans are seriously irked at this movie over one thing, for some white bleeding-heart liberal Hollywood screenwriter had manipulated history to try to manipulate the public into having a white liberal guilt-trip, inserting a storyline about how the white officers who commanded the code talkers were under orders to kill them rather than let them be captured by the Japanese, a storyline that implied that the Navajos were valued only as military tools and not as people or heroes; but this storyline hadn't ever happened, it was just the old white liberal guilt-trip bullshit denying the pride the military had taken in them and the pride they had taken in serving their country.

The standing ovation rolls on and on from block to block, and if you look around you can see people with damp eyes. The hundreds of Navajo children in the crowd, which is about one-quarter Native American, watch with special fascination, certainly noticing all the white folks cheering for Navajos.

The Navajos were good at marching, for they had been given plenty of practice at it. In the 1860s the U. S. army rounded up the Navajos to evict them from their Four Corners homeland and resettle them where they could be taught to live like Americans. To force the Navajos to surrender, the army practiced a scorched-earth policy, burning their hogans and crops and shooting their livestock. The Navajos were marched hundreds of miles in the middle of winter with inadequate provisions. Hundreds died along the way. By some accounts, those who could not keep up were simply shot. All of this was done for the Navajo's own good, just as it was for the Navajo's own good that generations of their children would be shipped off to BIA boarding schools to be dressed like white children, to worship the white man's god, and to speak—under threat of beatings—only the white man's language, for the Navajo language was primitive and utterly useless. All of this was done for the Navajo's own good because the Navajos were evildoers who for no reason at all were committing acts of terrorism against Americans. To solve this problem all it would take was a quick intervention of American military superiority and then the Navajos would be eager to become good Americans, living in towns and farming and running shops and practicing a miniature version of American democracy.

But someone neglected the postwar plans. The thousands of Navajos arriving at Bosque Redondo found seriously inadequate food, clothing, housing, firewood, and tools for farming. There were soon more people than the area could possibly sustain. When the crops repeatedly failed, the Navajos were placed on starvation rations and ordered shot if they tried to steal food or escape. Epidemics swept through the population. Adding to the trauma was the psychological stress of being forced to adopt starkly new lifeways and social structures, some of them based on serious misunderstandings of Navajo ways. It took several years for the U. S. government to admit it had bitten off more than it could chew and let the Navajos go home.

One of the traits the U. S. army had wanted to extinguish was the Navajo code of the warrior, in which fighting for your tribe won the highest honor. You could see this warrior pride still alive in these faces marching down the street, the pride of having fought the evildoers in Vietnam and Iraq.

If ever you wanted a symbol that combined all the power and pain and paradox of American history and identity and destiny, here it was, marching right towards you. You didn't have to be any kind of poet or historian to recognize this symbolism and feel its power. Its power was stirring this crowd of ordinary Americans to their feet, to stand there in awe before their national story made manifest.

Partly it was the power of guilt, not just the classroom guilt of knowing that someone had been wronged long ago, but the more personal guilt of standing next to someone whose utterly useless language had carried for 150 years the sorrow of an ancestor who had been forced to march to Bosque Redondo, a sorrow retold again in some lonely South Pacific island camp. It was the guilt of a redneck clerk who recalled having snubbed a Navajo customer in the store only last week and who now wondered if that slow, dumb old man had once done more for America than he ever would. It was the guilt of a liberal lady professor who saw the loyalty of Navajos to America and now wondered who she was to be so grudging and ungrateful.

Partly it was the power of gratitude, the religious gratitude of being forgiven for a heavy sin, forgiven to the point that now the Navajos would crucify themselves to save the white man.

But mainly it was sheer awe at the relentless centuries-old parade that had swept across an ocean and swept across an entire continent and swept the ancient mountains into iron horses sweeping the prairie night with a beacon looking ever forward and swept the iron despots from their fortresses and filled the poor world's eyes with visions of possibility and finally transformed itself into—and even transformed the long despairing march to Bosque Redondo into—this very parade of army uniforms proudly worn and flags proudly sweeping down the street. It was awe for the powerful march of American identity.

To get here from Lexington, American identity had marched nearly across a continent. It had marched into a different ecosystem yet brought with it lawns and parks like the Lexington green, even though here you had to force a green lawn to grow against the wishes of nature. From Lexington a town-square civic culture had rolled solidly through the Midwest, but here in the Southwest the town layouts were stretched thin by the railroad and then by Rt. 66, stretched thin by the incessant motion of Americans.

Yet Massachusetts was not so far away. Flagstaff owed its name to a group of fifty pioneers from Boston who camped here on the 4th of July of 1876. It was the American centennial and the rest of America was celebrating wildly, and these Bostonians turned a pine tree into a flagpole and raised their American flag. When they moved on they took the flag with them, but others started referring to this spot as "the flagstaff." Thus our 4th of July parades were also a birthday party for the town.

No one paid much attention to Flagstaff until another man from Boston came along, Percival Lowell, scion of the Lowell family that had built the textile mills and town of Lowell, Massachusetts. Percival Lowell decided that Flagstaff, with its high altitude and dry air, was the best location for building his astronomical observatory. In 1930 Lowell Observatory discovered the planet Pluto, and Flagstaff became world famous. Percival Lowell had initiated the search for a new planet as a way of redeeming Lowell Observatory from the ridicule it had accumulated due to Percival's obsession with the idea that Mars held an advanced civilization with an intricate planet-wide system of canals.

Back in Lowell, Massachusetts, I had walked between home and Kerry headquarters and I crossed the long bridge over the Concord River, just above where it merged with the Merrimack River. A thirty-two-foot falls on the Merrimack River was why Lowell was there. Water was diverted from the Merrimack and through an intricate system of canals to supply water power to the mills. I also crossed one of these canals, and sometimes I paused to look down at it. Like much of Lowell, its canals were a sluggish remnant of a once mighty energy. The canals that had once surged with a power that made hundreds of looms roar, that had once flowed red or green depending on what color of dye was being used that morning, were now dry or merely stagnant pools smelly with dead cats.

Percival Lowell too had plenty of opportunity to study the canals of Lowell. For several years Percival worked in the family business and his duties included making a weekly trip from Boston to Lowell to deliver the payroll. Percival saw one of the wonders of the industrial world, canals and mills roaring with power, pouring power and money and fame onto the Lowell family. It would have been natural enough for Percival to develop an unusual and strong personal identification with an intricate system of canals.

In the 1880s Percival was pursuing a career as an anthropologist when he was riveted by an astronomical report that the planet Mars bore strange markings. Percival was sure that these markings were an intricate system of canals, and he plunged into astronomy, building Lowell Observatory in 1894 just to study the Martian canals. The observatory sits on a mesa overlooking downtown Flagstaff, a mesa Percival named Mars Hill. Thus today's 4ᵗʰ of July parade was presided over by the Roman god of war.

Percival spent years observing Mars and drawing detailed maps of the canal systems. Astronomers back east complained that they couldn't see any such lines, and they decided that Percival was hallucinating.

Percival mapped out not just the canals but an anthropology of Mars. He started out with a theory of solar system evolution in which the farther out a planet was, the older it was, and thus Mars was older than Earth and its oceans had dried up and the only remaining water was locked in the polar caps. To survive, Martian civilization, which was also older than Earth's, had to build an intricate system of canals to transfer water from the polar caps to the rest of the planet. The canals proved several things about Martian civilization. First, Martians had plenty of Yankee ingenuity. Second, Mars must be ruled by an oligarchy, for only an oligarchy had the wisdom and organizational ability to carry out such a huge task. Mars could not be run by liberals and absolutely could not have labor unions, for labor unions would have disrupted the building and operation of the canals. Mars was, in short, just a giant version of Lowell, Massachusetts, or at least the company-town way the Lowells had tried to run it. Yet Percival supposed that the Martians had evolved beyond humans, their survival imperative forcing them to put aside warfare and contending nationalities.

Of course the real Mars was just empty plains, empty mountains, empty canyons, just blowing sand, just creeping and retreating frost, just dead volcanoes and dry river valleys. The dust storms were just a screen onto which Percival was projecting a movie. He turned the red plains red, white, and blue. He turned the boulder fields into a crowd of American oligarchs. Through him the huge momentum of American identity, which had already filled a continent and which after all was destined to fill the Earth, imprinted itself upon a whole other planet.

The writers would eagerly fill in the blanks. Edgar Rice Burroughs plucks his hero, Virginian and Confederate officer John Carter, out of the middle of a fight with Arizona Apaches and transports him to Mars to engage in cavalier adventures. Like Percival Lowell, Burroughs hated labor unions, and he wrote one novel in which liberals took over Earth and imposed universal disarmament only to learn their lesson when the Moon Men invaded Earth. H. G. Wells didn't see any reason why a superior civilization would sit on Mars and die when there was a perfectly good planet next door, so in the heyday of imperialism he sent the Martians to Britain to teach it a lesson.

Orson Welles had the Martians land in America in his 1938 nationwide faux-news radio version of *The War of the Worlds*. From coast to coast people panicked at the reports of invading Martians armed with WMDs (weapons of Mars destruction). In city after city hundreds of people massed in the streets and the churches and the railroad stations, their eyes and mouths wide with fear. From the cities cars poured out into the countryside, heads looking back to see if the cities were already burning. People wrapped their faces in handkerchiefs to ward off poison gasses. Several people decided that instead of waiting for a grizzly death at the hands of the Martians it was better to commit suicide. And while Americans were panicking in the streets, the dead red sands of Mars continued blowing as they always had, piling up in an hourglass of the eons and draining away again, completely oblivious of America. It was a ghost Americans were fleeing, the ghost of ourselves, a self-image projected onto the cosmos and mirrored back at us; it was our own national identity that terrorized us.

Thus in today's parade of American identities beneath Mars Hill, just between the Navajo code talkers and Percival Lowell's 1910 luxury car, we are presented with one identity that is so powerfully appealing that even the grandsons of those crushed by it were eager to enlist in it and proud to wear its uniform, and another identity that had passed beyond reason and become a Frankenstein driving its own people mad. Which of these identities was the truth of American history? Or were both of them true? Did Americans even know their own true identity? Or was it the ultimate identity of America that America had been born without any clear identity and we had been searching for it ever since?

On the original 4th of July even the most visionary of the men in Independence Hall weren't sure what democracy was all about. All Americans had to go on were the histories of Greece and Rome, which seemed too much like ancient history and too little like blueprints for the American future. The founders couldn't grasp the scope and potential of the continent we had beach-headed and they couldn't imagine how the technological inventiveness stirred by the challenges of settling that continent would generate a new world of economic power. At least, by whatever mixture of vision and luck, the founders created an open-ended form of government that allowed America to go on inventing itself anew. To a nation with an unknown identity came millions of immigrants who felt not just a national hunger for identity but a personal hunger, for they had left their old social contexts back in Europe and arrived in America naked of identity and eager to make one. Thus the national quest for identity was refueled by every new foot stepping onto Ellis Island.

Today's parade of American identities is taking place on the main highway of America's search for itself. The parade will go right past a hotel where a century ago Zane Grey lived and wrote, inventing the western, the largest myth of American identity. The parade will go right past another hotel where in the heyday of western movies many stars stayed while filming nearby, including John Wayne. The whole nation knows the name of our main street, Route 66, which is synonymous with journeying in search of America. Up our main street the Joads struggled in *The Grapes of Wrath* ("And then the tall trees began, and the cars spouted steam and labored up the slopes. And there was Flagstaff, and that was the top of it all")[4] in search of an American Dream still un-wrecked by greed. Down our main street Jack Kerouac passed in *On the Road* in search of a beatnik American Dream. A generation later the heroes of *Easy Rider* rode through downtown Flagstaff to the opening song "Born to be Wild," and a generation after that, Forrest Gump jogged through downtown Flagstaff on a coast-to-coast quest for something he couldn't define.

Thus today's parade is taking place in a mythic landscape. Not only that, this mythic landscape seems to be giving us an odd sign that the 2004 presidential campaign is fully a part of the archetypal landscape of America's search for itself. As the Easy Riders and Forrest Gump roll through downtown Flagstaff we glimpse only a few buildings, but they include the two future Kerry headquarters, for the primary and fall campaigns. Even more unlikely, the one block up which Forrest Gump jogs is the same block up which, a few weeks from now, John Kerry will walk from the train station to a massive downtown rally. The mythic possibilities of this situation invite us to pause for a moment and ask, at least, where Forrest Gump was going.

It turns out that Forrest Gump and the Easy Riders were heading for the same place, the same place where John Wayne hung out for years, Monument Valley, the unreal Martian landscape of Gothic red rock spires and buttes. Director John Ford was enthralled with Monument Valley and turned it into the quintessential landscape of the West, using it in classic movies like *Stagecoach* and *She Wore a Yellow Ribbon*. When John Ford made *The Grapes of Wrath* he probably would have made the Joads drive through Monument Valley if he could have gotten away with it. Tom Joad's son, Peter Fonda, understood the mythic dimensions of Monument Valley and rode into the sunset there just like John Wayne, if on a motorcycle instead of a horse. Forrest Gump had a moment of revelation there and, after jogging coast-to-coast several times in search of America and himself, finally decided he was finished running.

Yet if John Wayne and Jane Fonda's brother were in complete accord about the iconic value of Monument Valley, there were some unsettled issues. John Ford repeatedly hired local Navajos to play the bad guys who swept over the hills like demons, like red Martians invading America, requiring John Wayne and the cavalry to fend them off. Some of these Navajos had recently stormed the beaches of the South Pacific, and perhaps even been code talkers, but now they needed the bucks and so signed up to play Martians invading American destiny. John Ford had a tender social conscience but didn't shy away from the standard demonology regarding Native Americans.

Peter Fonda, on the other hand, was cruising a Rousseauan landscape of noble savages who could teach confused white people how to belong to the tribe and to the earth. Fonda camps in a Monument Valley ruin and communes with the spirits, and next he visits a commune in which suburban white kids are rather pathetically trying to live like Native Americans.

Like Mars, the spires of Monument Valley were oblivious of the national iconography that Americans were projecting onto them, projecting now from two different mental worlds.

If in 2004 John Wayne or the Easy Riders or Forrest Gump were to ride the road from Flagstaff to the setting of *She Wore a Yellow Ribbon*, they would indeed see yellow ribbons along the way, yellow ribbons tied to the signposts of Native American towns, yellow ribbons flapping in the desert wind to remember the Navajo and Hopi soldiers fighting in Iraq, and in one town they would see not just yellow ribbons but memorials for a local girl, Lori Piestewa, the first female Native American U.S. soldier to die in combat. Lori's roommate and best friend Jessica Lynch had become a national hero for surviving the same attack and being taken prisoner and rescued. Lori had been driving the humvee in which Jessica was riding when they were hit by a rocket-propelled grenade.

Now here was another mystery to add to the mysteries of American identity.

For a thousand years the Hopis had practiced the science and art of surviving in the desert. Actually it was far more than a thousand years, for the Hopis are the remnant of the Anasazi, who filled the Southwest with stone cities. At the founding of Rome, long before Christianity, when most of the world had never heard of monotheism and went on worshipping nature gods like Mars, Hopi ancestors were already farming in the desert. The Roman Empire rose and fell, Christianity arose, Islam arose, Christianity and Islam went to war over the true definition of monotheism, Jews were persecuted over the true definition of monotheism, Anasazi civilization rose and fell, and all the while the Anasazi/Hopis just went on farming in the desert, now at a few villages that had reliable springs; the name Piestewa means "people who live by the water." One day, about 1,500 years after monotheism really got going, the Hopis finally heard the news when some Spanish conquistadors and missionaries showed up in their villages. But the collapse of Anasazi civilization in a severe drought a few centuries before had left the surviving Anasazi even more obsessively loyal to the gods who brought rain, and the Christian god was seriously clueless about bringing rain, so the Hopis burned down the Christian church and tossed the priests over the cliffs and went right on with ceremonies to summon the rain gods, who lived in the mountains looming over the future Flagstaff. (Thus today's parade is presided over not just by Mars but by the benevolent Hopi gods of desert survival). One day the Hopis heard the news that the monotheists were at it again, this time all three branches of monotheism at once, for the Jews had gotten tired of being persecuted by the Christians and gone home to be persecuted by the Muslims, and now the monotheists were proclaiming God's universal love by crashing jetliners full of innocent people into skyscrapers full of innocent people, and thus Hopis like Lori were sent to another desert halfway around the world where survival required not kachina masks but gas masks, not cornmeal tossed into the sky but missiles; where directions were defined not by the sacred mountain on the horizon but by a GPS unit and a CD-Rom road map which still couldn't save the white commander from sending Lori down the wrong road and right into an enemy town where she was ambushed. What a strange fate and country where a Hopi ends up dying in a desert as distant as Mars to defend American identity.

This was the strange street up which John Kerry will be walking in a few weeks. As he walks he will pass several shops with Hopi kachina dolls and Navajo rugs in the windows. The kachina dolls, made from cottonwood roots gathered from sandstone canyon riverbanks, will stare at him with millennia of secret knowledge of the American land, and the Navajo rugs, made from sheep who know every green nook in Monument Valley, are spread out like coded maps of experience that white people can only try to decipher.

The debate over American national mythology, including its demonology of Native Americans, was also taking place on these streets, but not quite in the same way it was occurring elsewhere.

The healthy revisionist impulse that had started out a third of a century ago was still going strong, but because America's self-congratulatory myths were incredibly powerful and unyielding, the revisionist antidote and counterbalance had often hardened into nothing but an anti-image, an obsessive mirror image that offered only the negatives about America, and offered conservatives substantial mileage in attacking liberals as "America haters."

Elsewhere in America liberals who had never even met a real Native American were waging wars over the Indian mascots of college sports teams and accusing professors of racism for using the word "Indian" instead of "Native American." One of the hotels we will pass in today's parade was Democrat-owned and hosted the monthly meeting of a group of extra-liberal Democrats, chaired by a guy who was both black and gay and who served on every human rights commission in the state, and recently the speaker was a Berkeley-educated Navajo, a former Democratic candidate for congress, speaking in favor of affirmative action for Native Americans. Surely here of all places we would be using the politically correct "Native American." Forget it. He always said "Indian," and no one in the room took the slightest notice, for we lived in the real world where Native Americans are not just the team mascots of liberal righteousness but real people trying to live terribly complicated lives. For a Navajo candidate for congress to use the term "Native American" was to risk alienating Navajo voters by branding himself a product of a white world that still presumed to impose its good intentions upon Navajos for their own good. For the thousand-or-so Navajo college students in town, many of whom attended a Navajo high school with a fierce-looking "Warrior" mascot, the rich-white-kid fights over football mascots seem frivolous compared with their struggles to get through college.

Elsewhere, Bosque Redondo has become a leading exhibit in the case for America being a fascist empire. The arguments over Bosque Redondo have been especially vigorous because they center on Kit Cason, who in American myth is one of the most romantic heroes of national expansion. But it was Kit Carson who was in charge of rounding up the Navajos and marching them off to Bosque Redondo, so in revisionist history Carson has become a genocidal monster. Someone stole into his cemetery at night and painted swastikas on his grave and the grave of his wife—his Hispanic wife, not his nature-buried first two wives, who were Native American.

It's harder to find such righteousness on the streets of Flagstaff, for this is the real world of paradox and pain. When Kit Carson rounded up the Navajos and marched them off, the pueblo tribes, including the Hopis, rejoiced greatly, for they had been pleading to the U.S. government for years to stop Navajo raids against them. The Utes flocked to join Kit Carson to fight the Navajos. The Hispanics of New Mexico rejoiced too. When the Navajos finally left Bosque Redondo it started over a century of Hopi despair, for the Navajos started encroaching on Hopi lands.

There are also Hopi veterans marching in today's parade, but they won't be marching among the Navajos. The Hopi tribe is so determined to remain separate from the Navajos they they've arranged one of the most bizarre acts of congressional gerrymandering in American history. The Hopi villages, which are surrounded by Navajo land, are connected to the other end of the state by a thin, basically imaginary umbilical cord that snakes hundreds of miles across the desert and into the Grand Canyon and follows the Colorado River all the way through the Grand Canyon. The Hopis would rather share a district with Mormon polygamists and redneck ranchers than with their fellow Native Americans.

The Native Americans on these streets understand that the debate over Native iconography is only partly about them, and is heavily about white America wrestling with its own identity.

Today's parade will pass by an old downtown movie theater where once, with an audience largely of Navajos and Hopis, I watched *Dances with Wolves*. The movie had been out for many weeks and local whites had seen it, but the word was still spreading out on the rez so now Navajos and Hopis coming into town on weekends to do their shopping made up a large majority of the audience. They thoroughly enjoyed the parts of the movie depicting white people as crazy fools. But there was also laughter at scenes which the moviemakers had not intended to be funny, and there were scenes intended to be profound which evoked only a puzzled reaction. *Dances with Wolves* was aimed at a white audience, aimed to push the buttons of white liberal guilt and American loneliness at not knowing how to belong to a tribe and to the earth. A couple of scenes were intended to enthrall whites with the mystic oneness of Natives with the earth but brought a mixture of laughter and puzzled mumbling. This was a sensitive subject around here, for we were only thirty miles from Sedona, the national capital of Twinkee spirituality, filled with phony rent-a-shamans and cartoon versions of Native cosmologies. The scenes where Kevin Costner yearned to be a Native seemed dismally familiar here, and I could almost hear some of my neighbors wondering which was worse: being shot by John Wayne, or having your ancient and very private spiritual life looted by creeps? Then there were the scenes in which the Sioux/Lakota were fighting the Pawnee, and the audience was clearly expected to root for the Sioux, apparently just because the white hero has randomly attached himself to the Sioux and not the Pawnee. Many of the teenagers in the audience did indeed cheer for the good Sioux against the bad Pawnee, but this theater also held centuries of bitterness between the Navajos and Hopis, both of whom are now bitter at the white man for managing their conflict so poorly, and some viewers were not amused that even in a movie meant to expiate the white man's sins, whites still reserved the right to define who was good and who was bad by who gets in the way of a white man's destiny.

Native Americans were only the first of many peoples to get in the way of American destiny and be demonized for it, and it wasn't just a matter of race, although race made things easier. Europeans too were demonized, first the British, then the Spanish, the Germans, the Russians, and recently the French for doubting American destiny in Iraq. Then there were the liberals, demonized for a third of a century now for casting doubt on American destiny.

American destiny was more than just the Manifest Destiny of filling up a continent, and even our Manifest Destiny was held to be different from the expansions of European empires, which were only about power and wealth. America belonged to a handful of nations that had a larger sense of mission. Our Enlightenment confidence in remaking the world seemed amply proven by all the machines invented by American reason. Surely it was a sign of God's blessing that America was given a vast rich continent to make our own.

A few times America has collided with nations with a sense of destiny similar to our own. Marxism too was steeped in Enlightenment confidence about remaking the world, and after a further century of technological progress, it was even more confident about re-engineering the human soul. Yet while the American Enlightenment came from a land where anyone was free to wander west and make a fresh start, Marxism was born in a prison built by centuries of feudalism, where the only exit was to smash down the walls. America and Marxism confronted one another with such passionate convictions of destiny that both were quite ready to destroy the human race in the name of saving the human race. Nazism too had a strong sense of destiny, though its god was sheer power. And then there was Islam, whose sense of destiny was so intense that Mohammed, unlike the role models of other religions, was soon astride a horse and wielding a sword and leading armies against the infidels, armies that within a century would sweep across infidels for thousands of miles. When Islamic destiny literally collided with American destiny on September 11, all that President Bush needed to do was to define them as "evildoers" who "hate us for our freedom" to mobilize America's long-proven confidence that the world was only waiting to be remade in our image.

We don't have to look far for the evildoers, for as we Kerry supporters are standing here on a side street waiting for our turn to join the moving parade, a crazy sneering Muslim wearing a fez hat with a sword on it comes up to us and starts to urinate on the American flag. Well, actually, maybe I'd better explain this in further detail.

By chance the Kerry contingent has been placed to march right behind the Shriners, the guys in little cars making frantic circles in parades all over America. The Shriners were an offshoot of the Masons and they built their own elaborate ritualistic world out of Islamic raw materials. When the Shriners emerged in the 1870s America had had virtually no experience of the Islamic world and it remained strictly a fairy-tale world of magic lamps, genies, flying carpets, exotic dancing girls, and kings no more solid than King Arthur. Numerous fraternal orders sprang up in the late 1800s, often founded around a religious, ethnic, or occupational group, answering America's hunger for identity and community and social services; the Shriners built a network of charity hospitals. The Shriners, whose official name is "Ancient Arabic Order of the Nobles of the Mystic Shrine," built their temples to look like mosques and gave each one an Islamic name, such as the Bagdad Temple in Butte, Montana, and the Mohammed Temple in Peoria. On the long list of temple names the only anomaly is the Ben Hur Temple, named for the movie with a Christian gladiator hero, located in Austin, Texas, the gubernatorial home of George W. Bush. The Shriners adopted Arabic words as secret passwords and for a uniform adopted the red fez hat bearing a sword and the half-moon and star that appear on many Muslim national flags. Recently the Shriners have added a new feature to their parades, a six-foot-tall walking fez hat with a cartoon face and the name Fez Head Fred. Unfortunately Fez Head Fred couldn't join us today.

The usual contribution of local Democrats to the 4th of July parade is to carry a truly gigantic American flag that once flew over an Ohio car dealership to imply that patriotism required you to buy your car there. But recently a creative contingent of Howard Dean supporters has joined the local Kerry campaign and they've decided that the Democratic Party needs to be livened up not just ideologically but in the parade department too, so they've organized a Kazoos for Kerry band with Uncle Sam hats, and a Kerry impersonator. Some people have set their Uncle Sam hats on the pavement. A Shriner had been eyeing us with contempt, and now he walked over to one of the hats, pretended to unzip his pants and pee into the hat, and sneered at us and walked away.

Now here is an image worth contemplating: a man with an utterly cartoonish image of the Muslim world, combined with a firm faith in American destiny, is making a stinky mess of things for Uncle Sam.

Thirty-two years after I marched behind John Kerry in a 4th of July parade, here I was marching behind him again and passing out volunteer cards. Or at least, I was marching behind our Kerry impersonator, who wears a Kerryesque wig and holds up a Kerry photo-face on a stick, like a mask from a Greek chorus. Guarding him are two faux Secret Service agents with suits, sunglasses, and radio cords going from their collars to their ears.

The real John Kerry is marching in a parade in Iowa today, and in Dyserville he is playing baseball on the field used in *Field of Dreams*. It's supposed to be an all-American photo backdrop for the 4th of July, just like those happy picnicking families in Concord. But if you think about it, Kevin Costner was not a happy man in *Field of Dreams*, he was searching for something, something beyond the patriotic façade of baseball, just as he was searching for something in *Dances with Wolves*.

Just like the song says about getting your kicks on Rt. 66, I started to get a nostalgia kick from following John Kerry in a 4th of July parade and hunting for volunteers. But nostalgia has been known to kick back. Some of the memories being stirred up now by the reactions of the crowd are unpleasant flashbacks to 1972. I'm seeing angry facial expressions and thumbs-down hand gestures which might have been fingers-up gestures if not for all the children present; I'm hearing boos and accusations and even the old lines about Jane Fonda and going back to Hanoi where you belong.

A few weeks before, I'd marched in Flagstaff's Memorial Day parade, marched with some veterans for Kerry in uniforms and decorations. I was passing out flyers about Kerry's record on veteran's issues, searching the crowd for vets, and here too I'd met the old hostility. It was amazing how the feelings and phrases of betrayal had endured, even more amazing that vets too young to remember Vietnam had picked up the exact lingo about going back to Hanoi. No one mentioned Benedict Arnold; it seemed that Jane Fonda had thoroughly routed him. The hostility was all about Kerry betraying the code of soldierly heroism they needed to inhabit.

There were a fair number of Navajo vets in the Memorial Day crowd, and none of them barked at me. It wasn't because they didn't care about the code of soldierly heroism. On the contrary, whatever the economic desolations that pushed Native Americans into military careers, there was also a strong pull from an image of heroism that would finally bring respect both in American society and in Navajo society where being a defender of your people was highly honored. A few years of Bosque Redondo hadn't erased the Navajo code of the warrior, no more than a dozen years of Reconstruction had erased the Southern codes of military valor or white superiority—history lessons that might have tempered President Bush's confidence that the mere arrival of the American flag in Baghdad would quickly reconstruct ages of Middle Eastern society. The Navajos remembered not just their warrior code but the time when this code was not at the service of America but deployed against it, and they remembered that the American juggernaut was not always smart or kind or fair.

The still-bitter memories of Bosque Redondo here made it ironic that some of the standing ovation for the Navajo code talkers on this 4th of July was American self-congratulations that Indians with their famous warrior skills were now serving American identity, a proof of the totemic absorption Americans were aiming for by naming their attack helicopters 'Apaches' and their cruise missiles 'toma-hawks,' and when they yelled "Geronimo!" jumping out of planes. It was the same confirmation Americans received in the Cold War hack science fiction movie *Red Planet Mars* when the Martians radioed their superior wisdom to Earth and it turned out that the "reds" were actually Christians and probably Americans too, thus setting off riots throughout the communist nations. God was also on our side in the Cold War movie version of *The War of the Worlds*, in which even atomic bombs couldn't slow down the Martians but then Americans went to church to pray and in the next scene the Martians all drop dead.

The Islamic terrorist who had peed in Uncle Sam's hat was now driving a bit aggressively, as if he wouldn't mind running over the toes of some Kerry support-ers. This man was one of the thousand points of light in charge of charitable work in America. Let every other nation in the Western world have a rational system for caring for the health of their citizens; we didn't need it: our health care was in the hands of circus clowns.

Now I was having another nostalgia kick-back. I was following closely behind "John Kerry" so I could see who was applauding him and zero in on them to offer them a volunteer card. But I noticed that as "John Kerry" reached out to the crowd, some people were refusing to shake his hand. I'd seen this before.

It struck me as incongruous, but clearly some people were greeting the Shri-ners by waving their little American flags even harder. A few people were happily waving their Bush signs at the cartoon Muslims in the cartoon cars. If only there were cartoon tanks we could pretend we were parading triumphantly through the streets of Iraq.

We were now parading through downtown, whose main feature was a brick plaza framed by two red buildings, one of which was owned by the Hopi tribe. Unlike the many tribes that had opened casinos, the Hopis had rejected gam-bling, twice voting it down in public elections, out of fear that casino culture would degrade Hopi culture. The Hopis were just as poor as other tribes but their long physical isolation had left their culture much more intact and they were struggling to keep it intact. Instead of opening casinos the Hopis were investing their limited money in businesses in places like Flagstaff. In addition to this downtown building the Hopis owned two small retail malls in town, one of which was called Kachina Square. But in the white man's argument over Ameri-can identity Kachina Square had been turned into a symbol of evil. A quick tour: when you drive down Sunset Boulevard out of Hollywood, passing all the facto-ries of American dreams, you go down the Sunset Strip loaded with stylish cafes and clubs and cars and people, and then you drive into Beverly Hills with its mansions, and after a few miles of Beverly Hills you arrive at UCLA, and if you had walked into the ornate museum there a few years ago you would have found on the wall a large photograph of the Kachina Square sign, representing evil. This photo belonged to the revisionist/postmodernist movement, whose main project was to document how capitalistic values corrupted everything they touched, and the purpose of this exhibit was to show how noble Native Americans had had their sacred cultural symbols stolen by white capitalists to make a buck. UCLA hadn't done its homework. In effect, a college of rich kids, with parking lots full of BMWs and Mercedes, was denouncing the dirt-poor Hopi tribe for trying to preserve their culture.

It was a shame that Fez Head Fred had missed this parade, for now we passed something he could relate to. The Fez hat was named for a Moroccan town not far from Casablanca, and now we were passing the Monte Vista Hotel where part of the film *Casablanca* was filmed. Or at least this was the legend. You could find this legend not only in the hotel's self-publicity but in books on film history and Arizona history. The problem was that nothing in *Casablanca* looked anything like the Monte Vista. The Monte Vista also claimed that Teddy Roosevelt had stayed there, although Teddy had died a decade before the Monte Vista was built. Humphrey Bogart really did stay there, so maybe this got mixed up with *Casablanca.* Whatever its origins, the *Casablanca* story was just another projection that had gotten out of hand, which was appropriate since the Monte Vista owed something to Percival Lowell. The Monte Vista was funded through a public subscription drive headed up by Lowell astronomer Vesto Slipher. To prove his theories about Martians, Percival Lowell had set Slipher to work studying spiral nebula, which Percival thought were other solar systems in various stages of formation. Slipher recorded the red shifts of these nebula, which were actually other galaxies, and Edwin Hubble would use this work to discover the expansion of the universe. So let this be a lesson to you: when you project American oligarchs and canals onto Mars, you can end up not only completely changing the entire universe but also filling up an Arizona hotel with imaginary Muslims in Fez hats, with Nazis and the French resistance, with Rick the American café owner who isn't sure if he wants to serve cynical self-interest or the cause of democracy. And when you place the Martians in the hands of Orson Welles then you fill American streets with terror, terror that was really only terror at our own image projected back at us from a red mirror, terror at our own cynicism come out dominant.

Yet America had projected a monster that was even more dangerous than invading Martians, for this monster was much harder to recognize and could easily be mistaken for something innocent and appealing. This was a projection we had been viewing for two hours now. It was simply a crowd lined up on sidewalks and cheering happily and waving American flags at American soldiers marching with American flags. The danger was that if this parade made you so proud of American destiny that you projected this parade onto the rest of the world, onto the streets of Hanoi and Baghdad, then you would expect even there a warm welcome of cheering crowds and waving American flags. The danger was projecting the canal-veined Ellis Island patriotism of Lowell, Massachusetts, onto alien worlds that did not understand it. The greatest monster was not Martians but simply innocence, a Rosebud crystal bubble of innocence that we lived inside and could not see out of with any clarity.

Through the night the train headlight searched, picking out icons of the American imagination like images in a dream: a sandstone cliff, a cluster of horses, the stone ruins of a pioneer house, a Navajo hogan, a long-abandoned Rt. 66 café. The Kerry post-convention-tour train was heading west alongside old Rt. 66, and before that it had followed the Santa Fe Trail from Kansas City, heading into the iconic western sunsets that drew alike John Wayne and the Joads and Jack Kerouac. John Kerry too was feeling the power of the westering road, and at his last stop in Arizona he stood in front of a trackside Harley motorcycle mural with images of Rt. 66, and he told the crowd that as the train was paralleling a long still-intact section of Rt. 66 into the sunset he had yearned to be on his Harley and feeling the western wind in his face.

Perhaps the pull of national destiny was not so strong for some of Kerry's companions on the train as he headed into Flagstaff, for he was talking with the leaders of the Navajo and Hopi tribes, whose destiny was not to fill up a continent and save the world, but just to stand there and watch the corn grow for two thousand years. The tribal leaders got on board at Gallup and would get off in Flagstaff, where the Navajo tribe would officially endorse Kerry to the Flagstaff rally. The last presidential candidate to come to Flagstaff was Robert Kennedy way back in 1968, when he'd held a hearing on Native American problems and insisted that America had to do better at tribal health care. Now the tribal leaders were sitting in the 1948 give-em-hell Dewey-Defeats-Truman railroad car from which Harry Truman had insisted that America had to do better at health care, and they were hearing John Kerry insist that America had to do better at tribal health care.

The stop at Gallup had been especially busy, for it coincided with the Gallup Intertribal Ceremonial, one of America's most famous pow wows. I received a firsthand account of the Gallup stop from a Cherokee with a thick Mississippi accent and the name Bubba McCloud; he was the driver of a Kerry campaign bus, which he'd driven coast-to-coast to take volunteers to events. Now, if any readers have a problem with Native Americans having names like Bubba McCloud, it might be said that this is a great name for real Native Americans tying to live real and very complicated lives, for the "cloud" invokes the nature/spiritual heritage and the "Bubba" invokes the guys tooling around on their pick-ups with country music blaring. Bubba had lived in a Mississippi trailer without electricity or water. He'd also danced in many pow wows. Anyway, a crowd of thousands of Natives greeted Kerry at the pow wow arena tucked into a red rock alcove. The Natives were so pleased that a presidential nominee would pay any attention to them that they didn't even mind the lines at the Secret Service security gates. This was a new experience both for the Native Americans and for the Secret Service. The Secret Service probably had their mythic alarms go off at the sight of hordes of savages trying to get at a candidate, and when the actual alarms went off for people in full pow wow costume, the Secret Service had to figure out the unfamiliar landscape of all those feathers and bells. For the Natives it was an honor to be granted the same citizenship ritual as any white crowd, to be granted full equality in a society full of lurking, grievance-filled, sociopathic loners like Lee Harvey Oswald. The drummers beat out a rhythm that had filled the American land long before the train appeared to imitate it.

Through the night, through the red rock cliffs echoing its rhythm, the train rolled on towards Flagstaff, hours late now, but when it pulled into the station the crowd was still there, over 10,000 people completely overflowing the downtown plaza and filling the surrounding streets, and for many the Kerry-logo-painted train engine was surreal, adding to the surrealism of the empty streets, the strange glows and shadows from the floodlights, and the police cars with flashing lights blocking off Rt. 66; for this was the actual heartbeat of American democracy, which usually happened somewhere else and was seen only through a TV screen.

Walking across an empty Rt. 66 full of ghosts, walking up the block up which Forrest Gump had jogged on his way to Monument Valley, John Kerry passed the kachina dolls and the Navajo rugs in the windows, followed by the living leaders of the Hopi and Navajo tribes. He was heading for the tall sandstone building painted with the antique sign: "Babbitt Brothers: Ranchers, Merchants, and Indian Traders," which was now the Colorado Plateau's leading wilderness outfitters store. This was the other building, along with the Hopi building, that framed the downtown plaza. The Babbitts were to northern Arizona what the Goldwaters were to southern Arizona, the longtime leading mercantile family.

It was in front of the Babbitt building that Forrest Gump obliviously ran right through a big pile of dog poop and thus coined the phrase "Shit Happens." Forrest Gump too was a decorated Vietnam War hero who found himself joining VVAW and addressing an anti-war rally in Washington. Forrest Gump had gone off to Vietnam oblivious of what he was doing, and he went through the next third of a century of national turmoil oblivious to what was going on around him. Many viewers of *Forrest Gump* found it perfectly charming that someone could live inside a bubble of innocence as America was losing its innocence; others weren't so sure. Our only interest here is that John Kerry is walking straight towards a spot where a famous personification of a third of a century of American history could either pay attention and take one step aside, or obliviously splat into a mess and justify it with "Shit Happens." As in, Vietnam happens.

John Kerry did step aside, if only because he was heading into Babbitt's, the staging and press room for the rally, where he was greeted by Jim Babbitt. Back in 1967 Jim Babbitt had taken part in the march on the Pentagon that Norman Mailer had chronicled in *The Armies of the Night*, which had starred poet Robert Lowell of Percival Lowell ancestry. Robert Lowell had seen no Martians invading Vietnam. Back in the primary campaign Jim had given the Kerry campaign free use of an empty storefront in another century-old Babbitt building. Along with Jim were his brothers Bruce, President Clinton's Secretary of the Interior; and Paul, this district's Democratic nominee for congress.

John Kerry walked out the back door and into the plaza, which was lit by floodlights much brighter than the candles that had lit a memorial vigil for Lori Piestewa here. He climbed onto the stage and looked out at the red brick building owned by the Hopi tribe and at the hotel where Zane Grey lived and wrote American mythology and at the giant American flag that had flown over an Ohio car dealership. Looming above us in the dark was the mountain where the Hopi kachina spirits lived. Kerry couldn't see it in the dark, but the stage pointed him straight at Mars Hill and Lowell Observatory and the glass-domed tomb of Percival Lowell, his skull now filled not with glorious projections but only with Martian dust. Rosebud.

But I could see it. Kerry started talking, and maybe he was thinking of the scene in *Field of Dreams* when the ghost players emerge from the corn and ask "Is this heaven?," for Kerry joked "We're at 7,000 feet, and we're getting close to heaven." He was close to the Martian canals anyway. As Kerry talked I was looking up at Mars Hill, and I thought of walking to work every day a third of a century ago and pausing over one of the canals and gazing down. John Kerry sure had come a long way since that 4th of July weekend when we'd wandered around the Lexington fairground looking for voters, when Kerry had seen not a child's merry-go-round but a troubling vision of America's future and stood there pointing at it and looking so sad. Now a third of a century was gone, and that future was here, but it was as if no time at all had passed, as if we were living in the same damn moment. America had not come a long way in that third of a century, for the same shit was still happening; we were still living under the sign of Mars.

Yet the crowd was filled with hopeful faces, faces getting a huge kick out of this event, faces not looking down into the canals of Lowell. In one respect we were clearly a long way from Lowell; this crowd was full of Native American faces. We were standing in a landscape of American myth, not a field of dreams but a highway of dreams, for no one place but only a motion was the truest symbol of America, the motion of searching for a dream of something greater. Native Americans had been standing in their fields watching the corn grow for a thousand years when the people of motion appeared as a dust cloud and swept through and engulfed them, when the Martians invaded, and they had watched in utter fascination ever since, watched as hunted animals hiding in the rocks, watched as American heroes guarding the code of victory, watched as shamans who were supposed to heal lonely whites, watched from old pickups broken down along the highway of dream cars, watched as America landed men on the moon and landed itself in deep-shit trouble, watched as America redefined itself over and over. And they were watching with fascination now, for this was the white man's greatest ceremonial dance for defining himself. Soon the train would be moving on to somewhere else. And as it moved, there would echo from the red rock cliffs the steady drumbeat of a ceremony.

3

Le Ordinary Guy

It's the role of a lifetime, being president of the United States, if only you can guess what the script is. To get elected you have to fit the script of American history, for one of the most important roles of a president is to embody American history and identity. But the script is always changing, and no one can tell you what the script is supposed to be now. Quite a few presidents have gotten elected by embodying safe, ongoing scripts from the past, but there are also times when the American people want the script to change, usually only modestly, sometimes a lot. But the American people don't necessarily know how or how much they want the script to change until presidential candidates show them what's possible by embodying various scripts.

You can map out America's changing sense of itself by some large-scale patterns in what Americans have wanted in presidents. For the first thirty years of the presidency, Americans definitely didn't want ordinary guys.

For one thing, ordinary guys couldn't speak French. It was very important that presidents speak French, read French, think French, dress French, and be liked by the French. It was best if presidents had served as the American representative to France, like John Adams, Thomas Jefferson, and James Monroe. Jefferson, Madison, Monroe, and John Quincy Adams all served as secretary of state, as if international experience was mandatory, which it basically was in a world where America was still a baby nation vulnerable to European empires, where America wouldn't have been born at all if not for the French. Two more future presidents, Van Buren and Buchanan, would serve as secretary of state by 1845, which was just about the time America had become an unassailable nation, and then the office of secretary of state completely ceased being a stepping stone to the presidency.

In a world long governed by aristocrats, Americans seemed to feel more secure and respectable when their presidents were more aristocratic, including those silly wigs. Some of this was probably due to the voting franchise starting off with an aristocratic tilt. Some of the founders of the republic didn't trust the ordinary guy all that much, fearing mob rule. Their worst fears seemed confirmed when a mob filled the White House upon the inauguration of the first un-aristocratic president, Andrew Jackson. Jackson was a product of the log-cabin frontier and had zero experience of Europe. But the republic survived, and ordinary guys loved Jackson so much that the rules for getting elected president changed dramatically. Now it was a disadvantage to have an aristocratic background and such a plus to have humble origins that William Henry Harrison, who grew up on a Virginia plantation, pretended to have come from a log cabin, and Abe Lincoln emphasized his log cabin roots and not his prosperous legal career.

Yet Jackson had one qualification that was not ordinary. He'd been a very successful general, fitting a pattern that cut across class origins. Four of the first twelve presidents (Washington, Jackson, Harrison, and Taylor) were generals. But then generals went out of style and it took the greatest of generals from the greatest of wars, Grant and Eisenhower, to break through. Generals went out of style at the exact same moment that secretaries of state went out of style, as if the need for both had represented an insecurity complex that Americans finally got over. With Abe Lincoln, it became okay to be a completely ordinary guy.

After the Civil War, candidates started running as ordinary foot soldiers and ordinary guys, which was legitimate since some of them turned out to be all-too-ordinary presidents. But then something curious happened. American power grew beyond the point where we were safe from Europe and to the point where we could come out and play with Europe. When America found itself seriously re-engaged with Europe in the world wars, it seems to have re-engaged the old insecurities and the old aristocratic reassurances, for it turned to two presidents who were far from ordinary guys, Woodrow Wilson and Franklin Roosevelt. Wilson and FDR knew all about world history and they probably even spoke French. Whatever the coincidences involved in Wilson and FDR being in office during the world wars, Americans seemed reassured by their Euro-sophistication, so much so that when FDR died Americans were appalled that an ordinary guy succeeded him. Even Harry Truman was appalled. Yet the republic survived, and ordinary guys were back in style. Still, in the heat of the Cold War Americans seemed reassured by the Euro-sophistication of John F. Kennedy, who even had a Frenchie wife.

Even as the Euro-sophistication persona was back in demand, another powerful persona was gathering momentum through the twentieth century. Teddy Roosevelt started it off with a bang. Teddy Roosevelt grew up when Frederick Jackson Turner was worrying about how the closing of the frontier would degrade the American character, and when Buffalo Bill was thrilling crowds with frontier nostalgia. Teddy turned himself into a personification of the frontier, and not the domestic rail-splitting log-cabin settler but the most unsettled and vigorous aspect of the frontier, the cowboy and the hunter. The popularity of Teddy's cowboy persona was so strong that it transferred some of itself onto cousin Franklin even though Franklin lived in a wheelchair. The cowboy persona seems to have been given a big boost by the 1940s-60s golden age of movie and TV westerns. Dwight Eisenhower, having grown up in the quintessential cowboy town of Abilene, may have been a subconscious beneficiary of the cowboy persona, though he really didn't need it. But John F. Kennedy knew he did need it and wrapped himself in New Frontier imagery. The cowboy persona arrived for real in Lyndon Johnson. The cowboy persona took a serious hit over Vietnam, but it had too much power to be eclipsed for long, and Ronald Reagan brought it back in all its glory. George H. W. Bush tried his best to do the cowboy act, but it took his son, a real Texan with an accent and ranch and cowboy hat, to pull it off as well as Reagan.

The power of the cowboy persona includes being an ordinary guy and then draws upon the most basic archetypes of the American frontier experience to offer a strategy for dealing with a dangerous world. The cowboy persona says that all it takes is toughness and force. Cowboys could be even better than generals because generals had to be patient organizers while cowboys just went out on their own and got it done. Cowboys didn't have to fuss with the Euro-sophistication persona's knowledge of weird inferior foreigners, his time-consuming diplomatic skills, and his sissy hesitation over using force.

The crisis of September 11 and Iraq, which once again re-engaged America with a dangerous world, seemed to re-engage the old reassuring Euro-sophistication archetype. For decades the Democrats had been relying on country boys from the South and Midwest—Johnson, Carter, and Clinton; Humphrey, McGovern, and Mondale. But now the Democrats turned to someone who had grown up in Europe, the son of a diplomat. This set up a major showdown between the Euro-sophistication persona and the cowboy persona, really the most classic showdown in American history between these fundamental archetypes, which probably had a lot to do with why people kept saying it was such an important election. It wasn't just Kerry vs. Bush; it was America's European side vs. its frontier side.

Yet neither Kerry nor Bush could rest secure in his own persona; each needed to make inroads against the other's persona. Thus while Bush operatives made numerous aspersions to equate Euro-sophistication with un-American, Kerry chipped away at the well-known reckless-and-dumb side of the cowboy persona. Kerry also implied that Bush was really a spoiled rich kid and not an ordinary guy, and tried to show that he himself was an ordinary guy. This was the trickiest part of it for Kerry, for he had to be both Euro-sophisticated for dealing with a complicated world and an ordinary guy for relating to the blue-collar world. He had to be Le Ordinary Guy. Even trickier, he had to prove that at the same time he was Euro-sophisticated he was also enough of a cowboy to be tough. The combination of roles facing Kerry was so tricky that it wasn't surprising he got flak about it from all sides.

I watched with fascination as core American archetypes wrestled against one another. It was especially interesting to watch John Kerry being tested over whether he was an ordinary guy, because I'd seen this once before long ago. I'm going to do one more flashback to Lowell, Massachusetts, to take a look at the ordinary-guy archetype at work. Then I'll return to 2004 to watch this archetype at work in the presidential campaign.

Part One: Closed Doors

It was something out of Dickens, the tenements, the tenements always catching fire. The old unkempt wooden buildings burned fast, burning people alive or forcing them to jump from higher floors, shining an ominous glow for miles around. Not far from the tenements, at least in mileage, was a street lined with old mansions, yet mansions long neglected, abandoned, boarded up. Down by the canals the tall, mile-long, red-brick mills also stood abandoned and decaying.

It was literally out of Dickens, for back in 1842 Charles Dickens had come to Lowell to inspect it. He wasn't looking for an American Oliver Twist in the slums or for a Scrooge in a mansion on the hill. Those belonged in England but not in America. Dickens came to America with hopes of finding a democratic society better than Europe. In *American Notes* Dickens wrote that in England the industrial centers were "great haunts of desperate misery," populated by "degraded brutes of burden."[5] In Lowell Dickens couldn't believe his eyes. The workers, mostly young women, all looked healthy, clean, well-fed, well-dressed, and well-mannered. "I cannot recall or separate one young face that gave me a painful impression." He was especially impressed that the mill girls produced their own literary magazine, *The Lowell Offering*. Dickens held up Lowell as proof that industrialism could be civilized and that conditions in Europe were far from natural and inevitable.

The founders of Lowell were far from being utopians, but the very act of designing a new city from scratch, where, unlike European cities, buildings and roads were placed in the most rational locations, made Lowell a symbol of the Age of Reason. The founders had to find a large labor force but had no industrial class or Ellis Island immigrants to draw upon, so they drew upon the mass of unmarried New England farm girls. But given the terrible reputation of English mill towns, and given the time's restrictions on female freedom, New England families would never let their daughters go unless they were assured their daughters would be living cleanly, both physically and morally. Thus Lowell took care of its girls, requiring them to live in boarding houses that were locked at night and to go to church on Sundays. Farm girls had the extra advantage that they didn't need to be paid enough to support a family.

Utopia didn't last long. Gradually wages dropped, already long hours lengthened, workloads increased, conditions worsened, workers became restless, owners became repressive. By 1860 the Yankee farm girls were gone. To replace them the mill owners recruited in blighted, hungry Ireland. No one would complain if Irish workers were scruffy and overcrowded into decaying boarding houses. Now a large family had to live on wages intended for a single woman. From hardscrabble Quebec came French Canadians, and the Irish were no longer the bottom caste in town. Then the Greeks arrived and, like the others, built their own neighborhood.

Ethnicity determined not only where you lived but what kind of job you could get. Specific mill jobs were reserved for specific ethnic groups. If you were Greek you worked in the dye house. In small business too, getting a job or a bank loan or a city contract could owe less to merit than to ethnic loyalties. Ethnic loyalties even overrode religious loyalties; the Irish and French Canadians might both be Catholics, but the French Canadians stuck to their own churches and parish schools, their own language, rites, and saints.

One French-Canadian boy in the 1920s learned French Canadian first and only at age five started learning English. His father, Leo Kerouac, published a newspaper to look after the interests of the French Canadians in Lowell. Leo was fiercely combative about all the insults and barriers against French Canadians, and he called Lowell "stinktown on the Merrimack," where the entire commercial and political world was rigged and corrupt. When Leo's son Jean-Louis wasn't accepted onto the high school football team, Leo fumed that it was all political. But at least Jean-Louis got hired as a sports reporter at the city newspaper, where he signed his stories 'Jack Kerouac.' After finishing a story he spent the rest of the day typing away on his own *Ulysses* that would "delineate all of Lowell as Joyce had done for Dublin."[6] Decades later Kerouac still vividly recalled "all the despair, raw gricky hopelessness, cold and chapped sorrow of Lowell—Like the abandoned howl of a dog and no one to open the door."[7] Jack Kerouac's Lowell was a different world from Charles Dickens' Lowell.

Closed doors dominated the world of Lowell politics. Without upward mobility to stir it, the melting pot didn't work. With actual downward mobility, it became a fight to hold onto a job or a city contract. Political patronage became a matter of life and death, and ethnic groups fought over it savagely, and even within ethnic groups factions and families and neighborhoods carried on multi-generation feuds. Politicians were rewarded not for their intelligence, ability, or vision, but for their loyalty to their own clique, loyalties that often superceded the law, leaving a "stinktown" of corruption. And hopelessness.

Yet in the summer of 1972 a fresh breeze was blowing through Lowell. It had been nearly a decade since the death of President Kennedy, and now the teenagers who had heard the call of the New Frontier were young men eager to answer it. Kennedy had told them that politics was a noble profession, that youthful idealism could change the world, and that American government could do anything, whether landing a man on the moon or solving problems on Earth. The teenagers of Massachusetts were paying extra attention to Kennedy, and now a whole crop of them was entering politics at the same moment: Paul Tsongas, John Kerry, Michael Dukakis, Barney Frank, Ed Markey, and Robert Drinan, a rare cluster of talent that played a defining role in the national Democratic Party for a generation to come.

Nowhere in Massachusetts was this breeze from the New Frontier felt more than in Lowell. In 1972 both Paul Tsongas and John Kerry were living there and running for office. Tsongas was on the Lowell city council and running for county commissioner as a reformer. When Tsongas and Kerry spoke side by side that summer they stood out for their New Frontier confidence that declared in all seriousness that if we could land a man on the moon, we could put Lowell back to work. John Kerry had a stronger New Frontier confidence than did Paul Tsongas, for in growing up in Lowell Tsongas had seen that government could be powerless to steer economic forces and powerless to offer social services unless there was an economy to support them, and that in a downward economic spiral appeals to compassion and fairness wouldn't cut through the wall of fear.

The Lowell crowds reacted differently to Tsongas and Kerry. Tsongas was just a local boy, hardly known outside the Greek community, and no one would imagine him having a national career let alone running for president someday. By contrast John Kerry was already a national political celebrity. For Lowell youth who had thought that New Frontier confidence and the heady political energy of their generation happened only somewhere else, John Kerry had brought the hope and energy of the 1960s to Lowell. Kerry was untainted by Lowell parochialism and corruption, and he was young and smart and dynamic in a way that Lowell politics was not. Kerry was thinking big, not just about international affairs, but talking about the closed economic doors of Lowell and what he could do to open them. Elderly people too felt fresh hope, and they started calling up Kerry headquarters asking for help with problems over landlords and veteran's benefits and other government services, and soon the word spread that the Kerry campaign would help people out, and the campaign assigned a staffer fulltime just to deal with landlord troubles, and it put together and distributed a booklet about government services for the elderly, acts that were quite unusual for a political campaign.

Of course there were those who didn't see Kerry as a Camelot knight coming to the rescue but as an interloper who hadn't served any clique and hadn't waited in line for his turn and was causing trouble for good-old-boy slumlords.

As soon as the doors of the Kerry headquarters opened in Lowell, people who had long felt disenfranchised and hopeless started walking in and devoting themselves to the campaign, including kids from the world of the mills, kids whose parents had lost their mill jobs long ago and eked out a marginal survival ever since, obligating their kids to go to work at an early age, delivering newspapers or babysitting. These kids looked at their own futures with a bleakness that colored the rest of their self-confidence.

Kerry's promises about opening doors seemed already proved by the lack of social boundaries in the campaign. Irish names like Donahue worked alongside French-Canadian names like Doucet and eastern European names like Guzowski. Mill kids worked alongside the kids of successful lawyers who lived in the mansions on the hill. When the campaign held events or parties in those mansions, the mill kids could just walk right in, though for a century their families hadn't dreamed of entering those mansions even as thieves. The mill kids could also walk right into the stylish colonial homes of Lexington and Concord to attend campaign events with famous guests like Kurt Vonnegut. Even in the mundane job of answering the headquarters phone, mill kids found themselves talking with celebrities from Hollywood and Capitol Hill. With such magical possibilities opening up all around you, it was easy to believe that John Kerry was going to open more doors for you.

Still, there were doubts. When the mill kids' friends found out they were volunteering for John Kerry, the volunteers were given a hard time. Sometimes even their own parents gave them a hard time at the dinner table. Over and over they were told that they were betraying their own kind. John Kerry wasn't one of us.

The Lowell newspaper offered a steady supply of reasons why Kerry wasn't one of us. It attacked Kerry day after day, often over Kerry not being an ordinary guy. The newspaper fully understood the power of the ordinary-guy archetype in the American political psyche. This archetype and its contrast with the Euro-sophistication archetype was even more powerful in Lowell, which had long been polarized between the rich Yankees who owned and ran the mills, and the ordinary-guy workers. The newspaper emphasized everything that made Kerry a rich Yankee. He wasn't John Kerry, but John *Forbes* Kerry. Kerry had lived in Europe and gone to a prep school and Yale. He had money and wore nice suits. Kerry couldn't possibly understand or care about the lives of ordinary guys. His campaign was being paid for by fancy rich people in Hollywood and Manhattan. All of Kerry's talk about slumlords ripping off ordinary guys was just a big phony act to get himself elected, and after he'd used Lowell he'd disappear and forget all about us.

Kerry's efforts to establish rapport went nowhere, and sometimes worse than nowhere. One time he walked into a French-Canadian café and the advance man had told him that the ordinary guys inside were all speaking French so Kerry greeted them in French as if he was one of them, just an ordinary guy, except that Kerry spoke in Parisian French, which wasn't the same as French-Canadian French, and New England mill towns even had their own variations of French-Canadian French.

When seventeen-year-old Kerry volunteers were told over and over by friends, family, and the newspaper that they were betraying their own kind and helping out a phony who couldn't possibly understand or care about ordinary guys, it wasn't easy. It was enough to start you doubting your own perceptions.

Some of these kids had been the first volunteers to walk in the headquarters door, and Kerry had taken the time to get to know them. Yet as the campaign got a lot bigger and faster-paced, the Lowell kids saw less and less of Kerry, who zoomed in and out of the office. Some sour feelings were brewing among the Lowell kids, mainly because as Kerry seemed closer to victory the campaign was attracting some ambitious young Boston men who didn't care about Lowell or even about changing the world but who had caught the scent of power. These brash young men—very common in campaigns—found little outlet for their self-importance except the Lowell kids, whom they started bossing around and snubbing. The Lowell kids might put up with friends and even fathers snubbing them for working for Kerry, but to walk into Kerry headquarters and be snubbed was brewing resentments, even doubts about John Kerry. If Kerry didn't have time for them now, then what would happen when he was a congressman? If they showed up at his Washington office and said they were just Lowell mill kids, would his door be open to them, or closed?

It was a Saturday night and I and a few of the Lowell kids were attending some neighborhood event for the campaign. While their friends were out at the movies or partying, they were giving their Saturday night to John Kerry. As at many events in Lowell, you could observe the clannishness of Lowell, a tightness derived from families having known each other and gone through thick and thin together for generations, a tightness in which people felt kindred to strangers just because they were French Canadian, a tightness in which people did favors for one another, a tightness in which you could drop by a friend's house unannounced late at night and be welcome to the cold beer in the refrigerator.

It was late when we got in the car, and there was a brief discussion of whether we should go anywhere besides home. Then the driver suggested: "Hey, let's go drop in on John Kerry."

The suggestion hung there for a long moment, pregnant with consequence. It was clear he wasn't talking about dropping in on John Kerry at any public event. He was talking about dropping in on John Kerry at home. There were longtime paid staffers who hadn't been inside Kerry's home. I hadn't been there, and I wasn't expecting an invitation anytime soon.

"You mean," someone asked, "without warning?"

"Sure," said someone. "It's not far from here, and we can tell him we just happened to be in the neighborhood."

"Ah," I said nervously, "It's after ten o'clock."

"That's okay. We can just swing by and see if the car's there and the light's on. I've always wondered about John Kerry's house."

The others agreed that this was a good plan, and we were off. I was a prisoner in a car full of lunatics.

Actually I thought I understood where this impulse was coming from. Since I was the same age as some of the Lowell kids, we'd become friends. I was aware of the flak they were taking from friends and family, and I had started to notice their frustration at being stepped on in the office. They hadn't shared with me any doubts they might be having about John Kerry, but such doubts would be understandable enough. But it really wasn't necessary to sit around troubling yourself with doubts about what kind of guy John Kerry really was. It was easy enough to conduct a little test and settle the whole matter right now. Kerry was out there claiming to be enough of an ordinary guy to relate to the ordinary guys of Lowell.

Well then, he could just prove it. It was the perfect ambush: you'd have Kerry cornered, with no chance to fake it. Either he'd behave like an ordinary guy, or he'd behave like you were beneath him and he'd slam the door in your face.

In fact it wasn't far. We pulled to the curb. Kerry's car was in the driveway. The house was dark. Thank goodness, I thought, that's the end of that idea.

But it wasn't the end of that idea. It was even better now. It was nearly perfect. You wake up John Kerry. You get him out of bed. You invite yourselves into his house. You're seeing his true core now. A Lowell ordinary guy would welcome you into his house even after you'd woken him up. Now we'd find out for sure if John Kerry was really an ordinary guy. The driver opened his door to get out.

My first plan was simply to stay in the car, in fact to slump down where no one could see me. But these were my friends, and they'd always remember that I had abandoned them in their hour of greatest risk. And besides, I had to admit it, I was intrigued by this test, impressed by the sheer ingenuity of it. Maybe I didn't need to do this test for my own sake; in riding around with Kerry I'd gotten a fair sense of who he was, at least when it came to his sincerity on the issues. Still, even this hadn't offered such an ingenious test of whether Kerry in his private midnight heart was an ordinary guy or an ambitious snob.

We got out and walked up the sidewalk. It probably wasn't as bad as it looked: John and Julia were probably just in a back room watching TV. But it did look awfully dark in there. We stepped onto the porch. The ringleader reached out for the doorbell. He pushed it. Ding Dong. We stood staring at the closed door.

Lowell was doomed from the start. The whole idea of Lowell was that upstart American textile mills could compete with the almighty British textile industry because American mills were closer to the cotton. Instead of shipping cotton from North Carolina all the way to Britain to be milled into cloth and then shipping the cloth all the way to Boston, you could just ship the cotton from North Carolina to Boston. But the next inevitable step in this logic was to move the textile mills right into the middle of the cotton fields. The Civil War left plenty of Southerners desperate for work at any wage. Ungrateful Northerners who were complaining and unionizing had their jobs handed to North Carolinians. For the mill owners it was a big relief to be dealing with people who understood their place, partly just because they actually understood the English language and had proper American names, not those ridiculous Greek and Polack and Canuck names. Proper American names like Edwards.

There was no reaction from inside. The house remained dark. Time to give up and leave! The ringleader reached out and rang the door bell again. Darn that doorbell sounded loud. Loud enough to wake someone up. We stood there staring at the closed door.

It was the Edwardses of North Carolina who now had the open doors. They went off to the mill every day for decades to do the jobs that had been stolen from Lowell. While the sons of Lowell mill workers walked around in despair, an Edwards son walked off to law school and then off to the U.S. Senate, and then he ran for president.

A light came on in back. Oh no. They really had been asleep. We really were getting John and Julia out of bed way late at night. I started looking around for a shrub to hide behind.

When John Edwards ran for president in 2004, he talked a lot about being the son of a textile-mill worker. It was the first thing he brought up in his speeches. It was what defined who he was. The punch line of his speeches was "I still believe in an America where the son of a mill worker can beat the son of a president." Richard Gephardt talked a lot about being the son of a milk-truck driver. Dennis Kucinich talked about once being so poor he had to live in his car. They were outbidding one another in the contest of the ordinary-guy persona, leaving John Kerry standing there under the implication that he couldn't possibly relate to ordinary guys. Then Edwards talked about how the textile mills had closed and left their communities devastated, and he implied that a president needed to be able to relate to the despairing sons of workers of closed textile mills.

The porch light came on. The door started to open. I can't report on the look on John Kerry's face at that moment, for I was studiously looking away, making it clear that I wasn't to blame, letting me glance back with casual surprise: gee, look: it's John Kerry; imagine running into you in a place like this.

"We just happened to be in the neighborhood," said the perpetrators, "so we thought we'd stop by."

Now that the others had borne the brunt, I looked at Kerry, whose face said: *this is weird.* You could tell he was thinking: *it's way late at night; didn't you see that the lights were out?* But he also recognized some kids who had been with him for a long time. He invited us in.

We had to pass another test. Julia came out of the back, maybe not fully awake, and gave us the look: *this is weird. It's way late at night; didn't you see that the lights were out?* Even in the light of day Julia could be bluntly honest about all the nonsense that went along with political life, and our visit fell well beyond the call of duty. Yet Julia looked us over and she must have seen some faces that belonged to a realm beyond politics, for she welcomed us. She asked us if we were hungry and offered us snacks and went off to the kitchen to find cookies or something.

We stood there in awkwardness. I'm not sure the ringleader had planned on actually getting inside. We glanced around at the furnishings. We weren't expecting Kerry to be such an ordinary guy that he'd have tattered and yellowed newspaper posters of the New England Patriots duct-taped to the walls. The room was gracefully decorated, but nothing ostentatious.

"This is a nice house," someone said.

"Thanks. We like it." *This is weird.*

John invited us to sit down, Julia brought out snacks, and we sat and talked about ordinary stuff, about what somebody was doing at school or work, about the Red Sox, about life in Lowell, about the campaign. In truth it was a very ordinary conversation, or it would have been ordinary if not for the downright weird context. It was so ordinary that I can recall hardly any details about it. It was just like hundreds of other ordinary conversations going on in ordinary Lowell houses on an ordinary Saturday night. We were just like lots of other ordinary guys who had dropped by a friend's house unannounced and were welcome to the refrigerator.

Finally one of us said that it was getting late and maybe we should be getting along. We got up to leave and thanked our hosts, and John and Julia thanked us for dropping by, even as their faces still said: *This is weird.* They walked us to the door and bid us goodnight, even as their smiles still said: *This was weird.*

Back in the car the verdict was: *That was cool!* He had passed the test.

There was a bit more. A few weeks later another set of Lowell kids told me of their frustration about getting snubbed by the brash young politicos. I was disturbed by this because these kids included 'the Marines,' a group of high-school girls, two of them named Maureen, who'd been coming into the headquarters every day after school for a long time, to which I'd declare: "The Marines have landed!" For them to be ill-treated and unhappy was too much. I decided to talk with John Kerry about the whole situation. There was only three weeks left before the general election and he had plenty of other things on his mind, and by now the campaign was swarming with volunteers and a few less wouldn't be noticed. But Kerry sat down with the Lowell kids and listened to them and talked with them, and they were there loyally for the rest of the campaign, and crying on the night he lost.

I thought of this test during the 2004 campaign as Kerry was assaulted for not being an ordinary guy and as he struggled to prove that he really was an ordinary guy, to prove it through symbols and postures such as parading around carrying a hunting rifle. The campaign also tried to make a really big deal out of Kerry being ambushed in his swift boat and turning around and going back for a Green Beret who had fallen overboard. To tell the truth, I wasn't so impressed by the river ambush story. After all, the military has very strong codes about not leaving the wounded behind. But political campaigns don't have any codes requiring a very busy candidate to turn around and go back for a Marine whose girl's heart has been wounded. And when it came to ambushes that test a guy's character, I refused to give the Viet Cong more credit than the sons of mill workers whose ambush was so ingenious that John Kerry never even realized he was being ambushed by a very ordinary conversation.

Part Two: Dinner at Hemingway's

Jack Kerouac was only one of many in his generation of writers who found Ernest Hemingway an unavoidable icon, mainly because of the image of the writer as hero, someone living a life so outsized that the nation paid admiring attention, admiring itself in Ernest's adventures. This is the Hemingway who adorns the walls of Hemingway's Restaurant. Ernest holding his rifle proudly. Ernest beaming with pride over a dead rhino or lion on an African plain. Ernest posing with a monster fish bigger than himself. Ernest with trophy antlers. Ernest in a soldier's uniform near the front lines. Since this is a restaurant you might think that the walls would hold at least one photo of Ernest sitting in a Paris café, enjoying the movable feast. But no. There is no Paris cafe, no checkered table cloth with candles and French bread and French wine, no images of Ernest with books or artsy weirdoes like Gertrude Stein. No, this restaurant is devoted to Ernest Hemingway the tough guy, the runner with bulls, the lover of guns, the personification of American frontier virtues. And it's because this restaurant is devoted to American tough-guy myth that the wall holds another photo, right behind the reception desk, a photo of President George W. Bush right here, visiting Hemingway's, and next to him is a photo of his president dad visiting Hemingway's.

I was having dinner at Hemingway's mainly because it was right across the street from Kerry headquarters. The food was good too, but tonight Hemingway's was also giving me food for thought. I ordered a steak, well done of course, not rare of course because I was a squeamish liberal who refused to face the fact that blood is the lubricant and guns the pistons of American character and history.

The heads of dead African beasts stared at the diners, and leaping on the walls were giant fish that offered 'old man and the sea' epic connotations to the Friday fish buffet. Living fish swam in a giant aquarium behind the bar—of course there had to be a bar in a place called Hemingway's. I glanced at the bar half-expecting to see Ernest leaning into his huddle of bottles, trying to lose his deep insecurities in an alcoholic fog, boasting of what he had proven with his gun and his fishing rod and his pen, cursing the treachery of women, cursing the overwrought prose and reputations of Faulkner and Fitzgerald and Wolfe and just about everyone else, cursing his own powerlessness against his raging self-doubts. But there weren't any photos of the drunken and self-doubting Hemingway on these walls. This bar was devoted to the Hemingway of swaggering self-confidence. This was why the wall held a photo of President George W. Bush visiting Hemingway's.

I didn't spend long taking in the scene inside Hemingway's, for the view from Hemingway's was more engaging. I was sitting at the railing of the balcony, right next to the waterfall, gazing down maybe fifty feet. The waterfall plunged into an upper pool and then formed a cascade roaring white through the rocks until it settled into a lower pool. Several ducks were swimming in this pool, then they climbed onto a log and flapped their wings dry and began grooming themselves. On the rocky cliff beside the waterfall a bighorn sheep gazed outward. Nearby, a mountain lion crept. In a gnarled tree an American eagle was just now landing in its nest, its wings spread patriotically. A black bear was snarling at one end of a derelict rope-and-plank bridge, upon which a fleeing hiker was looking panicked as the plank beneath him snapped and he started to fall. I studied the hiker's plight and wondered if the designers of this diorama (the water and ducks were real) intended a moral lesson. Ernest Hemingway never would have ended up fleeing like this, for Ernest never would have been fool enough to wander around in bear country without a rifle. But this hiker didn't seem to have a gun. If he did he'd be holding his ground like a man and bagging a bear. Now he was going to be punished for not believing in guns.

A family stood in amazement before the diorama, pointing up at one thing after another, and then the father went fishing in his pockets and passed out coins to his kids, and the whole family tossed presidents into the water. What were they wishing for? The father was wearing a camouflage shirt and hat and the little boy was camo from top to bottom, and deer-hunting season was approaching, so maybe they were wishing for trophies. The presidents hit the water and twirled downward to lay distorted by the depths and the current—not the first images of American presidents or history to be distorted by wishes.

If only Teddy Roosevelt had made it onto a coin; this was his kind of place. Hemingway was his kind of writer. As a kid Ernest was enthralled by Teddy's books about hunting big game in Africa. When Ernest was eleven, Teddy came to his hometown of Oak Park, Illinois, and Ernest dressed up in a khaki hunting suit to cheer him through the streets. Decades later, Ernest was delighted to go on an African safari with the same hunting guide who had guided Teddy's safaris. Teddy would have been delighted to serve as the wish-bullet for the hunting dreams of a little boy at Hemingway's. But this wishing well would have to settle for the other Roosevelt, the March of Dimes cripple in the wheelchair. Franklin and Eleanor Roosevelt had once invited Hemingway to dinner at the White House, and Ernest found the meal appallingly unfit for a real man, consisting of "rainwater soup followed by a rubber squab, a nice wilted salad." Hemingway sized up Franklin and decided he was a girlie man, "sexless and womanly," less fit to be president than "a great Woman secretary of labor, say..."[8]

Since this was an American wilderness wishing well, George Washington the frontier scout was welcome, and Jefferson the sender of Lewis and Clark, and Lincoln of the log cabin. The presidents were dipped into the huge font of the American wilderness in a baptism that re-enacted the embodiment of national wishes that had propelled them to the presidency in the first place.

This was not just a baptism but a baptism in the greatest cathedral of American hunting and fishing culture. I do not use the term cathedral rhetorically. When you first walk in the main arch-framed doorway you face a grand nave five or maybe six or even seven stories tall. The nave is supported by massive pine logs, and the rafters and walls are giant logs too. From the ceiling hang huge rustic chandeliers decorated with wildlife scenes. This cathedral has a deceptively simple name: Bass Pro Shop. But make no mistake: this is a Vatican to which millions of pilgrims come from far and wide, dressing up in full camo just to go shopping here.

There was a strong geo-logic to the Bass Pro cathedral being located here in Springfield, Missouri, for Springfield was right on the edge of the Ozark mountains, where hunting and fishing were a stronger part of the culture than in most of America. In the stony, forested, hilly Ozarks the farming land was goat-poor, but the Ozarks were full of rivers and streams full of fish, and the woods were full of deer and rabbits, and a man with a good rifle and a good aim could manage to keep his family fed. Jed Clampett and his kin came out of the Ozarks, and there was some accurate sociology in the theme song of *The Beverly Hillbillies* presenting Jed as "a poor mountaineer barely kept his family fed, and then one day he was shooting at some food..." Shooting for food, not for blood sport. It was also decent sociology that the Beverly Hillbillies came out of the Ozarks and not the other enclave of hillbilly culture, the Appalachians, for in many respects Ozark hillbillies remained more isolated than Appalachian hillbillies. The Appalachians were immediately adjacent to the main population axis of America: roads and railroads had to go through it; millions of tourists made their way to mountain resorts and parks; and West Virginia coal mines lured billies out of the hills by the tens of thousands. In the Ozarks, it was only in the 1930s that the building of dams and lakes drew in tourists and paved the highways. Some Jed Clampetts discovered that they could set up a little shack and sell fishing gear to vacationers from Kansas City. But plenty of Jeds went on fishing and hunting for survival. There was a code of honor in a man being able to feed his family, an honor to having a better rifle and being a better shot and felling a bigger deer. Who would dishonor Jed for keeping Granny and Elly May from starving? Well, it sure seemed like out there in the incomprehensible world there were indeed people who had a righteous hostility against guns and who would gladly take away Jed's gun and leave Elly May to butcher her pet critters to keep Granny from starving. It was bizarre.

On the Interstate just outside of Springfield was a billboard featuring a fancy white French poodle, probably a girl with a name like Fifi. The headline read: "This dog won't hunt." The text was simply: "John Kerry has a 20 year record of voting against hunter's rights." Signed, the NRA. This billboard was up on highways all over rural America.

The phrase "this dog won't hunt" had a connotation that went well beyond hunting. It echoed a phrase, "that dog won't hunt," which Bill Clinton had used to—what? Fend off a Republican criticism? If people noticed the context at all they soon forgot. But they did remember that Clinton spoke the language of ordinary Ozarks folks. The national media, which was probably puzzled by this phrase when they first heard it, felt obligated to translate it for their readers and viewers. But ordinary guys in the Ozarks and elsewhere translated it like this: I'm one of you, just an ordinary guy; you can trust me to understand your lives. For the NRA to turn this phrase against John Kerry was to say: he isn't one of us; he's not an ordinary guy. Drivers chuckled as they imagined Fifi instead of a hound dog at Jed's side.

The Fifi billboard was one in a crowd of billboards near Springfield, most of which advertised shows in Branson. One reason Bass Pro Shop was thriving was because Springfield is the gateway to Branson, which had become America's number-one musical attraction, its shows drawing millions every year, more than Nashville, Broadway, or Las Vegas. Even more than music, Branson offers nostalgia—no, validation—for an America that many even in small-town America had thought was gone, an America of simplicity and self-reliance. The largest attraction in Branson is Silver Dollar City, which started out as a handful of craftsmen who made old-time things to entertain tourists as they waited for the next tour of a cave, but it turned out that the tourists were more fascinated by the craftsmen than by the cave, and today Silver Dollar City is a sprawling and crowded hillbilly theme park full of craftsmen making furniture, pottery, candles, baskets, clothes, candy, and horseshoes—frontier skills that died out in Boston 250 years ago.

Yet at the end of a day at Silver Dollar City, crowds flock to see Soji Tobuchi, a Japanese classical violinist turned wicked bluegrass fiddler, whose show is full of Broadway song-and-dance and Vegas glitter. Or they flock to the Moon River Theater to hear Andy Williams sing the theme song from *Breakfast at Tiffany's*, full of yearning for the glamorous life.

The mix-up of pioneer virtues and city sophistication, the difference between Branson and Boston, has been a powerful swirling current in American social history. It wasn't as if Ozarks folks had any objections to the material rewards associated with the city. It was also accurate sociology that Jed Clampett required very little persuasion to flee the Ozarks for Beverly Hills. Inside most country girls there was an Audrey Hepburn standing outside the window of Tiffany's, yearning for a life of glamour, even for a lovely dog named Fifi. In *Breakfast at Tiffany's* all of Audrey Hepburn's desperate pretensions of glamour were stripped naked when her jilted husband turned up on a bus from Texas and he turned out to be Jed Clampett, or at least the same actor, Buddy Ebsen, who reveals that Audrey's real name is Lula May and that she comes from a thoroughly rustic background.

The Moon River separating Audrey and Jed from the glamorous life was "wider than a mile." Now here was the problem. All of American folklore assured Ozarks folks that they were the true heroes of America history, that the qualities that had built America and that brought personal success in America were self-reliance and hard work and frontier toughness. Not just folklore, but geniuses like Hemingway had saluted the virtues of self-reliance and toughness. Even when the age of factories arrived, manly strength remained the crankshaft of success. But somewhere along the way the American Dream had fractured, leaving a disconnection between the virtues of American folklore and the rewards of the American Dream. Now it was weaklings, who were utterly useless with a gun or a hammer or a plow, who were walking out of colleges and getting the good jobs and buying the good cars and marrying the pretty women and walking Fifi down the streets of Beverly Hills or Boston, while the true heroes of America history labored on the loading dock at Wal-Mart with a despair that only deepened with the years and the debts. It was even worse that the weaklings looked down on the true heroes of American history, not only looked down on them as losers, which in economic terms was painfully undeniable, but looked down on them by refusing to acknowledge that they were in fact the true heroes of American history, looked down on them as ridiculous stupid hicks. You couldn't escape the belittling, for the weaklings made all the TV shows and movies, and you were lucky if the weaklings only showed their own kind enjoying the American Dream, for on the rare occasions when the weaklings even showed the true heroes of American history, they showed them as ridiculous stupid hicks. Worst of all, as if the weaklings hadn't already stripped enough masculinity from the true heroes of American history, now the weaklings wanted to take away their guns. If you finally got to the point when you couldn't take it anymore then the only thing left to do was to join the army where skill with guns still made you a true American hero, or just go down to the greatest cathedral of American hunting and fishing culture where your identity would be sanctified and where you could walk past a diorama portraying the punishment for not loving guns and you could say to hell with Tiffany's and to hell with the moon river wider than a mile and you could sit down to a bloody dinner at Hemingway's. And if while you were eating dinner at Hemingway's President George W. Bush showed up like a revelation, it would suddenly be clear to you that the vast sociological mix-up that had been flowing through American culture for centuries, the mix-up between pioneer virtues and city sophistication, between American myths and American rewards, had risen up out of the river of national intuition and perfectly embodied itself for the 2004 presidential election, embodied itself not just in Cowboy George but just as perfectly in his opponent Fifi.

The big news in Branson this summer was the opening of the Roy Rogers and Dale Evans Museum and Happy Trails Theater. It was a shrine to the mythology of the American frontier, filled with Hollywood and cowboy memorabilia. In movies Roy and Dale always wore white hats, and they had a white-and-black faith in America. The museum held Roy's collection of Remington guns; trophies from his real-life African safaris; and his parade car, a 1963 convertible decorated with bullets, pistols, horseshoes, and a saddle. The most popular exhibit was Roy's stuffed horse Trigger, rearing up on his hind legs and kicking just like in the movies; along with a stuffed Bullet, Roy's faithful dog; and a stuffed Buttermilk, Dale's horse. The museum used to be located near Los Angeles but it wasn't prospering, so Roy's son decided that Branson was the place it ought to be. Trigger, Bullet, and Buttermilk were loaded into a semi-truck and went for a great adventure, retreating up the exact route Jed Clampett had taken going the other way, which for Jed had been mom-and-pop Rt. 66 but which was now an Interstate clustered with impersonal franchises. Trigger, Bullet, and Buttermilk rode through the Mohave Desert as the mountains and the sage turned purple with a western sunset. In New Mexico they galloped through Gallup, passing the El Rancho Hotel where movie stars used to hang out while filming westerns nearby, its lobby adorned with signed star photos, its restaurant serving sandwiches named for stars, the Roy Rogers being a giant hamburger, the Ronald Reagan coming with a side of jelly beans. Trigger was getting his kicks on Rt. 66. Coming into Amarillo they passed Cadillac Ranch, the 1950s Cadillac tailfins sticking out of the ground; and leaving Amarillo they passed the Big Texan Steakhouse, where you'd get a five-pound steak for free if you could eat it in one hour. Going through Oklahoma they passed underneath the world's largest McDonalds, a giant archway spanning the Interstate. They passed near Bass Pro Shop and rolled into the Ozarks and climbed out of their truck and saw that their new home was right next to the Yakov Smirnoff Theater, home of the Russian comedian who told America-flattering jokes ending with his signature punch line: "What a country!"

Even at the entrance to the greatest cathedral to America's gun culture there was an acknowledgement that maybe things had gotten a bit ridiculous, a bit out of hand. The large sign over the Bass Pro Shop doorway says: "Welcome fishermen, hunters, and other liars." This raises the question of why people would want to lie about the size of their fish or the pursuit of their deer. The answer is confessed inside in the sale of t-shirts that say things like: "Fish Fear Me, Women Want Me." If hunting and fishing were just about feeding Granny, would guys sit around telling macho lies about it? The macho component in America's gun culture was further exaggerated by the enormous power of the national mythology of conquering the land. Now this macho culture was largely detached from the needs of family survival and entirely detached from the needs of national conquest of the land, but onward it went, onward like the long-dead Trigger and Bullet who still paraded macabrely across the land.

Hemingway biographers don't agree on exactly when his drive to personify America's frontier tough-guy culture began to drive Hemingway mad.

You can make the case that it all began long before Ernest was born, with a family that burdened him with expectations he couldn't possibly fulfill. It wasn't just that his mother was so severe and domineering that—Ernest was angrily certain—she drove his father to suicide. It was having a family history to live up to. Ernest's English ancestors included famous Oxford-degreed Stradivarius-playing musicians. His namesake grandfather Ernest was born in England to a respected silversmith and expected to go to Oxford but was removed to an Iowa farm. Grandfather Ernest joined the Union cavalry and was gloriously wounded in the Civil War, or at least, grandfather Ernest's daughter Grace, who idolized him, always told her son Ernest how glorious it was to be wounded in war. Grace had planned to be an opera star but ended up the housewife of a worthless husband. Ernest's father escaped the bitch for the woods, where he taught Ernest that the true measure of a man was his ability to shoot and fish. Now here were too contradictory imperatives, the European glamour life and the American hunting and battlefield tough-guy life. Ernest did ingeniously well at putting the two together, sitting in Paris cafes and drinking French wines and writing books about being an American tough guy on European battlefields and bull runs. But it was his internal bulls that were really driving him, driving him to prove that he was no ordinary guy. Yet could Ernest ever lift a gun without thinking of his father, who one despairing night had picked up the heroic ancient Civil War pistol and pointed it to his head and pulled the trigger? It must have been harder for Ernest when he recalled how he had hidden in the shed and aimed his shotgun at his father's head and pretended to pull the trigger. Certainly Ernest's brother Leicester was haunted by the suicide, and Leicester too would end up pointing a gun at his head and pulling the trigger.

Hemingway's was perched overlooking "America's Great Hunting Hall," a huge secondary nave separated from the entrance nave by a football field of merchandise, including the kind of tan outdoors/work coat that John Kerry wore throughout the fall campaign to prove that he was just an ordinary guy. America's Great Hunting Hall looks like a forest, for it's packed with camouflage clothing. At the far end of the hall is an archery shop with a long row of bows. Another wall holds a long line of rifles. There's a shooting range where you can test-fire guns. There's a gunsmith shop to fix your guns. There's a luxury gun shop that sells top-of-the-line rifles for over $5,000 and old collector's rifles for over $20,000. There's a knife shop in the form of an old mill, with a huge wooden paddlewheel actually turning in another waterfall, and inside are hundreds of knives including huge shiny $200 Bowie knives. Just below Hemingway's is "The Shoot'n Arcade," a laser-gun shooting gallery in the form of a hillbilly shack festooned with targets. Families came up and put in their fifty cents and picked up their laser rifles, and when they hit a bull's-eye they got an animated validation: a squirrel danced on a log, a mounted deer head nodded, an above-the-door horseshoe spun, or the front-porch rocking chair started rocking to the tune of "Foggy Mountain Breakdown." Now, I'm no expert on gun safety, but it seemed to me that it set a bad example for kids to be shooting at someone's house. But this arcade wasn't nearly as worrisome as the one at the Roy Rogers Museum. The laser shooting arcade there consists of a sheriff's office with a bad guy in a black hat in a jail cell and with Roy Rogers and Dale in white hats standing in front of the cell, and the laser bull's-eyes are so close that if you are even modestly off-target you could shoot Roy and Dale in the head. What kind of example does it set to visit a shrine to American frontier culture and end up blowing away the heads of American heroes?

At first and for a long time Ernest reveled in the American frontier tough-guy myth. Millions of guys longed to inhabit that image but had to settle for the smallest, most local kind of glory. But Ernest was a writer who could broadcast his glory to millions, and he became the image millions wanted to be. Thus the nation saw regular photo-spreads and reports of Ernest on safari in Africa, Ernest fishing in the Caribbean, Ernest boxing, Ernest at the bull fights, Ernest in jeeps and boats and planes and mountain lodges, Ernest surviving plane crashes, Ernest drinking, Ernest at the casino, Ernest with beautiful and daring women, Ernest on the front lines of the Spanish Civil War and World War Two. Most of it was actually true, but even at the start, when Ernest invented a myth about joining the Italian army in World War One, he realized how dangerously seductive the tough-guy myth could be. As the years passed and his health unraveled and he struggled to live up to his own myth and invented more and more, he realized that he had grabbed hold of something far bigger than himself. Worst of all, his myth began polluting his writing. Instead of the honest, complex, damaged characters that had made him famous, now he was writing characters who were versions of his own heroic myth, self-parodies that left the literary world shaking its head. As his self-doubts deepened into despair he drank more and bullied his wives more, behaved more erratically and self-destructively, and spoke more and more about killing himself. He not only spoke about it, he acted it out for his dinner guests. In his typical know-it-all manner he demonstrated how to commit suicide with a rifle. He sat in a chair and placed the butt of his Mannlicker rifle, the same make that would soon kill President Kennedy, between his bare feet on the floor; then he leaned forward and put his mouth over the mouth of the barrel, as if he was going to eat death itself. Then with his big toe he pulled the trigger, and his dinner guests all heard the click and watched Ernest look at them and smile.

My dinner arrived. It was a steak. It looked like a steak and it smelled like a steak. I picked up my big sharp knife and cut the steak. It was a tough steak. It was a tough steak but a good steak. It was a good steak because it was a tough steak. Because it was a tough good steak, it made me a bigger man than the wimps sitting at the next table eating pasta and salad.

Yet as I gazed down at the laser shooting arcade, with family after family stepping up and hitting their targets, I was reminded that I was just a liberal elitist sitting up in the literary heights and looking down, about thirty feet down, on ordinary Americans. When I first inspected the arcade I was curious enough to get out my fifty cents and give it a try. But I couldn't hit a thing.

Now here was the problem. If it wasn't for the true aims at Normandy and Gettysburg and Lexington and Concord and at stampedes of buffalos and Indians, America never would have existed at all or conquered a continent or become the leader of the world. The whole buffalo-stampede momentum of American history and identity validated a culture of violence, and it wasn't about to be invalidated by a mere 10,000 gun deaths a year or by weaklings sitting up in the literary heights and looking down on the true heroes of American history.

I don't usually play with rifles, but this fall it seemed okay. We liberals elites had something to prove. I could be just like John Kerry. It hadn't been enough for Kerry to walk around all fall in his tan outdoors coat he'd bought to prove he was just an ordinary guy. Now he was walking around in camo with a shotgun and smiling for the cameras to prove that he was just an ordinary guy and a tough guy too, to prove that this dog actually could hunt.

By the fall of 1960, as John Kennedy was running for president and trying to look tough, it was obvious to Hemingway's family that he was losing it. He couldn't write anymore. He would try for hours to write a brief tribute for Kennedy's inauguration, only to sit there sobbing in defeat. He had paranoid delusions. His wife took him to the Mayo clinic for electroshock therapy. On the private flight back to Idaho they landed in Rapid City, South Dakota, near Mt. Rushmore where Teddy Roosevelt had become a stone icon of America myth. But Ernest was still just flesh trying to wear a giant and impossibly heavy mask. As another plane taxied in, Ernest headed for the face-shredding propeller, but he failed again. It was only two days short of the 4th of July when he got up in the middle of the night and went down to the gun closet and got out his favorite double-barreled shotgun, bought at Abercrombie and Finch—who says you can't combine glamour and frontier toughness? He put in two shells. He sat down and placed his mouth around the gun barrels.

Like families, nations too can hold expectations or myths that are impossible to live up to. Or at least, if a nation tries to live up to its myths, the nation will drive itself mad.

But perhaps the madness of nations is too large a subject to digest over dinner, so let me simply relate how America's gun culture tried to drive me nuts one afternoon in Iowa in the fall of 2003. That morning and the previous evening Iowa newspapers and TV news had carried images of John Kerry carrying a shotgun through an Iowa cornfield. Led by Buck the pointer dog, Kerry had flushed a pheasant out of the corn and raised his shotgun and shot the pheasant down.

I was calling up undecided voters, and one guy announced that he had now decided to support Kerry.

"That's great!" I said. "What made you decide to support Kerry?"

"I'm a pheasant hunter, and I saw that Kerry is a pheasant hunter."

I waited for more. "I'm sure there must be other things you like about Kerry."

"Nope. I hadn't paid much attention to him before now. I'm a lifelong pheasant hunter, ever since I was a kid, and I like the idea of having a pheasant hunter as president."

You've got to be kidding. Listen buddy, we're talking about the presidency of the United States here. "Well, you know, John Kerry has been a hunter since he was a kid too. But are there any other issues you care about and would like to know where Kerry stands?"

"No, I just liked that photo of him standing with his shotgun."

"Of course." *Jerk.* "Anyway, thanks so much for your support. We'll stay in touch."

Not long afterwards I got a woman who declared: "I'm afraid I can't support John Kerry now. I used to like him, especially since he's the best environmentalist in the race. But I can't vote for someone who enjoys murdering harmless little birds."

"Oh, I guess you saw the newspaper."

"It was all over the news. He must have had a busload of photographers following him around. He probably didn't need a dog to scare up the pheasants."

"You know, John Kerry always eats what he kills."

"Ha! And now you'll tell me he puts Heinz ketchup on it. This guy is so rich he's the last man in America who needs to go hunting for food. That's what they always say. But everyone knows that hunting isn't about food, it's about guns and killing, and guns and killing are about little boys trying to feel like men."

"Did you know that Kerry has a long record of supporting gun control? That's why the NRA doesn't like John Kerry. The NRA *hates* John Kerry. Hunters *hate* John Kerry." I didn't give up on votes until they pried the phone from my cold, dead hands. But she was adamant about guys who murdered birds.

I could have told her how Kerry needed to prove he was just an ordinary guy, but this would be like saying that in order to cure our gun-crazy country he had to prove that he was just as gun-crazy as everyone else.

It was worse than that. The long masquerade ball of American presidential politics, which had periodically changed styles from French-speaking wigs to ordinary-guy frontiersmen then back to Euro-sophisticates and then to cowboys, was wavering in uncertainty again, the kind of uncertainty that seemed necessary to make it mutate into a different style. After America relied on the Euro-sophisticates to get us through the Euro-wars, it decided that the Cold War was basically a Wild West thing and we'd turned to the cowboy persona. But now America was confronting a new and strange and frightening challenge, a world of Islamic terrorism for which there was no reliable model. George W. Bush was insisting that the Wild West model was totally sufficient for dealing with Islamic terrorism. If the French rejected the Wild West model it was because they were city sissies, and we wouldn't defile ourselves with French fries or French's Mustard, even if French's Mustard was made by hunters on Mustard Way in Springfield, Missouri, right down the road from the Bass Pro Shop; and if during the Iraq war a Springfield TV station broadcast a recipe for French onion soup, viewers would let them know this was an act of treason; and we certainly wouldn't vote for a "French-looking" presidential candidate, which was the prefix Rush Limbaugh was using for John Kerry every day now. Still, many Americans found it worrisome that our longtime European allies were terribly disappointed in us and thought that Bush was a fool. Maybe it wouldn't hurt to have a president with more Euro-sophistication. But we didn't want a Fifi sissy either who would leave us at the mercy of crazy terrorists. We would grant you that the French-looking John Kerry was more Euro-sophisticated than Bush, but could the French-looking Kerry be as tough as Bush?

Thus the Kerry campaign faced the same dilemma that Ernest Hemingway faced when pressured by his mother to be a Euro-sophisticate and pressured by his father to be a frontier tough guy. But Kerry couldn't solve this problem by sitting in Paris cafes and writing novels about frontier tough guys. Such things weren't done by ordinary guys and Kerry needed to be an ordinary guy, not just an ordinary ordinary guy mind you, but an ordinary Wild West tough guy ordinary guy. Though the safety and reputation of the nation depended on America deliberating on its identity, much of this deliberation was mediated by a game of images, a game that everyone agreed was phony and often absurd yet which everyone took with the utmost seriousness, a game you couldn't escape from even when you weren't trying to play it.

When John Kerry went on vacation in Sun Valley, where he and Teresa had a home and where Ernest Hemingway had lived and gone mad from the absurd game of American images and killed himself, Kerry went snowboarding one day, which might have simply been his idea of fun, yet for months afterwards the political media fretted over whether snowboarding was a good image. Perhaps it did show that Kerry was a man-of-action tough guy, but was snowboarding a thing of ordinary guys? The same thing happened when Kerry went windsurfing. The Bush campaign, confident that ordinary guys didn't go windsurfing, began running commercials showing Kerry windsurfing, and soon the media reported that Kerry's campaign manager had forbidden him from going snowboarding or windsurfing again. To me, having decided long ago that the best method for determining whether a political candidate was an ordinary guy was to knock on his door late at night and get him out of bed and see whether he acted like an ordinary guy, all of this seemed terribly extravagant.

The image game turned even more absurd because the media, who generally were not ordinary guys, sometimes had a poor sense of how ordinary guys reacted to ordinary-guy imagery. For weeks the media proclaimed that Kerry had ruined his chances of winning Wisconsin by mispronouncing the name of the Green Bay Packer's stadium.

Yet amid the absurdities of the game of images, everyone understood it was serious business when Kerry the hunter reappeared two weeks before the election in the crucial state of Ohio; it made a good background image for his promise to "hunt down the terrorists and kill them." The Bush campaign understood that here was an image that combined both the ordinary guy and the tough guy, and they mobilized to brand Kerry the hunter a phony.

Even as John Kerry showed off his rifle and smiled for the cameras, could he avoid feeling in that rifle not just the weight of steel and wood but the weight of American history? Whatever innocence he'd once had about American history had been blown away long ago, blown away by the rifle that killed a president he'd idolized, blown away by the guns of Vietnam. Could he lift his rifle now without feeling the weight of the lost American innocence of his grandfather Frederick Kerry who had come to America to make a better life for his family and who had made three fortunes and lost three fortunes and finally couldn't deal with it any further and who walked into the men's room of Boston's Euro-elegant Copley Plaza Hotel and pulled out a handgun from his pocket and pointed it at his head and pulled the trigger?

Vanity of vanity, saith the preacher; all is vanity. The sun also ariseth, and the sun goeth down, and hasteth to the place where he arose. The sun also rises like a slow-motion version of 4th of July fireworks that appear as a red ball and explode outward, spraying the sky with red streamers. The fireworks also rise as a re-enactment of the rocket's red glare, the bombs bursting in air, that gave proof through the night that our flag was still there. The fireworks also rise just like a human brain exploding at the point-blank impact of two shotgun shells. Hemingway's skull was completely shattered and blown apart by the blast, and brain tissue was actually cooked by the energy of impact. His brain disintegrated into thousands of pieces and flew outward, pieces imprinted with African safari sunsets and with sentences from *The Sun Also Rises* and with memories of cheering Teddy Roosevelt and with pride in his favorite shotgun and with yearning to personify heroic American myth. Brain tissue and blood and skull fragments flew outward and painted the walls and ceiling and floor and furniture with a chaotic version of the 4th of July, the first in a coming decade of Jackson Pollock versions of American heroes. The shotgun pellets drove brain tissue right into the wooden walls, embedding it in lunar craters. His blood poured onto the floor and his remaining body turned pale, and when he had opened the fourth seal I looked and beheld a pale horse and a pale rider, and the name of the rider was Death, and Death was a headless horseman riding mindlessly across the American land.

When I had finished dinner and was ready to leave, I stopped in the Hemingway's men's room. I looked for photos of Hemingway on the walls, but they had missed a good bet here. They had missed the famous story of how when Ernest was staying at the Ritz in newly-liberated Paris he had flown into a drunken rage and placed a photo of his wife on a toilet and began firing at it with a captured German pistol, shattering the toilet and bringing the Ritz staff running in alarm. They had missed the infamous chapter called "A Matter of Measurements" in *A Movable Feast* in which over dinner a pathetic Scott Fitzgerald had confessed to Ernest that his wife found him inadequate as a man and he begged Ernest for his manly expertise and Ernest had led him into the men's room and taken his measure and pronounced him entirely adequate and pronounced Scott's wife a bitch who was just trying to make Scott feel unmanly. Some Hemingway biographers dismiss this whole story as just another act of self-mythologizing at the expense of a rival. But other biographers revel in this story, just as they hold that there was never anything wrong with Ernest, not even in the way his life ended. He was a man's man and he died like a man.

I had expected a bit more from the Hemingway's men's room after seeing the men's room at the store's main entrance. That room's entire ceiling held a huge elaborate map showing the route of the Lewis and Clark expedition. I stood there in amazement. It was like the Sistine Chapel of American exploration, lacking only a Thomas Jefferson reaching out an arm and finger of national creation to Lewis and Clark. The walls held forest scenes, and loudspeakers played forest sounds. The front of the long wash counter was inlaid with shotgun shells.

Thomas Jefferson was not surprised to hear that Meriwether Lewis had pointed a gun at his own head and pulled the trigger. Lewis had long been beset by dark self-doubts. But some historians have refused to accept that a hero of American frontier conquest could contain such weakness, and they've suggested that Lewis must have been a murder victim, since no one saw him commit suicide in his lonely tavern room. Similarly, many would refuse to accept that a manly hero like President Kennedy could be felled by a very ordinary guy or even by a stampeding culture of violence. Similarly, Americans were shocked to find that being the personification of American heroism wasn't enough to keep Ernest Hemingway happy and proud or even alive. Of course you could make the case that given his family history of manic depression and suicide, Ernest was doomed anyway, and grabbing hold of American myth helped keep him alive, just as having a great mythic challenge helped keep Meriwether Lewis alive. That's what national myths are for, to help people and nations live. But in the end it wasn't enough.

Shortly after the election, on November 22, the anniversary of President Kennedy's assassination, Americans saw news stories about a new video game that made you the assassin, letting you watch from the 6th floor as the motorcade approached and turned the corner, letting you aim at the back of the president's head and pull the trigger. If you were a winner the video rewarded you with rich colorful details of Kennedy's head exploding and his brains and blood flying out all over the car and all over Jackie. On the same newscasts Americans heard about a Wisconsin north-woods shootout in which hunters got into a dispute over possession of a hunting blind and opened fire, killing six hunters.

As I left Hemingway's I paused at the front desk to look at the wall behind it. Centrally placed was a large famous photo of Hemingway at his typewriter. This was the only acknowledgement on these walls that Ernest wasn't just a hunter and fisherman but a writer. This photo was taken at his home in Sun Valley, in the house where he was to kill himself. I couldn't tell, but I would be surprised if Ernest's typewriter wasn't a Remington. The Remington Company was the first to make a typewriter in America. This was the same Remington Company that made Remington rifles. There was a logical connection between firearms and typewriters, because the pulling/linking/striking mechanism of typewriter keys was rather similar to the mechanism of a gun trigger, so similar that Remington could modify its rifle-making equipment to make typewriters. Typewriters even sounded like guns. Writing used to be a very quiet art, but now a man could beat on triggers that went rat-a-tat-tat, rat-a-tat-tat. When you got going really fast it was just like a machine gun or a battle. Ernest was sitting there working on *For Whom the Bell Tolls*. And therefore—rat-a-tat-tat—never send to know—rat-a-tat-tat—for whom the bell tolls—rat-a-tat-tat—it tolls for thee.

Right next to the Hemingway photo was President George W. Bush, smiling happily, without any ambiguity, simply happy to be here at the greatest cathedral to America's gun culture. Now here was a man with nothing to prove. Here was an ordinary guy. That was why we loved him: he was the personification of the ordinary guy's faith in American myth. Believing in America completely was a no-brainer. Without any ambiguity, the president smiled.

4

Wilshire Boulevard

"Hello, I'm calling from the summit of the American Dream."

Actually I was calling from the top of a bank building in Beverly Hills, on Wilshire Boulevard, only a block from Rodeo Drive. That's Ro-*day*-o Drive. Don't even think of thinking of dusty cowboys here.

Looking out the window I could see far below a huddle of people staring into the window of Tiffany's at the corner of Wilshire Boulevard and Rodeo Drive. That's *day*, as in diamonds as bright as the noonday sun. It was as if the diamonds possessed the gravity of tiny stars too, for a steady stream of people were tugged from their trajectory down the sidewalk and into the orbit of Tiffany's, where they just stared into the window for many minutes. Few seemed to go inside; most seemed content to window-shop, for they understood their role as outsiders here, mere visitors to a glowing world they usually saw only through the window of a movie screen or television screen. Yet they had come here to claim some of that glow for themselves, to purchase some of it with their mere presence and desire, to cloak themselves in at least a t-shirt glowing "Beverly Hills" to the now-inferior folks back home.

Tiffany's was nestled in what had become the iconic Rodeo Drive scene, a fountain and a curving stairway leading upwards to a faux-Italian courtyard and cobblestone street. This stairway had been seen in so many movies and magazines that tourists had classified it as the stairway to glamour. People posed in front of the stairway for photos, for proof that they were glamorous. They walked up the stairway, then turned around and walked back down, then walked back up again.

I was calling from the board room of a law firm that had loaned their space to the Kerry campaign for a phone bank. Today was the California primary. But I had expected to be calling across the country to Georgia, for the national strategists had decided that California was a safe victory while Georgia was the closest race on this Super Tuesday. I liked the idea of calling Georgians, not just because I could make a difference in a close race but because of the mere idea of sitting atop a Beverly Hills bank and calling up some Appalachian hollow where Democratic loyalties went back to forgotten ancestors who had marched with Andrew Jackson. I liked the idea of telling hillbillies that I was calling from a Beverly Hills bank, for the power of American pop culture is such that the hillbillies would instantly get the joke. They'd laugh and say "Is Mr. Drysdale there? Be sure to say hi to Jed Clampett and Granny for us."

Maybe it was more likely that I'd be talking with African-American families in Atlanta, but I was ready for that too. I'd say: "You know that scene in *Beverly Hills Cop* where Eddie Murphy pulls up to that super-fancy hotel in his beat-up car and wearing his beat-up shirt and the hotel employees stare at him like he's a bag of garbage until he plunks down his money and they start treating him like a prince?" And of course almost every African American had known that scene even before *Beverly Hills Cop* came out, especially the part about being stared at like a bag of garbage and the dream about being treated like a prince. "Well, I'm looking out my window right now at that hotel, the Regent Beverly Wilshire." And they'd laugh and say: "No way!"

Or maybe I'd be talking with housewives in suburban Atlanta, and I was ready for that too. "You know that super-fancy hotel in *Pretty Woman* where Julia Roberts is treated like a bag of garbage until the prince falls in love with her and turns the hotel into her Cinderella Palace? Well, I'm looking right at it." And they'd laugh and say "Cool!"

Across all our miles and differences we would be instantly bonded by sharing in not just the American Dream but its ultimate address. Everyone I talked with would be charmed and tell their friends that they had been anointed by the glamour of Beverly Hills.

And yet, my Georgia friends would also fully understand that the American Dream was also loaded with unkindness. Mr. Drysdale might not treat the Clampetts like bags of garbage but he did treat them like bags of money. Eddie Murphy was only a prince until the hotel found out he couldn't pay his bill, and a greedy bad guy was trying to turn him into a body bag. Julia Roberts became Cinderella not because she was a nice woman but because she was a pretty woman in a town notorious for discarding the un-pretty. The glamour was all about the yearning to be treated nicely, yet people would commit any cruelty to get to where they'd be treated nicely.

Now I was watching a busload of Japanese tourists milling around the stairway to glamour. They may have gotten lucky and gotten an extra dose of glamour, for the Academy Awards ceremonies had been on Sunday night, and even today in Hollywood they were still rolling up the red carpets. The Oscar for best actress

went to a glamorous blonde wearing diamond earrings, a diamond ring, a diamond bracelet, and a diamond dress; she won for her sparking portrayal of a
grubby hooker turned deranged serial killer.

It was also possible that I'd be calling a little Georgia mountain town called
Mayberry, where I'd talk with Opie because his pa, Sheriff Andy Taylor, was out
doing some patient kindness for a total stranger.

Even in their goofiest forms American myths held strong powers to tug us into
their orbits. In the early 1960s American myth was grappling with the transition
between rural life and urban life for much of the nation, with nostalgic yearnings
for the kindnesses of rural life yet yearnings to be the simple folks who lived out
the American Dream.

The Beverly Hillbillies wasn't the first time that a hardscrabble Ozarks family
had overloaded several generations of kin and all their possessions onto a rusty
old truck and headed down Rt. 66 for California. You wouldn't guess it from the
film version of *The Grapes of Wrath*, which places the Joad farm on a flat plain,
but in the novel they came from the Ozarks fringe of Oklahoma, a dozen miles
from the Arkansas border. This means that if Tom Joad went up into the hills to
go hunting, he might have—brace yourself for a serious mix-up of genres—run
into a young Jed Clampett.

But the Joads were real, all too real; my father could tell you how real they
were since he grew up in dust-bowl Oklahoma and he saw them. *The Grapes of
Wrath* movie gives a glimpse of the Joads driving through downtown Oklahoma
City, and this was where my father grew up and saw the endless train of Joads in
old trucks trying to chase the American Dream down Rt. 66 to California. But
first came the tides of dust, massive boiling tsunamis of dust darkening the western sky and racing towards you, and my father and his brothers and parents cried
out a warning and raced about to get ready, to slam the windows and get the dog
inside and soak towels to stuff under the doors—but you couldn't stop it, the
dust came pouring in anyway and covered everything. This dust had been someone's farm and someone's American Dream come true but now the American
Dream was gone with the wind, gone because the American Dream could be
filled with unkindness, the unkindness of the land when you tried to take from it
more than it had to give, the unkindness of bankers and sheriffs taking your farm
at gunpoint and of bulldozers rolling over your little house and your family
graves. So the Okies packed their remaining dreams onto their rusty trucks and
did what Americans have always done when unkindness pushed and myth called:
they headed west, not just compass-west but mythic west, the direction of the
American Dream. But the road could be unkind too, the mother road could eat

her children: the tires popped and the radiators boiled over and the townspeople didn't want you to stop there; but sometimes the engine died and you were broke and wherever you were that's where your family would stay scrubbing restaurant floors for a generation or more. If you made it to California you found Hoovervilles and hostility but not the American Dream; you found yourselves lucky to get a job scrubbing restaurant floors for a generation.

Yet within a generation *The Grapes of Wrath* myth had been heavily revised. Now a hardscrabble Ozarks family overloading a rusty old truck and heading down Rt. 66 to California was a proof of the generosity of the American Dream. Absolutely anybody could strike it rich in America and end up living in a Beverly Hills mansion.

What was the truth about the American Dream? Was it primarily a great generosity, or was it primarily a ruthless competition? And if it was both a generosity and a heartlessness, which was the dominant theme and how did it get that way and how did the two interact? If they modified one another was it for the better or the worse? Did the generosity of the American Dream make Americans a more generous people, or did the heartlessness of the competition for the American Dream degrade the dream itself?

The Grapes of Wrath and *The Beverly Hillbillies* seemed to agree that the American Dream contained both generosity and ruthlessness. Even in the midst of their ordeal the Joads found and gave many acts of compassion, a sharing of food, a sharing of friendship, finally the notorious sharing of a breast with a starving man, which for some conservatives was obscene not just because of the breast but because the mere idea of a compassionate America where strangers helped one another was also obscene. Even in the midst of their bonanza the Clampetts were constantly beset by greed and insincerity, and most Americans took the show not first as a satire about sub-Mayberry country folks but as a satire of the phony and mean summit of the American Dream.

When I was a kid and *The Beverly Hillbillies* was a new hit TV show my father regularly drove me down to Oklahoma to visit the relatives, and our route took us through the Ozarks. Right along the highway were dilapidated cabins with old rusty trucks, some long abandoned and some not, but none of the trucks were heading to Beverly Hills anytime soon. I was seeing the difference between the American Dream and American reality, for many of these families had been stuck in poverty for over a century, and the abandoned cabins and trucks meant they had given up and moved to Springfield to scrub restaurant floors for a lifetime. Branson was a quiet little town back then, a real Mayberry that Americans would soon turn into the national capital of Mayberry mythology, yet just down the road Sam Walton was preparing to wipe out thousands of Mayberrys and spread nationwide Ozarks-style low expectations for the American Dream.

I was now being reminded of the discrepancies in the American Dream, for we weren't calling Georgia after all, just Los Angeles, and my voter list seemed to be some barrio neighborhood. All the names were Latino and most people didn't speak English. My rudimentary Spanish didn't get me far.

I assumed that I was talking with some Ellis Island neighborhood, recent enough arrivals that they hadn't learned even basic English, but they weren't illegal immigrants, for this was a list of registered Democratic voters. I guessed that many of these voters had taken considerable trouble to come to America and that they were drawn by the American Dream. They were the new Joads, taking the harvesting jobs and janitor jobs. They were eager enough to be part of America that they had registered to vote. But when I did find someone with good English and they started to talk about their lives, it was clear that many were struggling. One man told me how his mother got sick and of course they didn't have health insurance and they were staggered by the hopeless medical bills. One woman said sadly that the schools were bad and gang-infested and too many kids thought that the only way to succeed was by selling drugs. One woman complained about the bad public transportation, leaving her to walk miles to work on bad legs.

Listening to this as I kept an eye on the huddle outside Tiffany's, the *Beverly Hillbillies* myth lost much of its charm. I ceased thinking it might be fun to tell people: "You'll never guess where I'm calling from—the top of a bank in Beverly Hills!" Saying this now would place a thick barrier between me and the barrio, and could even sound like a taunt from a world they'd never enter no matter how hard they tried. Some of these barriered Latinos may have watched *The Beverly Hillbillies* in Mexico or the San Joaquin Valley and it had contributed to their deciding that Los Angeles was the real home of the American Dream. But by now they had discovered that the only way they were getting to Beverly Hills was by riding an hour or more on bad public transportation to scrub restaurant floors or mow lawns. Even the generosity of the America Dream became a taunt when it was barred from you.

Yet some barriers were more easily crossed. I thought of Lisa, an immigrant from El Salvador with whom I'd passed out flyers at the Santa Monica farmer's market on Sunday.

Santa Monica is another land of myth, like Mayberry and Beverly Hills. Santa Monica is the beach and the endless-summer fun-in-the-sun image of southern California. Moviemaking had barely started in Los Angeles before they started making beach movies full of pretty, carefree girls. Rt. 66 ends right at the Santa

Monica pier with its famous amusement rides, as if to promise the Joads and their successors that the beach would put an end not just to their travels but their travails too.

For me it was an easier drive, straight west on Wilshire Boulevard, through Beverly Hills, past the country club parked full of glamour cars, past the shops full of glamour clothes, past the cemetery full of glamour clothes on glamour corpses, dozens of big stars including Marilyn Monroe whose suicide declared that even the most glamorous summits of the American Dream couldn't save you from even deeper depths; down Wilshire Boulevard until I could smell the salt air and see the Ferris wheel turning and see the glorious beach and finally see the signs warning against swimming and fishing due to severe water pollution.

The Santa Monica farmer's market was an LA institution where people gathered not just for food and live music but for a gasp of community in the anonymity smog of Los Angeles. I took a handful of Kerry flyers and was heading for a good spot when I noticed a young Latino woman with her own batch of Kerry flyers and looking paralyzed, not even trying to hand anything to anyone. I figured she was just shy and went over to offer some teamwork. Lisa was studying nursing at a community college and was taking a course in social studies and her teacher assigned doing some volunteer work for a political campaign. As we talked I gathered that American politics was an alien world to Lisa; she wasn't even registered to vote. I figured Lisa was intimidated by the social barriers here, for the crowd was almost entirely white and well-off and ridiculously stylish for a farmer's market. Then Lisa started talking about how her parents had fled El Salvador to escape the civil war and chaos, fled to America for its famous safety, not for political freedoms but for freedom from politics. Her parents had always kept a safe distance form politics because politics was a very dangerous thing. Politics meant that your neighbor disappeared in the middle of the night and was never seen again. In El Salvador handing out political flyers in public meant that someone knocked on your own door at midnight. I coached Lisa about how to address a stranger in a crowd and showed her how harmless it was, and finally she spoke haltingly to a white guy and the guy smiled and she reached across the barriers of race and wealth and across an open trench loaded with bullet-ridden bodies.

The Latino neighborhood I was calling made quite a contrast with a neighborhood I had called earlier, where many answering machines had announced the names of moviemaking services, home-based freelance screenwriters or publicity agents or consultants about everything Hollywood. I seemed to have hit the bull's-eye of the moviemaking world. When I got real people on the line it wasn't really proper to go fishing into their personal lives, especially since these voters didn't talk about their personal lives in the way the Latinos did. Presumably they were doing fine financially. But they did live in the bull's-eye of American myth-making and they were worried about the fate of America's image and values. One man said how appalled he was that when Europeans thought of America now they thought of George. W. Bush. One woman worried about the public schools becoming tools of the religious right.

If the Latino neighborhood held the foot soldiers of the American Dream, who arranged their whole lives to follow orders from a mysterious mythic author-ity, then in the Hollywood neighborhood I was talking with the generals, the cre-ators of the images that guided a nation. It was they who decided whether a rusty overloaded truck heading down Rt. 66 from the Ozarks to California was a vision of the generosity or the travail of the American Dream, or what mixture of both. They created both the overblown glamour and the overblown violence that enthralled tens of millions every weekend. Yet even they were not the creators of the American Dream as much as its moderators, for they only gave new forms to old images that had been playing in the American mind long before the movies were invented. They couldn't even control whether the movies were mere fluff or very serious, for they too were in the grip of historical forces far mightier than themselves.

Take, for instance, the year 1939. It probably wasn't a coincidence that the historical moment when fascist myths were marching through Europe generated a burst of classic contemplations and proclamations of American myth. Ameri-cans sensed they were on the verge of one of their greatest challenges, and the national mythic unconscious was churning, measuring America against this chal-lenge and against America's own ideals. The year 1939 produced *Gone with the Wind*, *Stagecoach*, *Mr. Smith Goes to Washington*, *The Wizard of Oz*, and *Of Mice and Men*, and the years 1940–1942 produced *The Grapes of Wrath*, *Citizen Kane*, and *Casablanca*. Yet these myths were running in many different directions at once, openly denying one another. Americans couldn't even agree on the mean-ing of any one movie. In *Mr. Smith Goes to Washington* some people saw the democratic nobility of Mr. Smith and others saw the venality of the rest of the politicians in it. Hedda Hopper declared that "to me, *Mr. Smith Goes to Washing-ton* is as great as Lincoln's Gettysburg speech."[9] But one prominent U. S. ambas-sador telegraphed President Roosevelt urging him to ban *Mr. Smith* from overseas distribution since it made America look venal. Southerners adored *Gone with the Wind* for its romanticizing of the Old South, but liberals were dismayed by all those so-loyal slaves. *Stagecoach* gave America John Wayne and a classic statement of frontier tough-guy virtues triumphing over the attack of savages, while *Of Mice and Men* offered another John Steinbeck prescription of compassion for the Common Man. *The Wizard of Oz* might seem to be the movie least about America but it also offered the strongest contest between good and evil and proclaimed that there was no place like Kansas.

Abruptly, I decided that my phoning day was over. I made my escape because a photographer from *The New York Times* was heading our way, and not to document Kerry volunteers sitting and talking with Latinos about health insurance. The photographer needed something more dramatic, so she was going to stage an event, posing us on the street corner beneath the sign "Beverly Drive," having us hold up Kerry signs, with the caption: "Kerry volunteers rallied yesterday on a street corner in Beverly Hills."

That very morning *The New York Times* had carried the obituary of Daniel J. Boorstin, librarian of congress and Pulitzer Prize-winning historian. But perhaps his greatest contribution to American life, declared *The Times*, was his book *The Image: A Guide to Pseudo-Events in America*. Writing in 1961, when television was just beginning to change the way news was reported and the way politicians tried to make news, Boorstin bemoaned the growing domination of image over substance, the readiness of both media and politicians to stage events for the cameras. But Boorstin did allow that *The New York Times* was "a model of journalistic sobriety."[10]

Standing on a street corner and waving signs at passing drivers wasn't my idea of campaigning. I preferred a meaningful act of communication between human beings. Waving signs was just so California, all image and no personal contact, drive-thru campaigning, McCampaigning. There was no way I was going to be seen in *The New York Times* McCampaigning in Beverly Hills. So I fled.

The image. Along with the media and Hollywood, historians too shaped the images of the American Dream. The history writers were closer to Hollywood screenwriters than they'd care to admit in their freedom to define the American Dream as generous or cruel or anything in between, but like moviemakers the historians were in the grip of images and historical forces much more powerful than themselves. Just as Americans argued over the images in movies, they argued over the images in history books. Early in the 1960s California became the national center of attention for a fight over history-book images. Even before the 1960s revisionists really got going, long before William J. Bennett was railing against public schools for failing to teach traditional virtues, California state superintendent of public education Max Rafferty, a graduate of Beverly Hills High School, was railing against public schools for promoting un-heroic images of America, for promoting a *Grapes of Wrath* indictment of the American Dream and not a *Beverly Hillbillies* glorification of it, for promoting an *Of Mice and Men* compassion over a *Stagecoach* toughness, for promoting Mr. Smith the liberal windbag over Scarlet O'Hara the noble victim of liberal gone-with-the-windbags. Max Rafferty became a national hero to conservatives determined to defend the John Wayne image of America against the onslaught of the hippies, and in 1968 he beat a moderate incumbent U. S. senator in the Republican primary.

I'd already done my share of sign waving in front of Kerry headquarters, which was upstairs in another bank on Wilshire Boulevard, just outside of Beverly Hills. I had a green 'League of Conservation Voters for Kerry' sign, and once when a Hummer stopped at the traffic light I pointed my sign at him and used my finger to underline the word 'conservation,' and he started using his middle finger back at me. If I had a Hummer, I'd Hummer in the morning, I'd Hummer in the evening, all over this land. I'd Hummer out the meadows, I'd Hummer out the wildlife...

The LA Kerry volunteers were more energetic than me about sign waving. We were led by an actor who had played one of the students in *Dead Poet's Society* and he was putting on an energetic show. Quite a few of the volunteers had Hollywood stories, and one of them seemed to know all the stories about Hollywood for he was telling me the film history of the spot where we were standing. We were standing on the Miracle Mile, which, before Rodeo Drive, was once the most glamorous shopping address in LA. We were standing in front of a former classy department store with a huge art deco golden cylinder in a black frame. Heddy Lamarr starred in a movie set in this store, playing a washed-up star who had to go to work in the lingerie department—No, wait—that wasn't a movie. Heddy Lamarr really was a washed-up star, and she really was arrested in this store for shoplifting lingerie or something. It was Bette Davis who starred in a movie set in this store, playing a washed-up star who had to go to work selling lingerie. But Heddy Lamarr couldn't have stolen lingerie from Bette Davis because one was real life and one was a movie, right? A mile or two up Wilshire Boulevard was the creepy mansion where they'd shot *Sunset Boulevard*, with washed-up star Gloria Swanson playing a washed-up star who couldn't tell the difference between real life and the movies, who was crazy from trying to live in the past. And wouldn't you know it, the classic depiction of Hollywood phoniness was phony about the mansion being on Sunset Boulevard; it was really on Wilshire Boulevard, a long-abandoned mansion when they'd used it in the movie, later torn down to make a parking lot. Just to get this straight: Sunset Boulevard was the phony address of phoniness and Wilshire Boulevard was the real address of a phony depiction of real phoniness.

To pick up a few dozen League of Conservation Voters for Kerry signs I'd driven miles down Wilshire Boulevard to the other side of Beverly Hills to the very modest office of the California League of Conservation Voters. I'd driven through the world capital of conspicuous consumption, through streets full of luxury cars including Rolls Royces, past $100-a-dinner restaurants, past $1,000-a-dress clothing stores, past $10,000-a-necklace jewelry stores, past $100,000-a-car dealerships, past $10,000,000-a-home realtors. I'd picked up these signs for an environmentalist event featuring Teresa Heinz Kerry. It was held at an Audubon center right across the Arroyo Seco from the home and museum built by Charles Lummis. A century ago Lummis was the leader of an Arroyo Seco colony of artists and writers who believed that southern California would redeem America from material values, inspiring instead a Walden simplicity and Native American affinity with nature. Today the Arroyo Seco is encased in cement. Though it was a beautiful day at a beautiful site, only three dozen people showed up. The next day a $1,000-per-person fund-raiser with Teresa at a movie mogul's house in Beverly Hills brought out such a crowd that it caused a traffic jam on Sunset Boulevard.

There were quite a few Hummers on Wilshire Boulevard. One of us was holding up a sign saying "Honk for Kerry," but none of the Hummers honked. The demographics of honking was intriguing. Kerry might be losing the Hummer vote but he was doing quite well with the Volvo vote. This seemed a scientific confirmation of the phrase "Volvo liberals." This phrase of course was intended to compliment liberals for their life-affirming values. While American auto makers were building cars with little regard for safety, cars that needlessly killed thousands of Americans every year, Volvo was building safety-loaded cars as if human life was valuable. A Volvo liberal, then, is someone who believes that people matter. Yet in their typical confusion conservatives seemed to regard "Volvo liberal" as a pejorative term. In their lexicology "Volvo liberal" had evolved from "limousine liberal," a 1960s term for liberals who prescribed lofty ideals for urban troubles only to drive home to safe neighborhoods. By the 1980s conservatives had noticed the proliferation of Volvos in faculty parking lots and they largely replaced the limos with Volvos, implying not just the economic elitism of limos but an un-American cultural elitism. Silently included in this indictment were thousands of successful Jews who were seriously disinclined to send their money to Germany for BMWs or Mercedes.

To my surprise quite a few BMWs and Mercedes were honking, but then they were probably Hollywood liberals, another now widely-used phrase for doubters of America. We were also honked at by blacks and Latinos in dented pickups loaded with lawnmowers. We were honked at by two LA city buses—were they allowed to use city property for political purposes? But the bus drivers couldn't match the train driver who'd walked into our Flagstaff office, only a block from the mainline of the Santa Fe railroad, looking for a Kerry bumper sticker for his locomotive.

When I fled the photo pseudo-event on Wilshire Boulevard I headed for the anonymity of Rodeo Drive. I had become curious about what the crowd at Tiffany's was staring at. I stared into the eyes of the hypnotist: the diamonds arranged into every constellation of ring, earring, necklace, and bracelet; the gold watches and cuff links and candle holders; the $100 silver baby spoons; the $600 silver piggy bank in the shape of an elephant.

I glanced into the famous fountain, full of coins wishing for Rodeo Drive dreams. I walked up the famous stairway, slowly, savoring every step. If only my friends could see me now. I was entering the innermost sanctum of glamour, the home of the gods Gucci, Chanel, Armani, Cartier, Versace, Vuitton—and those were just the plebian names: to get into Bijan, where a suit cost $15,000, you needed an appointment. I window-stared at the $25,000 dresses, intended to deny that humans are the same basic biology even as they declared the extravagant outcome of the quiet evolutionary decision that among humans it would be females who needed to be decorated to attract attention and prove their value. I saw in these windows the reflected faces of people from all over the world, from Paris and Rio and Bombay, San Francisco and San Antonio, and their craving eyes made hard to deny the universal human craving for wealth, which ultimately was a craving for what wealth bought, for not just valuable objects but for the value they bestowed upon their wearers, for not just looking good but for being looked upon as good. A dress or a diamond necklace could serve the same void as did the constellations in the sky, a sky into which humans looked with such gravity of craving that they shaped gods who guaranteed the endless value of human life.

I went into only one store, an art gallery with western landscapes. They didn't have any paintings of rodeos or cowboys.

History had played a joke on Beverly Hills by giving its most pretentious street the same name as a dusty, dung-perfumed, beer-soaked cowboy show. Beverly Hills couldn't evade this irony by pronouncing it Ro-*day*-o, which was actually the proper Spanish. Perhaps history had even endorsed the American Dream with this name, for the American Dream held that the distance between a cowboy rodeo and Rodeo Drive was not so far after all, so close that anyone could ride off into the sunset to go live on Sunset Boulevard. The fascination of window-shopping on Rodeo Drive included a mythic fascination with the idea that class barriers in America were window-thin and as easily crossed as opening a Rodeo Drive door. The Hollywood mythmaking machine was very aware of the power of this myth and continued turning out hit varieties of it. These hits gained deeper resonance for coming from the famously democratic Hollywood where any lingerie sales clerk could step off a bus and be discovered and become a star, a Hollywood self-myth that had produced its own genre of hit movies.

Even in the depths of the Great Depression, when families skimped all week to save the dimes to go to the movies on Saturday to see a dream of glamour and success, Democrats were playing with fire when they questioned the reality of this dream, when they implied that the door between the rodeo and Rodeo Drive was locked shut. Even those who most needed the help of the Democratic Party would accept it only if it was a key to opening that door and reject it if it was a pin to burst their bubble. When Democrats spoke to the rodeo about Harvard sociological truths, they helped turn Harvard into an un-American word that the Bushes could use against Boston presidential candidates, and they turned Harvard-educated, Volvo-driving Hollywood filmmakers, who should have been the first symbols of success, into snobbish enemies of the American Dream. They helped drive the rodeo into the hands of Rodeo Drive conservatives who proclaimed an unwavering faith in the American Dream and eagerly invoked Hollywood-sanctioned rodeo symbolism, such as Bush's cowboy hat and ranch and chores. Volvo liberals seemed to think they were insulting Bush by calling him a cowboy, when they were only confirming his power in American myth.

When the east-coast polls closed, it soon became clear that Kerry was winning almost everywhere, essentially clinching the nomination. I headed many miles down Wilshire Boulevard in sunset rush-hour traffic to the Wilshire Grand Hotel downtown, where the California Democratic Party was holding its election-night party. But no California Democrats were there yet, as the local polls were still open. In a huge empty ballroom there were only four of us Kerry workers watching the big-screen coverage of east-coast returns and cheering the state-by-state victory projections. But the Kerry victory party in Washington D. C. was packed. Ted Kennedy was cheerleading. Originally Kerry was supposed to be in Florida tonight and California senator Barbara Boxer was supposed to be here, but both stayed in Washington to vote on the assault-weapons ban, which the NRA was vigorously opposing as a violation of the right of Americans to murder spouses, clerks, and presidents with assault rifles instead of just cheap handguns. Ted Kennedy introduced Kerry, and the huge crowd cheered, and four of us cheered in a huge empty ballroom, and Kerry gave his victory speech. A dozen cameras surrounded us. Eventually enough Kerry workers arrived to impersonate a crowd, and the press photographers prompted us to put on a show, coaching us to move closer together and wave our signs and cheer, but still only half of my face and League of Conservation Voters for Kerry sign made it into *The Los Angeles Times* the next morning, which in LA meant that I was only half real and half unreal. We cheered for the emptiness and the fullness of democracy in America.

The crowd continued building through the evening until the ballroom was full. Kerry won big in California. I would have stayed much later, but something else was tugging on me, something that would not allow this night to be complete.

I headed back down Wilshire Boulevard. Since Wilshire was a major business street it was a canyon of lights. But finally, after thirty blocks or so, I came upon a void, a large zone of darkness. I parked and walked back. I stared through the chain-link fence, which was topped with some serious barbed wire. The lawn was long un-mowed and strewn with litter. A long way back from the street was the main building, completely dark except for one vertical chain of lights, probably mapping out a stairway, ready for an emergency evacuation in a building that had been abandoned for fifteen years. Even the darkness couldn't hide the decay. I walked up to one end of the property, where a row of bungalows ended near the sidewalk. The bungalows had broken windows, peeling paint, missing roof tiles. A faded billboard announced that the property was available for filming, so apparently some interiors had been maintained in their old grandeur, saving moviemakers from having to build sets of a grand old hotel.

For decades this had been one of the most glamorous addresses in America. The rich and famous from Europe and the east coast vacationed here. Out-of-town stars lived in the bungalows while making movies, and Hollywood stars and directors lunched at the Coconut Grove. Ordinary folks saved their money for years for one honeymoon or anniversary night here. Famous singers and bands performed in the ballroom.

The Academy Awards ceremonies for 1939 was held here, and the stars turned out in all their elegance, the ladies filling the ballroom with the diamond glitter of Rodeo Drive and the Miracle Mile, all in honor of tales of ordeals and ideals and grim endurance as the American mythic imagination worked very seriously and created *Gone with the Wind, The Wizard of Oz, Stagecoach, Of Mice and Men, and Mr. Smith Goes to Washington.*

From London, Ambassador Joseph P. Kennedy had sent telegrams to President Roosevelt and to the state department urging that *Mr. Smith Goes to Washington* be banned from overseas distribution because it "will cause our allies to view us in an unfavorable light."[11] Then he wrote to the head of Hollywood's self-censorship board declaring that *Mr. Smith* was "one of the most disgraceful things I have ever seen done to this country."[12] It was "criminal" that Europeans were seeing it. Kennedy sent a copy of this letter to Roosevelt. To the president of Columbia Pictures Kennedy complained that its *Mr. Smith* portrayed "a governor, senators, the press and radio…taking orders from crooks."[13]

We can suspect that Roosevelt and everyone else was amused by the irony of Joseph P. Kennedy, of all people, worrying about venality blotting America's image. Kennedy was a master at using venality in pursuit of the American Dream, making his fortune from prohibition bootlegging with the aid of organized crime, from manipulating the stock market and leaving ordinary folks the losers, from shady dealings and back stabbings as a businessman and as a Hollywood mogul. But was it just America's image that Ambassador Kennedy was upset about? Perhaps as part of his master plan to win the American Dream status chase by getting one of his sons elected president he had tried to inspire his sons about political careers by taking them to see *Mr. Smith Goes To Washington*, only for them to be confronted by a depiction of politicians as stupid, dishonest, self-serving hacks. Naturally Ambassador Kennedy would see only the venality, not allowing for the possibility that his sons might see Mr. Smith as challenging American democracy to rise to its ideals.

But Ambassador Kennedy certainly grasped the mythmaking power of movies. He had founded RKO Pictures and lived on Rodeo Drive and taken Gloria Swanson as a mistress for three years. Kennedy had hired director Eric von Stroheim to make a Gloria Swanson movie, but Swanson decided that Stroheim was crazy and walked out on the movie and it was never finished—but scenes from it showed up decades later in *Sunset Boulevard* to show the younger years of the crazy washed-up actress played by Gloria Swanson, who really was a washed-up silent movie actress. The crazy washed-up director-turned-servant in *Sunset Boulevard* was played by Eric von Stroheim, who kept forgetting that he really was a crazy washed-up director and kept trying to direct *Sunset Boulevard*, which was all about crazy people living in the past, except that the ultimate movie about Hollywood unreality wasn't really filmed on Sunset Boulevard but here on Wilshire Boulevard, only half a mile from the Ambassador Hotel. Kennedy had used his venal political skills to pursue an Oscar for his mistress, and she was nominated twice, but she lost twice in Academy Awards ceremonies that were both held here in the ballroom of the Ambassador Hotel.

For the 1939 Academy Awards the center of attention was *Gone with the Wind*, which had captured the national imagination. David O. Selznick had stoked this imagination by holding a nationwide talent search for a star, a democratic search for an undemocratic heroine. A third of a million fans lined the streets of Atlanta for the premiere. The Nazis banned *Gone with the Wind* for romanticizing endurance of invasion. Liberals denounced it for romanticizing tyranny, but then their sympathies perked up when Hattie McDaniel became the first black nominated for an Oscar. Then she became the first black seated at an Academy Awards ceremony. She was seated at a segregated table at the back of the ballroom. Hattie had given a strong performance as Mammy, who was utterly loyal to Scarlet O'Hara and the social codes of the Old South, enforcing the codes for dominant white ladies even when the ladies themselves found it all silly. When Hattie won the Oscar for best supporting actress she cried out "Hallelujah!" and pledged to "always be a credit to my race."[14]

In the movie itself and in the world itself, the battle for human equality was fought not with golden statues but with blood, with armies of millions marching across America for four years. The bright lights in the streets of Atlanta had been the torches of Sherman's march to the sea. Some of Sherman's men were Irishmen who had left the land of their family, church, and hearts because they hated the feudalism the British had planted deeply into the Irish earth, left it for an America that had fought a war to free itself of British feudalism and give birth to the American Dream. They endured a long miserable sea voyage and a long miserable trek to Illinois to find the farmland that certified they were free of feudalism. Yet with a sense of betrayal they had realized that the British had planted feudalism deeply in America too, too deeply for one revolution and one constitution to eradicate. When Lincoln called upon them to march, the Irishmen in their long enduring outraged memory of betrayals had marched, marched to Shiloh and Vicksburg, to Chickamauga and Missionary Ridge, and then they marched on Atlanta. (Vivien Leigh, after carefully considering what dress would look best with an Oscar, had selected, according to *Variety*, "a full-skirted flowered dress, covered with long ermine robe, heavy antique bracelet and huge precious stone pendant around the neck."[15]) They marched singing "The Battle Hymn of the Republic" with its line about trampling out the grapes of wrath. They marched through Appalachian hollows where hillbillies whose grandpas had marched with Andrew Jackson stood with Gettysburg amputations. They marched through plantations where the slaves cried out "Hallelujah!" and swarmed around them. Like the hollowed faces in the concentration camps eighty years later, these black faces didn't doubt they were being delivered from evil by the armies of justice. This was America at its best, the clearest possible enactment of the founding dream of America as liberator of a world of tyranny.

Not here was the border between good and evil blurred by Manifest Destiny or manifest stupidity; it was as sharply defined as the barbed wire fence at Treblinka or the stone fence at Gettysburg.

Except, of course, that in the Civil War both the good and the evil were American.

The Civil War was only the armed interlude in a civil war that had raged from America's beginning and hardly stopped with Appomattox, a civil war in which the best and the worst in the American soul contended for mastery, contended to define and steer the American Dream. It was fought out in the motivations of the first settlers, some of whom came for freedom and some of whom came for greed. It was fought out from wilderness pulpits and political stumps as people sought to define what we were doing here and what America should be. It was fought out in the Continental Congress, when America finally had to codify itself. It was fought out in campfire homespun tales of folk heroes, and in novels and philosophies written in Concord libraries. It was fought out in presidential campaigns that allowed a protean nation continually to redefine itself. America defined its ideals with the words of Jefferson and Lincoln and Martin Luther King, even as America worked to sabotage its ideals. The shallowness of the American soul never ceased to mock the depths. (Olivia de Havilland wore "a voluminous black evening dress with lace inserts and white-ermine jacket.") It was fought out in Hollywood, where the meaning of America was debated by Scarlet O'Hara, Mr. Smith, John Wayne, a phony wizard, and displaced men dreaming of their own land; where Joseph Kennedy and Hedda Hopper argued over whether Mr. Smith was another Gettysburg address. It was fought out on the balcony of Ford's Theater (Mrs. Lincoln, always eager to impress Washington society, wore a low-cut, light gray, silk spring dress, along with gloves, a dark bonnet with tiny pink flowers, a necklace, bracelet, and earrings), where a man who had sought his value on Sunset Boulevard, in the phony identities and the applause of the theater world but who found that it wasn't enough; and who had sought his value in a nation that had declared that human life had no inherent value and that then ceased to exist—he crept quietly up the stairs, and paused at the door, and pulled out his pistol, and pushed the door open, and aimed the pistol and pulled the trigger and tore apart the loom of the Gettysburg Address, leaving the Gettysburg Address bleeding its words and ideals onto the illiterate floor. Still, the ideals refused to die. They had not yielded to Lee's charge at Gettysburg and they would not yield now. They would live on and become the Lincoln Memorial to which Mr. Smith paid an awed visit upon first arriving in Washington: Mr. Smith stood there reading words no longer dissipating on the floor but raised high and turned giant and enduring above him. The ideals that refused to die—perhaps it was this and not the venality of politics that caught the imagination of Ambassador Kennedy's sons when he took them to see Mr. Smith standing there in awe.

Then again, there were those who preferred *Stagecoach*. The combination of storyline and dashing new star John Wayne struck an archetypal frontier chord. The next year, *Stagecoach* director John Ford would create *The Grapes of Wrath*, and people started to wonder how the same man could offer such contradictory American Dreams, both a celebration of toughness and Native dispossession, and a call for compassion for the dispossessed; and they would wonder even more as Ford turned out more John Wayne cavalry movies. The answer was that John Ford was an Irishman who embodied centuries of Irish toughness against British and Boston Yankee violations, and also a centuries-old tender heart at the sight of poor farmers being exploited and thrown off their land.

In this regard John Ford was a lot like Robert Kennedy. Kennedy went from *Stagecoach* toughness to *Grapes of Wrath* compassion not in one year but over several years, and he changed more fundamentally. Robert Kennedy started out with a full share of his father's ruthlessness, yet while his father ruthlessly pursued the American Dream, Robert Kennedy pursued Jimmy Hoffa, organized crime, communists, and his brother's political rivals. Mainly he made himself the instrument of family ambitions to win the American Dream contest by getting a Kennedy elected president. He belonged to the same ruthless side of the American Dream that incited Americans to crave glory at any cost to their fellow Americans, including the glory of an inferior actor and an inferior book depository clerk who killed presidents—the inferior part of the American Dream triumphing over the better part that called out for malice towards none and for asking not for yourself. Yet Oswald's bullet had ricocheted unpredictably and become the momentum that turned the inferior part of the American Dream in Robert Kennedy into the better part which could better sympathize with loss and injustice, which could recognize his own sense of dispossession in the lives of the modern Joads picking grapes in the San Joaquin Valley or in the eyes of slum dwellers in Los Angeles. If the American Dream was always more driven inside Robert Kennedy then it inherited a higher intensity when it inverted itself from its ruthless side to the side of compassion. It was as if the historical moment had responded too, as if the American mythic unconscious was churning to produce an answer to a time in which the meaning of the American Dream was being passionately debated on angry streets and campuses, as if in Robert Kennedy the American Dream had mutated to show America how its destructive side could be inverted into the compassionate side America needed and was now passionately reaching out for.

Through the streets of Los Angeles they reached out for him. Through the neighborhoods the colors of the hands changed from black to white to brown but they all reached out with passion. Hundreds of people jostled around his car, trying to press closer, reaching out their arms even when they were much too far away to touch, reaching out anyway simply to offer gratitude and hope. The motorcade could barely move in the throng. The faces too reached out, faces black and white and brown, faces young and old, faces stylish and plain, all of them filled with hope. Those on the press bus who had covered presidential campaigns for decades had never seen such passion. Into the night the motorcade rolled, leaving him a silhouette against the streetlights.

Passion filled the ballroom of the Ambassador Hotel on the night of the California primary. Two thousand people filled the ballroom, clustering around televisions and cheering as the incoming results indicated a Kennedy victory. Among those faces were some celebrity friends of Robert Kennedy, a remnant, four decades later, of Joe Kennedy's fixation on celebrities as proof of his social success, a fixation that would leave Joe's granddaughter Maria Shriver married to a movie-star governor. Yet there were many more faces whose color rendered them worse than anonymous in American society.

At last a cheer went up, and the band struck up a triumphant song, and Robert Kennedy stepped up to the podium and the hands reached up again. He started by noting that he had also won the other primary tonight, in South Dakota, a state so different from California that it proved that "I think that we can end the divisions within the United States...what I think is quite clear is that we can work together...We are a great country, an unselfish country and a compassionate country. I intend to make that my basis for running."

The crowd cheered and cheered, finally convinced that America was an unselfish country and a compassionate country, that the American Dream was not finally about ruthlessness but about hope, that the long wrath of violence had finally been vanquished by gentleness. Yet the crowd held one man who was a failure at the American Dream and who, like Booth and Oswald, now hated the winners; he now waited in the kitchen to prove with finality that America was not after all a compassionate country, to prove how easily the American Dream could be inverted once again, how one little bullet could tip the scales back from the hopeful dream to the nightmare; he now waited to leave American compassion bleeding onto the floor; to leave a dismayed young man standing there the next morning holding his mop and bucket and remembering how he had come to Los Angeles because he had believed in the American Dream only to find that for him the passage to Wilshire Boulevard was merely a long ride on bad public transportation in order to get down on his knees to scrub a kitchen floor, scrub it clean of the hemorrhaging American Dream.

Journalist Jack Newfield was at the back of the ballroom, and in his memoir on Kennedy he recalled:

> Numbed, I tried to find a television set, and wandered into another ballroom, where the victory celebration for Max Rafferty, who had won the Republican senate primary, was going on. There was no panic and no tears here. Older people, all of them white, were blowing noisemakers, cheering and dancing. Steve Smith suddenly appeared on the television to ask very calmly for a doctor. Kennedy was clearly shot, but the Rafferty party went right on as if nothing had happened.[16]

They went right on as if nothing had happened. They went right on celebrating the worst side of the American Dream. They went right on celebrating the old national story in the history books and the movies, the old heroes like John Wayne and Scarlet O'Hara, as if nothing about them was incomplete. Not just here but all over America, not just tonight but for decades to come, they went right on as if nothing had happened. They went right on as if ruthlessness was all that was required in the American Dream and as if America wasn't paying a terrible price for its failures of compassion. They went right on as if a nation of people treating one another as worthless to prove their own worth added up into a worthy society. They went right on as if the ghettos hadn't burned and as if in a nation of many races there was no need to build a bond of common humanity. They went right on as if Vietnam had never happened and as if the American military could do anything it pleased. They went right on as if the assassinations and the daily local murders had never happened and as if guns and violence were the glory of American history. They went right on as if Earth Day had never happened and as if the endless frontier would go right on supplying endless resources and absorbing endless waste. They went right on as if nuclear weapons hadn't been invented and as if America could go right on acting out westerns in the Dodge City streets of the world. They went right on as if the world's deepening resentments of America only proved how small those nations are for not appreciating how great we are. They went right on as if the Gilded Age and the Great Depression hadn't offered any warnings about polarizations of wealth and runaway faith in stock markets. They went right on as if *The Beverly Hillbillies* was real and *The Grapes of Wrath* was a slander from someone with an insane hatred of John Wayne's America. They went right on living in an unreal world, rejecting all the intrusions of reality. They went right on living in the past, rejecting all the signs of a failing future. They went right on living in the past just like Gloria Swanson in *Sunset Boulevard*, her eyes and smile and thoughts and actions crazed from being hypnotized by a glorious and powerful past, when all the time she wasn't on Sunset Boulevard at all but really on Wilshire Boulevard only half a mile from the Ambassador Hotel, when all the time America was really living in the unrealities of Wilshire Boulevard.

I stood there in the darkness and in the silence. I listened for some echo out of time, and I heard a distant cheering, and then a distant screaming, and then a voice echoing in a cathedral, singing "The Battle Hymn of the Republic" with its line about trampling out the grapes of wrath. Then I was back in the silence, back in the architectural decay that denoted a greater desolation. Was I too living in the past? No, simply in a future that had never happened.

The Ambassador Hotel had become a giant ghost house. The kitchen passageway where Kennedy was shot lay in ruins, full of decaying fixtures and litter and dirt and spider webs. The only memorial was a sheet of plywood taped to the floor to prevent anyone from prying up floor tiles as souvenirs.

Yet the Ambassador was still a battleground over the American Dream. After the hotel went bankrupt from old age, Donald Trump bought it to tear it down and build the world's tallest skyscraper or maybe a super shopping center. But the LA Public School District was desperate for land in this area and tried to claim the property, resulting in a long court battle. A small citizen's group advocated restoring the hotel, but they were motivated by its Hollywood glamour history, not out of any concern for Robert Kennedy. Two years from now, the Ambassador would be torn down.

I lingered there for awhile, wandering up and down the sidewalk and inspecting the ghostly decay. I was trying to remember something, Kennedy's favorite lines from Tennyson, which I had memorized long ago but which I now found had also decayed. I was trying to redeem at least something from the decay in case it turned out that tonight's celebration didn't redeem it. I stared into the darkness. *The lights begin to twinkle from the rocks.* Once I gazed up at the stars. *The long day wanes: the slow moon climbs: the deep moans round with many voices.* But the stars were hidden by the glare of Los Angeles. It was getting late. *Come my friends, tis not too late to seek a newer world.*

5

Righters of the Purple Sage

If you wanted to find a good place for thinking about community in America, about the strengths and serious weaknesses of the American social bond, you couldn't do much better than a small isolated pioneer Mormon town in Utah. Among themselves the Mormons have a stronger social bond than almost anyone else in America, but when it comes to outsiders, the Mormons have a weaker social bond than almost anyone else. But this wasn't why I decided to hang out in Kanab, Utah, to watch the Democratic National Convention.

I also wasn't thinking about how I'd be watching the Democratic convention in one of the most Republican spots in America. Utah was Al Gore's worst state in 2000, giving him only 27% of the vote. Kane County, which included Kanab, gave Al Gore only 17%. Next-door Garfield County gave Gore only 10%, nearly Bush's best county in America. It was only when I was approaching Kanab with its dramatic backdrop of tall red cliffs that it occurred to me that Utah was our reddest state not just geologically but politically too and that without intending to I had set up an inquiry into the political cliffs and canyons that separated Americans.

There are quite a few of us who live in the West because red rocks and canyons and mountains and rivers are the real world, the primordial and creative world that speaks the deepest poetry to humans. Yet this poetry can easily be drowned out by the incessant, seductive, fashion-crazed, usually meaningless chatter from Hollywood, Madison Avenue, and Washington D. C., and so we avoid owning a television. But I didn't want to miss the Democratic convention, so I decided to find a motel home base for having some adventures by day and watching the convention by night. Kanab made a good base because it was surrounded by beautiful landscapes.

Kanab had remained a quiet little town for decades after its founding in the 1860s. It was very isolated in the heart of canyon country, with the Grand Canyon blocking access from the south and terrain like Zion and Bryce complicating access from elsewhere. This was just fine with the settlers, for the Mormons had come to Utah to put a political Grand Canyon between themselves and the rest of America. Yet the Mormons remained thoroughly American in their dedication to pioneering the frontier, and in being punished for acts of hubris against nature. When they first arrived here they tried to set up farms along Kanab Creek, and when even normal cycles of drought and flood bedeviled their irrigation needs they built a dam and reservoir, but the dam turned a spring flood into a tsunami when it broke, sweeping away fields and cows and houses, digging the streambed forty feet deeper. The citizens of Kanab took up ranching.

In the 1920s Hollywood discovered Kanab, the Hollywood that celebrated American myth with western movies. Tom Mix himself, the original cowboy hero, decided that Kanab-area red rock landscapes were a great backdrop for heroic adventures. A hundred movies and hundreds of TV western episodes would be filmed around Kanab. An enterprising local family, the Parrys, worked to make Kanab a good base for moviemaking, building a lodge where the stars and crews stayed and supplying food, movie sets, props, and townspeople for extras. A large portion of Kanab's population became images in American myth. The Old West remains the dominant theme in town, with restaurants and shops filled with western movie images, with a Frontier Movie Town of buildings used in movies, and with a Little Hollywood Walk of Fame on the sidewalk.

I started my Kanab visit by having lunch with a friend who was an actor in the real drama of the American frontier. Marietta belonged to the most famous family of American archaeology, the Wetherills, who discovered Mesa Verde and other major sites in the late 1800s. The Wetherill name remained clouded in the archaeological world, for they'd been too ready to ruin ruins to find relics to sell to collectors. Marietta had become a professional archaeologist devoted to protecting ruins, as if doing penance for the bad karma of the Wetherills. You could also say she was doing penance for the bad karma of America, the karma of a value system that placed the individualistic pursuit of wealth above all else.

Marietta was continually involved in the struggle to reshape American values into a greater respect for the common good, for she was one of the master planners of the new Grand Staircase-Escalante National Monument. The creation of the monument had ignited a ferocious controversy, and eight years later passions still ran strong. President Clinton created the monument in the homestretch of his 1996 re-election campaign, and he did so by using the Antiquities Act, which meant he by-passed congress. Indeed, Clinton gave no warning at all to Utah officials. Even environmentalists were stunned, and they ended up regretting the political context and fallout of the monument. Utahans were enraged, and none more so than the citizens of Kane and Garfield counties, for the monument included half of Kane County and a third of Garfield County. Anger over the monument had a lot to do with why Gore did so badly here. The authorities of Kane and Garfield counties had now devoted years to sabotaging the monument, not just with lawsuits but with bulldozers, carving pointless roads through monument lands to retain county authority and prevent lands from getting wilderness status. Even within the monument staff there were philosophical schisms, for this was the first national monument placed under the jurisdiction of the Bureau of Land Management (BLM), which traditionally regulated resource extraction—timber, grazing, mining—on public lands, so it was a culture shock for the BLM to suddenly have a mandate for wilderness preservation.

I could relate to these controversies, for half a century ago my uncle's brother-in-law Max was the BLM administrator for the monument lands and quite a bit more of southern Utah. In his BLM pickup Max had patrolled some of the most rugged backcountry in America, stretching from the Colorado River in still-undammed Glen Canyon to a town of polygamists hiding in plain view because they were too isolated to bother anyone and too isolated for the authorities to bother with them. The polygamists had fled just across the Arizona border when Utah banned polygamy to win statehood. The polygamists probably feared and hated federal authority more than any other group in America. For them federal authority was named Max, who showed up and told them how many cattle they could graze on what had once been wide-open Mormon lands, and how much timber they could cut on the plateau above. The polygamists had their own lumber mill because they wanted to be self-sufficient in everything, with zero obligations even to other Mormons. Max was the enemy of this self-sufficiency for enforcing the alien word "ecology."

Even before Max was rattling over the horrendous backcountry roads, my uncle Nils was a certified expert on the subject of how southern Utah Mormons interacted with federal authority. At the University of Oklahoma my uncle wrote his history masters thesis on the 1858 federal military expedition against the Mormons in the aftermath of the Mountain Meadows massacre, which happened on September 11, 1857 and had some of the same shock impact on the American public as our September 11, for it was a massacre of a wagon train of innocent civilians by religious fanatics. But the federal expedition was poorly planned and executed, and finally the army quit and left. A century later the families responsible for the massacre still lived in southern Utah and still possessed jewelry taken from the massacred, and now Max had to personify the federal government to them and impose BLM restrictions they viewed as a form of vengeance against a righteous people on their own God-given land. It was taken for granted that many locals were cheating on BLM restrictions—overgrazing, over-logging, poaching—and thus it was an ever-present possibility that as Max came around a corner in his federal truck he'd suddenly come upon federal-haters standing with rifles over a poached deer. In such a world self-righteousness was not a helpful social skill, but striking up a bond of common humanity might be.

For a decade Max and his wife Marjorie were one of very few non-Mormon families in Kanab. Even their house was symbolic of living deep inside Mormon-dom, for it was built by the family of Jacob Hamblin, the Daniel Boone of the Mormon world. Their neighbors were always cordial, but never cordial enough to invite them into Mormon homes or events. But Max and Marjorie invited a polygamist wife into their home as their housekeeper, for the authorities finally raided the polygamist town, dragging the men off to jail and forcing the wives to fan out and find jobs.

Max and his BLM colleagues had to fight not just the Mormon social bond but the myth of the endless frontier. The BLM was trying to save Utah from self-destruction, for grazing in the Southwest is an inherently unnatural activity. When the pioneers first arrived they did find grasslands reminiscent of Kansas, but the soil and rainfall and recuperative power of vegetation were far poorer than in Kansas, and when the pioneers tried to plant Kansas-style herds on those grass-lands they doomed their grandchildren to despair. These grasslands had sup-ported modest herds of buffalo, but the buffalo had no fences and had enough sense not to chew on the same watershed for months until it was devastated. The job of the cowboy was to serve as artificial buffalo instincts to keep the eco-unprogrammed cows moving from place to place. That's right, the real Marlboro man was an environmental adaptor. But all that living around campfires and roaming as free as the wind made the Marlboro man hate anyone telling him what to do or not do. The southwestern forests too, if mistaken for quick-grow-ing Appalachian forests, would quickly retreat for good.

Max and Marjorie saw the frontier myth being acted out in another way, for they were in Kanab for the golden age of western movies. They saw the movie stars downtown and the Wild West store fronts with nothing behind them and the Heinz ketchup used for blood. The national myth celebrated by those movies was also a picturesque store front with a great emptiness behind it, not just the emptiness of devoured landscapes but the emptiness of a society that devoured people too.

Marietta and I discussed current local feelings about the monument. She said that it would now be safe for Bruce Babbitt, the brains behind the monument, to visit here without being shot, but if Bill Clinton tried to visit, there was still a high risk of him being shot. This was not hyperbole. When the monument was created, both Clinton and Babbitt were burned in effigy. Clinton hadn't dared set foot in Utah to sign the monument into law but had gone to the south rim of the Grand Canyon, with the canyon protecting him from the Mormons. During the signing ceremony cars bearing license plates from Kane and Garfield counties were refused entry into the park. I asked Marietta if my truck would be vandalized at some lonely trailhead for having a Kerry sticker and a Babbitt for Congress sticker, and she said no, though BLM employees remained very cautious about putting liberal stickers on their personal vehicles. The real vandalism problem came from the county authorities, who had recently removed the signs from a monument road, prompting the BLM to prosecute.

At the heart of the Mormon hatred of the monument was the weakness of the American social bond, which was weak enough in the 1800s that Americans refused to view the Mormons as fellow Americans to whom they had any obligations, and they persecuted the Mormons until the Mormons fled to find their own land. Now the Mormons felt very low obligations to other Americans and hated to admit that their lands also belonged to people from Virginia or California. Mormons not only didn't want Virginians and Californians hiking around Utah feeling it was their land, they felt little obligation to send their tax money to help Virginians or Californians. This was the leading reason why Utah was the most Republican state, for the Republicans were happy with a weak American social bond.

But liberals too may have some weaknesses with the American social bond. Before Marietta's job was stopping conservatives from vandalizing public lands, her job was stopping liberals from vandalizing public lands. She was in charge of the Sedona area, where she once took me for a ruins hike and explained all the ways New Agers were damaging archaeology sites, burying their lucky charms in walls, removing artifacts for lucky charms, constantly rearranging rocks into medicine wheels, feeling no obligation to living Americans or dead Native Americans but only to a loneliness so crazed that they prayed for UFOs to land and for alien shamans to take over America and teach Americans how to care about the earth and one another.

The owner of the cafe came over to talk. Victor had moved to Kanab a couple of years ago to recover from his career as a cameraman for CBS News. He had covered six national political conventions, including the two that nominated George Bush Senior. He was wearing a golf shirt bearing the emblem of George W. Bush's Crawford ranch, which Victor had visited many times. One time Victor's helicopter crashed in the middle of Texas nowhere, but it wasn't the crash that nearly killed him, it was the sun of a Texas summer afternoon. I asked him what it was like covering the conventions, and he sighed over the ever-shallowing shallowness of news coverage of American politics. Victor spoke of Lee Atwater, the first Bush's hatchet man, with such loathing that I supposed that Atwater had done something nasty to Victor, but Victor said no, it was simply that Atwater had debased the dialogue in political campaigns to comic book levels, and now Karl Rove was following Atwater's example, and the networks went along like sheep. Victor could barely stand to turn on CBS coverage of conventions these days because it was so superficial.

When I turned on my TV the next day, the first thing I saw was a photo of John Kerry in a NASA dust suit for inspecting the space shuttle. The network commentators were going on and on and on and on about whether this photo had destroyed Kerry's chances of being elected president. Was it the equivalent of the Dukakis-in-a-tank images that Lee Atwater had used to ruin Dukakis? The Kerry campaign retaliated by releasing photos of Bush in goofy costumes or picking his nose. Now I fully sympathized with Victor's career change to a Kanab café with walls of photos and art of red rocks that were undeniably real. Yet perhaps Kanab wasn't so remote from the center of American political life. For a century now liberals and conservatives had waged an enormously consequential dialogue on individualism vs. the common good, and if this dialogue hardly showed up in the TV convention coverage, it was going strong in café conversations in Kanab, Utah, here on the front lines of the battle for the heart of America.

After lunch I wandered around town, and my first stop was a voting booth that was already open. The owner of a t-shirt shop had printed up toilet paper wrappers that featured Bush and Kerry. In the interests of fairness both Kerry and Bush rolls bore the same motto: "It's rough, it's tough, it's an all-American pain in the butt!" They were displayed alongside his longtime bestselling John Wayne toilet paper: "It's rough, it's tough, it doesn't take crap off anyone!" I assumed that the Kerry toilet paper was far outselling Bush here in Kanab, but the shop owner, John, said that in fact the Bush toilet paper was the runaway favorite. This wasn't due to locals, who were too practical to spend $3 for any roll of toilet paper. It was due to European tourists, who were delighted to find such an acknowledgement of their feelings about Bush. They repeatedly complained about Bush being a cowboy who treated the world as a western movie with white and black hats and an imperative for force. Thus a t-shirt shop in Kanab, Utah, hosted more sophisticated discussions of America's role in the world than you could find on the TV coverage of the Democratic convention.

John confessed to being one of Kane County's rare Democrats, a thing even rarer in his former profession, where "99.99% are very conservative." For twenty years John had been a uranium prospector. Though such work was now very high tech, John could fill the role of the grizzly-bearded mule-and-pick prospector in a western movie. He said that if you asked the 99.99% why they were conservatives they would cite government regulations, but John didn't consider this a sufficient explanation. Most mining regulations made obvious sense, and for uranium miners in particular, who dealt with highly concentrated ores, compliance wasn't difficult. But occasionally regulations were ridiculous. At one mining site John had been obligated to place plastic buckets over one species of cactus to protect them from dust on the premise that this species was rare and endangered. John showed the BLM biologists that this cactus was actually plentiful in the area, and they removed the bucket rule. I didn't ask John about the irony of the U. S. government covering cactus with buckets even as it was uncovering uranium to turn whole cities and bio-zones into radioactive deserts. John said that bucket-type regulations drove some of his colleagues "over the edge," into the realm of conspiracy theories in which some ominous force was plotting to destroy America's freedom, prosperity, and world power.

Mining and its grizzled strike-it-rich prospector iconography had a lot to do with hostility against the monument. John said that local residents had been looking to a major coal deposit under monument lands to rescue them from a bad economy. The local economy used to depend on uranium mining and logging, but the uranium mining had ceased and the local timber mill had closed. Depending on who you listened to, this was either due to the free market, which dropped the price of uranium and rendered a small, remote, antiquated timber mill hopelessly uncompetitive, or due to deranged environmentalists. Many Kanab families had left town or settled for tourism jobs. In John's professional assessment, the coal deposits under monument lands had been very unlikely to be developed due to their extreme inaccessibility and high costs. But locals had fixated on the coal as their salvation, and when Clinton locked up the coal, locals took it as a deep betrayal.

I wandered over to the 1895 Pioneer House Museum, whose yard full of fruit trees and kitchen full of fruit jars and butter churns and other tools symbolized the Mormon code of self-sufficiency. Some of this code was the same code shared by a West where physical isolation and the challenges of building towns and ranches from scratch generated a strong ethos of self-reliance. This Western code has much to do with why federal authority and environmentalism are resented throughout the West. But Utah's code of self-reliance is also substantially different from the rest of the West. Whereas the rest of the West is the epitome of individualistic values, Utah is a stronghold of community values, of a civic code of people taking care of one another.

It started with the Mormon religion, which asserted that Mormons are God's chosen people who will build the ultimate Jerusalem for Christ's return. This alone gave Mormons a very unique identity and social bond, and this social bond was powerfully reinforced first by persecution, with the Mormons being driven out of place after place by mobs and civil authorities, and then by their trek west and the challenges of pioneering a tough desert. While pioneering elsewhere in the West was done by lone prospectors or lone mining companies trying to strike it rich for themselves, the Mormons made pioneering a community project, with pioneers being supported by and benefiting the whole Mormon community. This pioneering was very successful, establishing hundreds of towns. In an era when millions of Americans were abandoned to hunger and sickness in New York tenements or Mississippi shacks, the Mormons set up a strong social network to look after one another. In the 1870s Mormon leader Brigham Young had enough confidence in the Mormon social bond to launch America's most ambitious experiment in communism. More on this later.

The museum host was sewing a quilt, but in one respect it was very different from pioneer quilts. The Mormons came to Utah dreaming of establishing their own nation, but this quilt featured patriotic bald eagles.

The host said that she used to love wildlife but now if she saw an owl or goshawk she would gladly shoot it or run it over, for they were to blame for the timber mill closing. Her husband had worked for the mill for forty years but been thrown out of work with 500 others because the federal government cared more about stupid birds than about the people who had built Utah out of nothing. The government had called in effete college kids to comb the forests with bird calls to find endangered birds and shut down logging, and they did so out of vicious malice against Mormons. She hoped that the forests on Cedar Mountain in Garfield County caught fire and burned down the fancy homes of the rich California environmentalists there. John Kerry was "scary" because he was an environmentalist. Environmentalists were all crazy: just this morning there was a newspaper article (it made the national news) about an animal rights activist who set fire to a pile of cardboard at a Brigham Young University farm, thinking the farm was used for animal research, but he had actually set fire to the BYU recycling center.

Her hostility was about something bigger than just environmentalism. In the 1800s Mormon leaders fought against mining in Utah just as adamantly as environmentalists fought mining today, for back then mining brought in outside mining companies and non-Mormon miners, and the Mormons resisted every intrusion upon their autonomy.

I headed over to where the environmentalists hung out, a combination outfitters store, book store, and coffee shop. It was run by Victor's hiking buddy Charlie, who wore a ball cap saying 'CBS News: Election 2000.' In Vietnam Charlie served on a boat with a machine gun so huge it took six men to work it, patrolling some of the same rivers John Kerry patrolled. Charlie was talking with Bart, a local Marine who had served years in Asia and was on his way to Quantico to become an officer; he was looking forward to going to Iraq to finish the job. Charlie and Bart were talking about how the BLM was managing the monument, and they agreed that the BLM was a bunch of wimps. The BLM should be aggressively moving to restrict ATV use in the backcountry, which was permanently scarring fragile and beautiful canyons. ATV users were a bunch of lazy wimps who should put on boots and backpacks and see the backcountry the honest way, the pioneer way, the Marine way. Charlie was contemptuous of the talk of rights and freedom to excuse destroying public lands: "The ATVers think that just because they bought an ATV, it gives them the right to go anywhere they want: it's like saying 'I bought matches so I have a right to burn down the forest.'"

The bookshelves in Charlie's store were full of celebrations of the beauties of southwestern desert canyons, not just the aesthetic beauty of sinuous red rock but the deeper existential beauty in which the accumulated litter of a human life could be flash flooded away to leave only the foundational rock of the human soul, a beauty in which the ancient elements of the earth could finally be heard speaking of all they had been doing for ages before humans were created. Once you heard these voices it was unforgettably clear that humans belonged to the earth and that all the fences and contracts in the world could never bind the earth to humans, that there were places where the earth was so sovereign, so powerfully itself, that they could never belong to the sovereignty of a county or state or company or even all the people of a nation.

Because of the time zone difference between Boston and Utah I had to be back at my motel by 5 PM to catch the convention coverage. In one other respect you could say that Utah and the West were behind the times. Boston and the rest of the Northeast and industrial Midwest had gone through a long perplexing struggle over how to combine the Jeffersonian ideals of agrarian democracy with the realities of masses of poor immigrants funneling into Gilded Age capitalism. In the East the dialogue about freedom vs. the common good was rarely conducted over cattle or natural landscapes but over whether the American people would be treated like cattle. The long struggles over monopolies and labor unions and urban slums and ethnic discrimination had evolved a mental universe of concepts and language about how to practice the common good in a high-powered capitalist society. The West had largely missed out on this experience, as had most of the South and rural Midwest. In most of the West the code of self-reliance and of extracting a living directly from the land had gone on working. Perhaps it had failed in the Great Depression and then westerners were ready to hear FDR saying that self-reliance didn't always work, but still, self-reliance was obviously the real and ideal American universe. Thus when folks in southern Utah or western Kansas turned on their TVs and heard Boston politicians saying that Americans could succeed only if government gave them a helping hand, it was a message from an alien universe. Likewise, when Boston shanty Irish or Chicago blacks turned on the Republican National Convention and heard a celebration of self-reliance, it seemed quite uncomprehending of their lives.

I turned on the TV and there was Bill Clinton praising Al Gore and saying how all Americans want good jobs and a clean environment. A few sentences later Clinton repeated the importance of the environment. At that moment someone walked past my window and I realized that a good citizen of Kanab could have caught me worshipping the devil himself committing eco-porn. I closed the curtain. Clinton went happily on and on about how Democrats wanted to build an America of "shared responsibilities and shared benefits," about how "we're all in the same boat," as if being in the same boat with Boston liberals and California environmentalists wasn't the worst nightmare of Kanab Mormons.

In the morning (my truck was un-vandalized) I headed up the road to the town where the Mormons had practiced "shared responsibilities and shared benefits" far beyond anything Democrats had ever dreamed of.

These days the Mormons hate to use the word "communism" when talking about the United Order. And in truth the United Order was usually just a cooperative in agriculture, manufacturing, or retailing. But some towns took the United Order more seriously and citizens, while retaining private homes, deeded their farms and businesses to the Order. A few towns went all the way to "The Gospel Plan" and wholly abolished private property, living in shared dwellings and eating in communal dining rooms, working as teams in the field and sharing their profits equally. The model town for the Gospel Plan was Orderville, two dozen miles from Kanab. Communism lasted ten years in Orderville, though it was gradually fizzling out for the same reasons communes usually fizzled, because some people worked harder and other people took more, and surrounding market-oriented towns were more prosperous. In most towns the United Order fizzled out within a year. The United Order originated with Mormon prophet Joseph Smith who envisioned Mormons living in Christ-like harmony, and in 1874 Brigham Young tried to implement this vision statewide. Quite a few utopian communes sprang up in nineteenth-century America, often religiously based, often encouraged by practical frontier necessities, but almost all were solitary units. The United Order was a much larger experiment, and it attracted widespread attention, helping to inspire Massachusetts author Edward Bellamy to write the utopian classic *Looking Backwards*. It also drew severe condemnation from American conservatives, being one more proof that the Mormons were dangerously un-American.

The Mormons represent a paradox that cuts right to the heart of the question of American community values, or our lack of them. The Mormons felt such a powerful sense of community among themselves that they could give outright communism a try, yet such a weak sense of community with the rest of America that a president would be risking his life to come to Utah to proclaim part of it the proud property of all Americans. This mixture of community values and Wild West individualism applied to the land too: it was the United Order that started most of the livestock herds in Kane and Garfield counties, meaning that it was commie cows out devastating the future Grand Staircase-Escalante National Monument, serving Manifest Destiny just as loyally as all-American cows. The Mormon paradox has had important national consequences. When the Great Depression struck, Utah Senator Reed Smoot decided that the answer was Mormon-style self-sufficiency and he pushed through a strict tariff act that only worsened the crisis, but Utah banker Marriner Eccles decided that the answer was Mormon-style community values and he became the first chairman of the Federal Reserve and helped talk FDR into aggressive routing of economic elites and into government leadership of the economy.

Since the heart of the Mormon social bond is religion, the Mormons offer the strongest proof of the conservative argument that religion can give great strength to society. Yet the Mormons also illustrate the limits of religion as a basis for a national social bond. The Mormon social bond is strictly rationed only to Mormons, and when it comes to people of other faiths the only obligation is to convert the poor devils to Mormonism. The Mormons also paid for their social bond with the worst case of theocracy in America. The same boundaries occur in varying degrees in other sects, with churches applying social duties mainly to their own flocks and often making little effort to assert a social duty that covers all Americans, and indeed sometimes demonizing outsiders. America's religious diversity becomes a source of weakness when it comes to building a social bond for all Americans. Americans are supposed to be bonded by a love of freedom, but what happens when freedom of religion becomes the freedom to preach that other sects are devils? The evangelicals who insist that religion is a sufficient basis for an American social bond seem oblivious of the history of American evangelicalism, which early in the twentieth century largely abandoned social gospel duties in favor of saving souls, a change so dramatic that historians of evangelicalism gave it the name "the Great Reversal."

The boundaries that arise from religion are multiplied by boundaries arising from other sources, including geography, history, race, and ethnicity.

Unlike European countries where a substantial portion of the population lives in one big city like London and the rest of the population can easily visit London, Americans inhabited a vast continent where regions could have little contact with other regions. Very few New Yorkers ventured into rural Utah or rural Mississippi, or vice versa, and when they did there was little chance for people to get to know and care about one another as real people; American's perceptions of one another were heavily mediated by images out of history or pop culture, often negative images. Like American geography, American history too was sprawling, leaving lots of disconnections. Kanab Mormons didn't want to send their tax money to the Illinois that had killed their prophet; Chicago blacks didn't want to send their tax money to Mississippians flying the Confederate flag; and Mississippians didn't want to send their tax money to Yankees. When you add race and ethnicity to this map you have boundary upon boundary that make it hard for Americans to identify with one another, boundaries that reinforced disconnections, the Catholic Italian New Yorker having three reasons not to identify with Kanab Mormons, and vice versa. So what exactly is supposed to unite Americans?

The saga of American history is supposed to unite us, and it's certainly a dramatic story, the pioneering of a continent and the building of a great nation, with lots of dynamic heroes. Yet if this pioneering saga had generated any social values or moral lessons it was first of all the value of rugged individualism, of heroes heading away from other people and doing things on their own for their own benefit.

America's democratic values are supposed to unite us, our love of freedom, but as with freedom of religion American freedom can be full of paradox and centrifugal force, for it includes the freedom to not give a damn about other Americans. Freedom of speech and of the press and of voting includes the freedom to declare that Americans shouldn't give a damn about one another. America's civic culture is heavily defined by rights, protections of the individual against King George III, but it is much weaker in the matter of responsibilities, offering few justifications for why Americans should care about distant strangers, or even neighbors.

When you combine America's diversity of land and people and religion with a history myth that promotes individualism and with a civic culture that promotes rights but not responsibilities, you end up with a sharp anomaly in the Western democratic world, the only nation with a social bond too weak to support national health insurance or paid maternity leave, among many other examples. While the rest of the democratic world sees no unworkable contradiction between civil liberties and social responsibilities, in America the political dialogue is so tilted that we define the question not as "big compassion" but as "big government," and conservatives think that all they have to do is label something "socialism" to settle the argument.

I drove into sleepy Orderville, but its small history museum was closed and there were few other chances to meet and talk with locals. I was on my way to go hiking so I didn't stop, and besides I suspected I wouldn't get far by asking loyal Republicans about their commie ancestors. In Colorado City the social bond was so severely ingrown that locals were very reluctant to speak with outsiders at all.

That night the curtains-drawn Democratic convention featured Barack Obama of Illinois declaring that "we are all connected as one people," as if he'd forgotten how an Illinois mob had murdered Joseph Smith and forced the Mormons to abandon their hard-built town and bountiful farms for the desert, as if he now expected Kanab Mormons to identify with Illinois, as if a culture of family values and self-sufficiency would sympathize with Chicago unwed mothers living on welfare. Kanab Mormons even loathed the married Mormon white women of Colorado City living on welfare. Ted Kennedy said: "America is a compact, a contract. It says that all of us are connected. Our fates are intertwined," and he went on and on about government being a good thing, as if Kanab Mormons were Boston Irish who couldn't succeed on their own. Al Gore and Teresa Heinz Kerry spoke about "the global environment" as if Kanab was on the same planet as Los Angeles or something.

The next morning I headed out for another hike in the land of red rocks and purple sage.

The Kanab area was the setting for Zane Grey's *Riders of the Purple Sage*, the book that often gets credit for establishing the western genre. Zane Grey traveled extensively in the Southwest and used real locations and real people in his books; he befriended the Wetherills and they took him to remote places like Monument Valley. The villains in *Riders of the Purple Sage* are the Mormons, whom Grey depicted as demons, and the hero is a mysterious loner gunfighter named Lassiter who hates Mormons and is bloodthirsty to shoot them. Grey fully expected his readers to go along with this demonology, and they did, turning the novel into a 1912 national bestseller. Liberals didn't complain about anti-Mormon bigotry and were rooting for Lassiter to blow away the Mormon devils.

While liberals were rooting for Lassiter, Utah was electing a liberal Jew as governor to spearhead progressive social reforms. Utah was only the second state to elect a Jew as governor, the first being Idaho, another heavily Mormon state. The Utah progressive movement was similar to the national progressive movement in seeking to rewrite the social contract with industrialism, especially mining in Utah. But the Utah progressive movement was unique in that it drew upon Mormon community values and nostalgia for pioneer solidarities. Governor Simon Bamberger, a railroad and mining magnate, described his political philosophy as "One fundamental rule of free government—where property rights and human rights conflict, human rights must always prevail."[17]

Liberals were rooting for Lassiter to blow away the Mormons about halfway between 1896, when Utah gave William Jennings Bryan 86% of its vote, and 1932, when Utah gave FDR 69%. Utah was quite ready to apply its community values on the national level, also backing Wilson, Truman, and even Lyndon Johnson against next-door Barry Goldwater who emphasized western-style self-sufficiency. But Johnson was the last Democrat Utah supported, and support for Democrats soon plunged off a cliff, Reagan winning 72% and 73% of Utah's vote. Utah was the most extreme case of the mountain West's abandonment of the Democratic Party.

What happened to take Utah from 86% for Bryan in 1896 to 25% for Clinton in 1996? Utah was a silver state, so silver-advocate Bryan represented self-interest. FDR too represented self-interest to a nation in economic crisis. As long as the liberal agenda coincided with self-interest, Americans would support it. Most New Deal programs benefited most of America, beginning with building a more solid foundation under the financial system, and building a safety net that applied to all. Yet by the 1960s the Democratic Party of LBJ had seriously overstepped the boundaries of the American social bond, asking Americans to support programs that applied only to minorities, with whom other Americans didn't identify. While other Western nations continued expanding social democratic values and policies, American liberalism stalled out on the unique barriers that discouraged Americans from caring about one another. Utah had thicker barriers than any other state.

American liberalism also stalled out at responding to this situation, for liberalism too was infected with the weakness of the American social bond. Liberals too were steeped in a culture of individual rights, and often they barely knew how to speak the language of social responsibilities. Liberals framed their whole agenda in the language of rights, advocating the rights of blacks and not the responsibilities of whites to blacks; the rights of labor and not the responsibilities of corporations to labor; the rights of owls and trees and not the responsibilities of humans to the earth and future generations; the rights of New York City women or San Francisco gays and not the responsibilities of Utah Mormon men to respect their fellow Americans. When liberals did address the weakness of the American social bond they often did so with their own form of that weakness, with the furious self-righteousness of political correctness, seeing not fellow Americans suffering from a chronically weak social bond, but demons. Just as liberals rooted for Lassiter to blow away the Mormons who were electing a liberal Jew to champion community values, liberals continued being trapped within their own failures of identification.

I can illustrate this point with some family history. After growing up in dust-bowl Oklahoma my father fled to New York City, specifically Greenwich Village. After H. L. Mencken and Sinclair Lewis had branded the Midwestern common man as a moron, an Oklahoman moving to Greenwich Village was fated to be viewed as a hick. But soon after my father arrived in New York came the premieres of *The Grapes of Wrath* and the Broadway musical *Oklahoma*, and, with further help from Oklahomans Woody Guthrie and Will Rogers, Oklahomans suddenly went from being hicks to being noble proletarian heroes. Yet Greenwich Village liberals still weren't identifying with Oklahomans as real human beings or Americans, merely as political symbols. Gradually the celebration of the Common Man faded, and by the 1960s the champions of the Common Man—Steinbeck, Sandburg, Grant Wood, Thomas Hart Benton—saw their academic reputations plunge. Steinbeck's compassion for the humanity of the Common Man was now dismissed as sentimentality, and the Joads were replaced by anti-heroes full of cynicism, irony, alienation, and self-destruction. When race became the defining political question, poor rural white Oklahomans just like the Joads were now scorned by liberals as redneck trailer trash. But they were still just the Joads, the same people all along, transformed from hicks to heroes to trash by the fads and failures of liberal identification.

In the summer of 1932, with FDR running for president, with a decade of Okie migration to California underway, with dusty overloaded trucks rolling down Rt. 66 near my father's house, my father helped load up the family Model-A Ford. My grandfather built a fold-down kitchen on one side of the car, and they rigged washtubs and spare tires and water cans and camping gear and suit-cases anywhere they'd fit, and they headed for California.

Unlike all the Joad families who were heading to California out of despera-tion, my grandfather was just a school teacher taking his three sons on a family vacation, including the Olympics in Los Angeles. But to others they looked like just another Okie refugee family. Californians spotted their Oklahoma license plate and glared at them with hostility. Our family camped on the edge of towns with other Okie families and heard the stories that became *The Grapes of Wrath*.

The movie *Grapes of Wrath* ends with two famous tributes to The People. Not just people. *The Grapes of Wrath* was made before it was clear how much grief and moral bankruptcy Marxism had rendered by caring about The People but not people. But it should have been warning enough that John Ford ends *The Grapes of Wrath* just like he ends all his John Wayne movies. A caravan of Okie trucks rides off into a western sunset just like a wagon train, and Ma Joad pro-claims: "We keep a coming, we're the people…They can't wipe us out, they can't lick us. We'll go on forever, Pa, cause we're the people." And just before that Tom Joad proclaims his oneness with the proletarian oversoul: "I'll be all around in the dark; I'll be everywhere, wherever you can look. Wherever there's a fight so hungry people can eat: I'll be there. Wherever there's a cop beating up a guy: I'll be there…And when the people are eating the stuff they raise, and living in the houses they build, I'll be there too." Today liberals watch the Joads riding off into the sunset and think: those were the days; they don't make proletarian heroes like that anymore. They see the Joads as eternal symbols. But how many stop to won-der what became of the real Joads after the movie ended?

Some real Joads drove back east on Rt. 66 and tried to make lives in dust-bowl Oklahoma. My grandfather went on teaching but his school district was so broke it could pay him only in script that only a few stores would accept. My father gave up on Oklahoma, taking his engineering degree to work for Bell Labs, living in Greenwich Village alongside famous radical folk singers sitting on front steps and singing Woody Guthrie's "Tom Joad." One of my father's brothers trained to be a journalist but ended up working in the only Oklahoma business that was thriving, becoming an oil business journalist. My father's other brother Nils got his masters in history and tried to become a history teacher, but the school dis-tricts were too broke to pay a history teacher enough to support a family, so after awhile Nils too gave up and joined the oil business, becoming an exploration geo-physicist. He became the administrative assistant to a geophysical company presi-dent, Herbert Hoover, Junior. He settled in Midland, Texas, where my cousins grew up in the 1950s and 60s. Does this begin to ring any bells? Hold on a second.

Ding-Dong. The doorbell rang at the Lago house. The table was ready for the fried-chicken birthday party of my cousin Phil, who was the same age I was when we rang John Kerry's doorbell in Lowell. The Lagos opened the door, and standing there smiling was Laura Bush. Still Laura Welch. Laura went to school with my cousins, who say she was very gracious and caring. Laura's mom Jenna taught Sunday school alongside my uncle Nils for years at the same Methodist church where Laura and George were married. When Laura flew off to college at SMU, she was sitting next to my cousin Phil heading to Baylor. Phil can't quite recall, but he thinks it's possible that when he went trick-or-treating as a kid he rang the bell at the Bush house. This is what became of the Joads after they rode off into the sunset: they did their best to survive.

They were still the Joads, the same people all along, and they had a cousin who was now ringing John Kerry's doorbell to make sure Kerry could identify with people like the Joads. But it seems that many liberals never cared about the Joads as human beings or Americans, but only as symbols of opposition to capitalism. If the Joads were going to survive by working in the oil business, one of the deepest circles in liberal hell, and even hang out with the Bushes, then the Joads went from being heroes to demons.

My father and his oil business brothers did drift apart politically, but they didn't allow their political differences to define their entire identities or override what they had in common. Family values, you know. American values, you wish. My uncle Nils admired Adlai Stevenson and took Texas pride in LBJ in 1964 but was so disappointed in Johnson that he never voted for another Democrat for president. My cousins Phil and Diane became compassionate conservatives, the old Joad sympathies stirred by being teachers in under-funded and over-burdened public schools. Phil served as assistant principle in an inner-city school plagued with gangs and other problems, and then he decided that being a baseball coach offered a better chance for personal mentoring, turning kids from every racial and economic background into united and successful teams. American values, you wish. Phil and Diane remained proud of the hometown kids Laura and George who made good, but we made it through the 2004 campaign with hardly a ripple.

On my way to go hiking in Escalante country I made several stops in Garfield County to talk with residents and explore the mindset of Bush's nearly-best county in America. In the world according to Garfield, America had hundreds of years of oil reserves and the only reason we had to import any oil was because of environmentalists blocking domestic drilling. Thus the environmentalists were to blame for American soldiers dying in the Middle East. They were also to blame for 125 of Garfield County's 6,000 residents serving in the military, many in Iraq, for the environmentalists had shut down the local timber mill and left no jobs for the young. But the California tree huggers on Cedar Mountain would learn their lesson when the forests they didn't want cut caught fire and burned down all their homes. The only reason Clinton created the monument was to pay off the Sierra Club. The only reason Clinton stopped the coal mine was to pay off a huge illegal campaign contribution from Indonesia where they wanted to export coal to America. The Heinz Corporation ran facilities in fifty-seven countries so Teresa won't let John Kerry attack any country that has a Heinz facility. John Kerry is taking orders from some secret ominous America-hating source—the Trilateral Commission, the Masons, the Illuminati. No, it's Skull and Bones, and Bush too is part of the conspiracy. Jet contrails are actually mind-control drugs.

It was curtains for John Edwards that night. What was John Edwards supposed to say to Garfield County? He gave his basic "two Americas" speech, empathizing with those who were struggling economically, and promising "We can build one America," and "We believe in bringing people together." I had a vision of Garfield County Mormon loggers and San Francisco lesbian Sierra Clubbers sitting around a campfire and roasting marshmallows and singing Woody Guthrie: "This land is your land, this land is my land…"

The next day, John Kerry's big day, was a very Wild West day. After breakfast in a Wild West theme café, with John Wayne looking me over, I looked into the Parry Lodge, whose lobby was full of autographed photos of movie stars who had stayed there, including John Wayne and Ronald Reagan. Then I visited Frontier Movie Town, a gathering of buildings used in movies around the area. A life-sized cut-out of Clint Eastwood looked me over. Several of the buildings had been used in *The Outlaw Josey Wales*, a typical Clint Eastwood vengeance story. One of the employees told me proudly that he had been in this movie and been shot off a horse by Clint Eastwood. He'd also been in a John Wayne movie but sadly he hadn't been shot off a horse by John Wayne.

On my way back to Flagstaff, where I was going to watch Kerry's acceptance speech in the Zane Grey Ballroom, I stopped at the Paria movie set, a Wild West town with a dramatic red cliff background, built in 1962 and used in various westerns over the years. The movie set was authentically Western in how its builders obliviously built it in the middle of a drainage where it was guaranteed to get swept away by a flash flood someday. It finally happened in 1998, turning the main street into a huge ditch. But Kanab-area residents were fond of their fake Western town so they rebuilt it on higher ground, a fake fake Western town, a perfect shrine to the myth of rugged individualism, perfect because it didn't include any people at all.

The area around the Paria movie set contained many hoodoos, boulders balanced atop eroding pillars of stone and dirt, and they reminded me of Zane Grey's solution to the problem of America's weak social bond. The climax of *Riders of the Purple Sage* finds Lassiter and his true love fleeing the demon Mormons, and they retreat into a secret valley accessible only by a narrow slot canyon, and Lassiter rolls a huge balanced rock into the entrance, sealing the Mormons out "forever," and sealing themselves alone forever.

It's called the Zane Grey Ballroom because it was once a hotel suite where Zane Grey lived and, according to legend, wrote *The Call of the Canyon. The Call of the Canyon* features a soldier who came back from World War One disillusioned and hurting and headed west to restore his vitality. Zane Grey's heroes were often Easterners escaping the softness and fakeness of the East and embracing the vitality of the West. But *The Call of the Canyon* was unusual in that it didn't oppose a hero and a demon and settle it with gunfights. Instead the heroes wrestle with inner demons. Imagine that: American myth in which America faces its own inner weaknesses. *The Call of the Canyon* was not Zane Grey's most popular novel.

Into the Old West décor of the Zane Grey Ballroom came big-screen John Kerry from the soft and fake East. The Democrats cheered. Kerry started by talking about what his parents taught him, a subtle way of saying that he believed in family values, but then he blew it. Of his mother he said "she gave me her passion for the environment. She taught me to see trees as the cathedrals of nature." The many environmentalists here smiled, but up in Kane and Garfield counties they were gagging at the thought of a Boston Catholic converting Mormon Wild West trees into cathedrals.

The curtains here weren't closed, and in fact the windows were open to welcome the evening cool, but this also meant that since we were right next to one of America's major train tracks, with several trains an hour that could speed for days between New York and Los Angeles and still be filling the lonely night with longing, every so often Kerry was drowned out by a train whistle, every so often his appeals for the unity of Americans were drowned out by a loud proclamation of the vast distances between Americans, his mouth moving and moving but saying only motion, the endless motion of Americans. We were also right next to Rt. 66, the track of another form of the endless motion of Americans trying to belong somewhere or belong nowhere, so every so often a Harley or a truck rebelled against a traffic light that dared to try to stop this motion and filled John Kerry's mouth with an old longing to belong somewhere or belong nowhere.

Kerry tried various ways of saying that Americans should care about one another. He tried sociology, pointing out the social costs of America not having national health insurance and other measures; he tried personal sympathy, naming individuals and describing their struggles; he tried ideals, talking about "the American family," about how in Vietnam he served with men from all over America: "No one cared about our race and our backgrounds. We were literally all in the same boat. We looked out, one for the other—and we still do. That is the kind of America I will lead as president—an America where we are all in the same boat."

Yet Kerry's speech was also heavily imprinted with the weakness of the American social bond. He seemed to think that the ultimate way to justify national health insurance to Americans was to declare emphatically that it was "a right," as if Americans who cherished their rights to be left alone by their fellow citizens and by their government could be tricked by a mere word into a duty or a passion for caring about their fellow citizens. He acknowledged that it took something as traumatic as September 11 to create a strong if brief national bond: "How we wish it had stayed that way." He insisted that liberals who criticized America's lack of caring weren't being unpatriotic.

After the red, white, and blue balloons had buried the smiles and waves, I stepped out onto Rt. 66 and saw another train thundering by. In ten days John Kerry would be arriving here to declare—in the middle of southwestern dryness and purple sage—that we were all in the same boat. Yet it would take much more than a metaphorical boat and millions of railroad ties to tie together the American people in all their distances.

Since Rt. 66 was a mythic road it wasn't hard for me to recognize the mythic shape emerging from the darkness and the east, pursuing the mythic sunset to California. It was a battered old truck overloaded with people and possessions, a truck still wearing a map of the dust bowl—it was the Joads. And looking the other direction I saw emerging from the darkness and the west the shape of a Model-A Ford heading back to Oklahoma, heading to both Greenwich Village and Midland, Texas, heading to the doorbells of both John Kerry and the Bushes. As the two vehicles approached each other someone recognized something more than just Oklahoma license plates, more than just a shared ordeal, more than just the loneliness of the American road, and from their windows they reached out arms and waved at one another as they passed, waved just because they recognized their common humanity, and that was all.

6

The Human Comedy in the Theater of the Ages

1: The Theater of the Ages

The eons called out a warning.

The eons called out that if humans couldn't figure out their place in nature, they would be crushed. To be more specific: ancient plants that were now petroleum burst into flame inside the train engine and became the energy of the train whistle wailing out a warning as the train approached a road crossing. Any pedestrian or even a car foolish enough to remain on the tracks would be crushed. But humans wouldn't be foolish enough to stand in the path of such power, would they?

The train broadcast its geological power not just with a whistle but with a thick black smoke plume roiling high into the air, visible from miles away. As the smoke rose it dissipated until it was no longer visible to the human eye, but it was still there, the carbon of it, still rising high into the atmosphere where it would remain for years, soaking up sunlight, warming the atmosphere, the ghosts of extinct species haunting the cities and packed highways of humanity.

The train blew its whistle several times as it emerged from the woods and approached the station, and tourists looked with surprise at the big blue engines bearing 'Kerry for President' logos. The train stopped a few hundred feet from the rim of the Grand Canyon.

Even at the Grand Canyon it's possible to get a flawed perspective on the place of humans in nature. When you arrive at the rim hotels and gift shops and jammed parking lots and crowds, you could get the impression that this place is all about human entertainment. Interpretative signs tell you about the coming of the pioneers and the building of the historic buildings and the trails into the canyon, as if this was just another episode in the American conquest of the West.

But there's also the perspective from the bottom of the canyon, the perspective of a lizard sitting on a boulder by the river as lizards sat for ages before any humans showed up, the perspective of looking up at a mile of rock, layer upon layer of compacted time, eon upon eon of mountain ranges rising and eroding away again, eon upon eon of species arising and thriving for eons and dying out when environments changed. From the bottom you are looking up through nearly two billion years of change, of biological annihilation, and atop all of that the human presence is a very thin and new deposit. But occasionally, even from down here, when the wind is just right, you can hear the whistle of the train arriving on the rim, the whistling of the long-imprisoned sunlight and wind that knew these rocks when the rocks were living jungles, a whistle calling out a warning.

2: The Human Comedy, Act One

We'll have to use a bit of imagination to flesh out the following event, since the whole incident was hushed up by the Secret Service and other authorities.

Two Navy pilots were flying planes back to their base in California and passing over the Grand Canyon. Hey, one of them radioed to the other, wouldn't it be cool to fly inside the Grand Canyon? But, replied the other, we could get into trouble for that. No one will ever know, answered Maverick: we're a long way from the tourist areas; just look down there at the empty desert for miles around. I'm with you, Maverick, let's go for it!

The planes swooped down and dropped below the rim, the cliffs streaking past their windows. They dropped nearly to the river, skimming over it at about 150 feet, veering back and forth as the river and canyon walls veered.

It used to be more common for jet fighter pilots to go joy-riding into southwestern canyons. The Air Force might not approve of its planes being risked for stunts, but then the Air Force seldom heard about it. As river running and backpacking soared in popularity in the 1970s, aircraft intrusions into places like the Grand Canyon became more of an issue, but the National Park Service had no authority over the air space over national parks, so aircraft could fly anywhere they pleased. Then in 1986 a tour helicopter collided with a tour plane over the Grand Canyon, killing all two dozen aboard. The helicopter pilot, John Thybony, had been a helicopter pilot in Vietnam and had marched with John Kerry in VVAW's march on Washington. This collision prompted Senator John McCain to go up against the air tour industry and push legislation transferring from the FAA to the Park Service the authority over air space over national parks, which the Park Service used to ban aircraft from flying below the rim of the

Grand Canyon. Still, temptation was sometimes too much for young jet pilots who had fantasized being Luke Skywalker dodging through the canyons of the Death Star. Let the force be with you, Maverick. One Maverick tried to fly through Taos Box Canyon and he turned a bit too slowly and slammed into a cliff, exploding into a fireball.

Hey look, Maverick, there's a raft trip camped just up ahead on the right. Won't they be surprised! ZOOOOM! Right past them! Look at those guys running up the beach! What the hell? Isn't that guy pointing a gun at us?

Eight miles downriver the pilots came close to colliding with an incoming Park Service helicopter.

When the pilots got back to base the FBI swarmed in, looking for the utter losers who had gone joy-riding in the Grand Canyon at the very place and moment that the vice president of the United States had been doing a raft trip. The Secret Service agents on the beach had gone nuts, yelling into their radios, fearing a military coup. The careers of those two pilots were over.

Vice President Gore's raft trip was camped at a large creek delta once farmed by the Ancestral Puebloans (a.k.a. the Anasazi); perched hundreds of feet up the cliffs was a famous Puebloan ruin, a set of granaries. We can assume that like most rafters who camped here Al Gore hiked up the steep trail to the granaries. Occasionally, in spite of warnings from river guides, some tourist leans against a granary wall and it collapses, and the Park Service has to rebuild it again. There had been no rebuilding Puebloan society when it collapsed 800 years ago; the Puebloans had abandoned the Grand Canyon for good. We can imagine Al Gore sitting on the ledge in front of the ruins, gazing downriver at a famous view of the Colorado River swirling back and forth for miles between straight red cliffs. The Puebloans too must have sat here admiring the view. They must have felt their vulnerability in such a difficult environment, yet even they probably didn't imagine that the entire southwestern environment could collapse into a severe drought and take down their whole society with it. For 800 years now the wind had whistled through their ruins, calling out a warning. But it was hard to hear the mourning wind over the screaming jet fighters of a brash young nation proving that it was the master of nature.

3. The Theater of the Ages

A few weeks before the Kerry post-convention train tour arrived at the Grand Canyon, I had spent a week searching for Puebloan ruins on the canyon rim, part of an ongoing Park archaeological survey.

When most people think of the Anasazi they usually think of the impressive architecture of Chaco Canyon and Mesa Verde, and they often assume that Chaco and Mesa Verde represent a mighty, long-lasting civilization. The Puebloan people have indeed been long lasting, but for almost all of their history they have lived far more modestly than on the scale of Chaco. Chaco represents a relatively brief flourishing, actually a violation of the natural order, an unsustainable consumption of a temporary bounty of resources. It's ironic that today Chaco is a pilgrimage site for educated whites unhappy with America's lack of an earth ethic and seeking Native American role models for living in harmony with nature. Native Americans do have a lot to teach us, but Chaco is about the last place to go looking for it, unless you are looking for a model of a society that brashly misjudged its abilities and then couldn't turn and slammed into a canyon wall.

Chaco was the apex of an inherently unnatural idea: farming in the desert. For the first 10,000 years or more after humans arrived in the Southwest they survived by hunting and gathering. Sometime around 2000 B.C. corn arrived in the Southwest from Mexico, making a farming lifestyle possible, but people were very slow to adjust to this possibility. Hunting and gathering was backed by 10,000 years of success, and it was a huge change to build permanent villages and sit there helping crops grow. Gradually farming caught on, creating a distinct Puebloan lifestyle, but it remained limited to especially favorable sub-environments such as canyons with a reliable water supply. Then, about 1,000 years ago, when the Puebloans had a few centuries of success to give them confidence in their lifestyle, the climate began to grow wetter, and large new areas became cultivatable. The Puebloan population spread out and grew dramatically, and Chaco and other centers arose. The western edge of Puebloan society was along the Grand Canyon.

Out here there was no grand architecture, only small pueblos inhabited by a few families. But there were lots of them. Today the ruins are hidden in a pinion-juniper forest, but back then the forests were cleared back and this landscape showed house beyond house, cornfield beyond cornfield. This rural settlement was much more typical of the Puebloan world than was Chaco. Such settlements were surprisingly extensive in the Southwest; even inside the Grand Canyon every drainage that had reliable water and soil held a Puebloan community.

But not for long. Even before the climate changed back, some Puebloans were ruining things for themselves. The Chacoans deforested Chaco Canyon so thoroughly that it is still bare today, and they had to go fifty miles for wood. On the rim of the Grand Canyon the land was more marginal for farming to begin with, and even subtle changes could tip the balance.

When the southwestern climate changed back, it didn't just return to normal, it dropped into a severe drought, catching the Puebloans with a vastly expanded population and social structure trying to live on now untenable and degraded lands. The population and society collapsed. The Grand Canyon settlements were among the first to go. Region after region was abandoned, and there are ample signs of chaos and warfare. At the Grand Canyon the period of collapse saw the building of odd, heavy structures, some perched atop pillars jutting out from the rim, which are less logical as houses than as forts.

One evening around the campfire, surrounded by ruins, Chuck the longtime backcountry ranger told us stories about the endless parade of fools who showed up at the canyon and tried to hike it but were grossly unprepared for it. The core problem was a failure to understand the environment, the severity of it, the demands it placed upon the human body, the scarcity of water. The most dangerous hikers might not be the city folks who had never been hiking before but the veterans of the Alps or Rockies, where the air was humid and every drainage flowed with water, who were brimming with confidence but who had zero experience at hiking in a desert canyon. The canyon taught constant lessons in humility.

Chuck and a few of us talked about going over to the Hopi mesas in a few days for the kachina ceremonies. Some of the Hopis were descended from the Puebloans who had lived in the Grand Canyon a thousand years ago. The Puebloan collapse had left Puebloan remnants like the Hopis and Zunis with a deep cultural memory of drought and an obsession with rain and ceremonies that brought rain. But our plan fell apart when Chuck got an emergency call. A marathon runner from Boston had disappeared in the canyon. She was a serious athlete and was viable to make the U. S. Olympic team. It was her dream to proudly represent America, to stand there on the podium with a gold medal around her neck as they played the national anthem. But she was seriously lacking in Hopi respect for drought. She had tried to run thirty miles into and through and out of the canyon in one day in the worst of the summer heat. Instead of starting at first light to beat the heat, she had waited until late morning. She had carried an absurdly inadequate supply of water and food. Now she was indeed proudly representing America, at least in its hyper-confident disregard for the realities of nature. The realities of nature soon exhausted her resources of water and food, and then they exhausted her, many miles from water or help. She stumbled onward in 100+ degree sunlight. When she finally got desperate for water she decided to follow a side canyon down to the Colorado River, though she had no idea whether this side canyon allowed access to the river or ended in a cliff. If only she'd kept going for another two miles she would have reached a much busier trail and an emergency phone. She started down this side canyon and then she came to a ledge that was tall enough that if she dropped over it she would never be able to get back up, and if there was a cliff between her and the river she would be trapped, and no one would be able to guess where she'd gone. She was proudly representing America now as she dropped over the ledge anyway. This was where Chuck would find her, after circling and circling in the park helicopter, find her trapped and dead. As she was dying did she hallucinate that she heard the national anthem playing and the crowds cheering for the gold medal around her neck like a hangman's noose, cheering a mad pursuit of gold that proudly represented America's attitude towards nature? Several times every summer, Chuck and other rangers recovered the bodies of dead hikers from the canyon.

4. The Human Comedy, Act Two.

When the Kerry train pulled into the station I went out to greet the press and the Kerry staffers who worked with the press. I had assigned myself to the press detail to pay back a debt I had incurred back in the Iowa caucus campaign. The advance man who was now in charge of the national traveling press had saved me from a lynch mob. It was all about humans not knowing their proper place in nature.

One of my Iowa projects was to build a crowd for a debate-watching party at a Des Moines diner. The campaign scheduler had promised me that John Kerry would stop by the diner after the debate, so I was promising everyone that here was a great chance to meet John Kerry, and people were indeed eager to come.

On the Sunday of the debate an ugly blizzard moved in, the streets turned seriously icy, the cars piled up in the ditches. But fifty people came out to the diner anyway to meet John Kerry. When the debate was over I asked Lars the advance man how soon we could expect Kerry to show up, and Lars reacted with surprise and informed me that in fact Kerry wasn't scheduled to appear here. Damn. I looked at the fifty eager people around me. Someone was going to have to tell them that some fool had gotten them out in a dangerous blizzard for no reason. I was going to be lynched.

I started thinking of how I could break the news in a way that would save my neck, and I toyed with an environmentalist angle, something like this: "I'm sure you all appreciate that John Kerry is the best environmentalist in the race. Environmentalism means that humans respect nature's power. It's foolish to burn up fossil fuels without any thought of tomorrow, and it's foolish to go driving around in dangerous blizzards. I'm sure you are supporting Kerry precisely because he's no fool." I was going to be lynched.

Luckily for me Peter Yarrow was there and started singing to entertain the crowd while we waited for Kerry to arrive. This was a real treat for the crowd, but still, they hadn't gone out in a blizzard to hear about Puff the Magic Dragon. When I meekly told Peter that Kerry wasn't showing up after all, he saw the answer, my friend, blowin' in the snowy wind. Peter, a longtime Kerry friend, looked at Lars and told him that he should go out in the hall and call his advance boss at the TV studio and get John Kerry to come over here. Lars looked at Peter like he was a lunatic, but Lars did dutifully call up his boss and told him that Peter Yarrow was staging a sit-in at the diner. Soon the campaign bus pulled up and John Kerry came in and talked with the crowd.

When Lars and the press stepped off the train at the canyon I led him and the rest of the staff to the press room, which might well be the most spectacular press room in the entire history of presidential politics. It was set up in the meeting room of one of the lodges right on the rim, the only meeting room with a view of the canyon. But now, as the press was sitting down at the rows of tables and plugging in their laptops, I saw something bizarre. The advance person who had set up this room had arranged the chairs so that the reporters were sitting with their backs to the canyon. They could have been looking out a huge window at the canyon, but instead they were staring into little windows filled with up-to-the-minute political chatter. I stood there wondering whether this was an act of insensitivity or a stroke of genius, for if the reporters had seen the chatter of politics framed against the eons, they might have been struck dumb by the revelation that human affairs could look incredibly puny.

5. The Theater of the Ages

Not long after the railroad was built to the Grand Canyon, President Teddy Roosevelt arrived on a special train. He took a mule trip into the canyon. He was awed. Teddy had seen a great deal of the world, and he declared that the canyon was the world's most impressive natural wonder. Standing near the rim, he gave a speech that would end up on a plaque in the park visitor's center: "Leave it was it is. You cannot improve on it. The ages have been at work on it, and man can only mar it."[18]

Roosevelt did what he could to protect the canyon, making it a game preserve and then a national monument; national park status would take a bit longer. The game preserve included hiring wardens to eliminate the predators from the north rim forests so the deer wouldn't be wasted on varmints. Teddy himself went hunting mountain lions on the north rim. The wardens wiped out 800 mountain lions, 550 bobcats, and 5,000 coyotes. The deer population exploded from 4,000 to 100,000. The deer decimated the forest vegetation. Over one bad winter, tens of thousands of deer starved to death.

Even an environmental visionary like Teddy Roosevelt was caught in the presumption that Americans could do as they pleased with nature. This temptation seems to be ever-present for human societies, but some societies indulge in it much more than others. Few societies have had as much self-confidence as America. This confidence is a fairly accurate codification of our national experience. From the first pilgrim footsteps onto America, there was always more, always more land to inhabit, more forests to cut down, more wildlife to hunt, more and better farmland to claim, more mountain ranges full of minerals, more oil hidden somewhere. America also came of age during an explosion of technological invention in which there was always a better idea over the next horizon. The combination of ever-more land and ever-more resources and ever-more technology gave Americans a deep faith in an ever-more economy: America would always grow richer, and so would companies and stock prices and household income. It was no big deal if either families or the nation got into debt, for we would always grow our way out of it.

America's enormous success was codified into social values. America did offer a much stronger correlation than Europe between reward and individual initiative and ability. This led to the belief that individual wealth was an accurate measurement of personal merit, an ethos reinforced by the Puritan belief that God blessed the righteous with worldly success. This ethos was applied to the nation as a whole: America was a success because of our initiative and because we were God's chosen nation. No doubt the Puebloan priests too assured their people that their enhanced rainfall and fast-growing society was a proof of god's blessing.

In truth, America's success was owed first of all to an utterly unique circumstance in human history. Never before had a vast temperate zone continent loaded with agricultural and mineral resources sat virtually wide open to a technologically empowered society. Democracy and capitalism undoubtedly facilitated the settling of the continent, yet even if America had been a kingdom or a communist dictatorship it would have been a trick to stop America from becoming a huge economic success. Though Americans have long been aware that we received a unique bounty, this was usually invoked as a proof of national destiny and not as a warning that this bounty might run out or that our unique pioneer history might be a faulty predictor of the future or a resented basis for judging the worth of other nations.

If we had interpreted our prosperity as a gift from a very unique environment and historical moment, our success might have made us the world's staunchest believers in the importance of the environment. At least our awesome landscapes impressed us, and thus America gave the world the concept of the national park. Our awe-inspiring land gave ample encouragement to visionaries like John Muir and empowered the strong start of mass environmentalism with Earth Day in 1970. For awhile American environmentalism was a role model for the world. But American environmentalism had to compete against America's now nearly religious faith in the ever-more. When environmentalists tried to describe a world with limited resources, which would start to run out alarmingly soon, they were speaking a foreign language. Environmentalism was definitely un-American. Americans might have embraced environmentalism if they could have their canyon and eat it too, but only a few years after the first Earth Day Americans were enraged by the Arab oil embargo, which left their trophy cars waiting in long lines and costing a lot more. Americans proved quite ready to turn their backs on environmentalism and turn to a prophet of the old-time religion of the ever-more, Ronald Reagan.

6. The Human Comedy, Act Three.

When President Reagan's secretary of the interior James Watt took a raft trip through the Grand Canyon he said that by the second day he was bored with the canyon. By the third day he was wishing that the motor on the raft was bigger so it could get him out of the canyon quicker. On the fourth day he was "praying for helicopters" to get him out of the canyon. [19]

The bubble in which James Watt lived and worked was not just a bubble of personal insensitivity to natural wonders. It was also the bubble of American national destiny, which was seriously out of touch with the realities of nature. Like all animals, humans test and define reality by what behaviors work and what don't work, and for over 300 years Americans had found that the ever-more was not only real but enormously rewarding. This has left us living in a bubble so opaque that it's difficult for natural realities to penetrate national realities.

American national reality was performed brilliantly by Ronald Reagan, who had personified it in movies about the ever-more frontier and as a real-life rancher. As president, Reagan channeled the old confidence in national destiny, which was the mainspring of his popularity, just as it had been for FDR and JFK. Reagan, a former Democrat, was fond of saying that he hadn't changed, the

Democrats had changed, and he was right. But instead of allowing that liberals might be learning from history, he took liberal doubts about American destiny as a mysterious and outrageous betrayal, at least a failure of character and quite possibly a sign of loyalty to something un-American. Jimmy Carter had tried to introduce a new tone of humility into America's self-image and consumption habits, but Americans rejected it. Reagan rolled back many of the environmental initiatives of the 1970s, and James Watt openly hated environmentalists.

George W. Bush was a good fit for the Reagan image and faith in American destiny, and he assured Americans that they could go on believing in the ever-more. Now the environmental stakes were much more serious, not just the despoiling of specific public lands but global threats like ozone depletion, global warming, and mass extinctions. Yet these ideas too had a hard time penetrating national reality. The first President Bush ridiculed Al Gore as "the ozone man" for worrying about the ozone layer, and global warning was even more alien to national reality, leaving America alone in rejecting the Kyoto treaty. Like Al Gore, John Kerry had enough sense to frame the need for alternative energies in terms of a great American technological adventure in the spirit of Apollo, but he was still working against the religion of the ever-more. The word "religion" here is not rhetorical. American national experience was already enough to make Americans true believers in the ever-more, and this faith was reinforced by America's unique style of Christianity.

In 2003 Grand Canyon National Park began selling in its bookshops an attractive book that gave no warning on its cover that it was a creationist version of the Grand Canyon. Hundreds of tourists must have bought this book on a casual glance and only later noticed the illustration of Noah's Ark bobbing on the flood. The book declared that the Grand Canyon was carved by Noah's flood and that the world was created in the six days of Genesis. The book repeatedly said that the Grand Canyon declared God's glory, but it also warned that the canyon fossils were trillions of animals that had to be sacrificed because Noah's generation didn't believe in God. The book sparked a national controversy. Many park employees, European tourists, and national science organizations were appalled by it, but evangelical networks spread the word and demanded that the book stay on sale.

The creationist agenda of course was not ultimately about the origin of rocks, but about the meaning of creation for humans, and for America. In creationism the world was created for human use and would be discarded when Christ returned. It was inconceivable that the divine plan could be thrown off course by something like global warming, which was concocted by the same egghead scientists who concocted evolution. Some fundamentalist sects were founded on the conviction that the Second Coming was imminent, including Pentecostalism. James Watt was a Pentecostal, as was John Ashcroft. The early Pentecostal church strongly disdained worrying about politics. The early Pentecostals asserted that only they would be raptured at the Second Coming, while all other so-called Christians were left behind to suffer the chaos of the tribulation. Thus James Watt and John Ashcroft would be raptured right out of a cabinet meeting, leaving Ronald Reagan and George W. Bush, their eyes and mouths wide in shock, left behind. Most Pentecostal public officials, including Watt and Ashcroft, were quite circumspect about admitting if or how their belief in an imminent Second Coming colored their planning for America's long-term future. But if you were serious about it then you had to believe that America's abundant resources were God-given, part of a divine plan in which America was God's instrument, and in which running out of resources was nothing to worry about and probably part of God's schedule.

A Duke University scholar of Pentecostalism, Grant Wacker, found that "holy spirit-filled believers not only lost interest in politics but also proved oblivious to many of the day-to-day recreations that most people considered simple and legitimate pleasures in life…even commonly sanctioned satisfactions such as dropping a fishing line or watching a parade faded in the glow of the heavenly light."[20] Or, rafting through the Grand Canyon. "If Pentecostals discountenanced the routine pleasures of life, they were equally prepared to forgo the bonds that tethered them to earth. That outlook helps explain why one could dismiss digging a storm shelter as a "habit of the flesh."

Thus we are allowed to imagine James Watt on the second day of his Grand Canyon trip, already bored to death, perhaps entertaining himself by looking for seams of minerals to strip mine, and looking up to the sky and praying for a helicopter to rescue him from mere nature, or far better than a helicopter, praying for heaven itself to finally open up and the angels to descend and raise him up even as they cast environmentalists into hell, Teddy Roosevelt not excluded.

7. The Theater of the Ages

After a campaign luncheon in Iowa Teresa Heinz Kerry figured out that I had some sort of connection with the Grand Canyon and asked me about doing a raft trip there. She explained that she and her first husband John Heinz had been scheduled to do a Grand Canyon raft trip when Heinz was killed in a plane crash, and Teresa had cancelled that trip. I could tell that the whole subject was haunted for Teresa, for now she couldn't go down the river without seeing the ghost of the trip that had never happened. But still she was interested in going.

I told Teresa that one of the Grand Canyon rafting companies, AZRA, was owned and run by the husband of a former Arizona congresswoman, Karan English, who was a strong environmentalist and a longtime admirer of Teresa's environmental work. AZRA had taken Al Gore down the river when he was vice president, so AZRA had experience at dealing with security issues. I didn't tell Teresa that she might be buzzed by daredevil Navy pilots. A few weeks later at the Iowa victory celebration I told Teresa I'd talked with Congresswoman English and she said she'd put together a special raft trip for Teresa and John Kerry. Teresa smiled and said "But maybe not this year."

Ten days later, on the eve of the Arizona primary, Teresa was in the home of Karan English in Flagstaff. The home was packed with Grand Canyon-themed art, and tonight it was packed with Grand Canyon-themed people, with river guides, park rangers, archaeologists, professional photographers and writers, and nationally-known environmental leaders. The house was so packed that Teresa had no where to stand where she could see or be seen by the crowd. Then she spotted two tall wooden stools and placed them in a corner and climbed atop them, one foot on each stool, a precarious and uncomfortable perch even when the stools weren't trying to scoot apart. But Teresa stood there for an hour and a half, talking mainly about environmental threats to human survival. She said in more detail what would become one of John Kerry's most reliable applause lines in the fall campaign: "We need a president who believes in science." Everyone seemed to understand what this meant.

An hour and a half is a long time for a four-year-old girl to stand there listening to such ideas, but Wendy was fascinated by the lady atop the tower, who seemed to enjoy being up there. Wendy started wondering what you could see from way up there. Wendy's parents were both longtime Grand Canyon rangers and they had already taken Wendy on many adventures. Ranger kids tend to become very adventuresome. So Wendy decided to have an adventure and started to climb up the stools. In any other living room in America the adults would have quickly intervened, but not this living room, for this room was full of very adventuresome women who had been scolded as little girls not to be so adventuresome, little girls who were now rangers who threw on an eighty-pound medical backpack and raced up a trail in 100+ heat to save a life, little girls who were now river guides whose muscles and judgment could match the raging chaos of Crystal Rapid at its worst, little girls who were now archaeologists who climbed cliffs to find a message from the Puebloan past. Now all eyes were on the little girl having an adventure, and Teresa suspended her talk and started encouraging her, obviously charmed by a kindred spirit. Wendy summited and the two of them stood there looking very precarious for another half hour, Teresa's hand on Wendy's shoulder.

I once did a Grand Canyon raft trip with Wendy's parents Randy and Sharon. It was a trip of Grand Canyon rangers on vacation, and though between them they'd done over a century of interpreting the canyon to visitors, none had ever rowed a raft in the canyon before, so I was along as the guide. Mostly I just let them figure out things for themselves, but even a century of interpreting the canyon doesn't prepare you to grasp the tricky dynamics of particular rapids, so a few times when they were about to make a mistake, such as at Crystal Rapid, I intervened. This was a lesson our pioneer ancestors, whatever their faith in the evermore, understood far better than Hollywood cowboys like Ronald Reagan: either you comprehend the workings of nature, or you are going to die.

I'd also neglected to warn Teresa that rafting down the canyon could leave you clutching a little cage hanging by a thread from a helicopter hovering over a rock island in the middle of Crystal Rapid after your raft had careened out of control down the rapid and gotten stuck. A few years previously an AZRA motor raft had smashed its motor on a submerged rock at the top of Crystal and ended up stuck in the rock island with twenty people aboard. The Park Service sent a helicopter to the rescue, including Chuck and me, and after the passengers had been helicoptered to shore and out of the canyon and after the raft was extracted, the helicopter headed out, leaving me behind to spend ten days alone at Crystal Rapid. I was there as part of a long-term park study of the impacts of Glen Canyon dam, which had been built decades ago without any thought for its damaging ecological impacts on the Grand Canyon downstream. I was studying boating accidents at various water levels at key rapids. The clear lesson of this study was that the best river runners were those who "believed in science," who had a strong comprehension of the workings of nature, while the "accidents" belonged to those with a poor grasp of hydrology, often combined with foolish self-confidence. (The AZRA accident, it became clear, was a rare and honest stroke of bad luck).

On a rock mesa a hundred feet above Crystal Rapid was a Puebloan ruin. Sometimes in the evening I wandered up there and sat for a long time and looked down on the rapid. The Puebloans had farmed in this creek delta, the same outwash that formed the rapid. Here the Puebloans had prayed to their gods, and for awhile at least, their gods answered loyally with good rain and good crops. For the Puebloans who were born here in the canyon, living here seemed normal, and for awhile they noticed that conditions were even improving, opening up new areas for settlement. When this confidence proved shockingly wrong and the drought began, nothing came from the sky to rescue them, not rain or helicopters or angels.

Usually I look at Puebloan ruins with an abstract regret, as a lesson in the rise and fall of civilizations. But on my final evening at Crystal I looked at the ruin with a more personal sense of dread. Perhaps this was mainly because tomorrow I was hiking out alone in the worst of the summer heat and thus the canyon dryness really was a personal threat to survival. In any case, the ruin now felt like a personal message from the Puebloans to me, a warning that in the Grand Canyon and in the grand scheme of nature humans and human societies are tiny and very vulnerable things.

8. The Human Comedy, Act Four

As the Kerry family was driven along the rim of the canyon they passed a huge ruin perched right on the rim. It was not a Puebloan ruin, but the ruin of our own civilization. It was a tall steel tower, closed off by a chain-link fence bearing signs warning of radioactivity. This mine had harvested one of the richest lodes of uranium in America. Uranium from the Grand Canyon now waited in atomic bombs, waited for the order to inflict Grand Canyons upon the cities of the world.

The Kerrys stopped at an overlook near the mine, and they could look east and see its tower like a hangman's scaffold.

The Orphan mine was originally opened as a copper mine by Dan Hogan, who had served in Teddy Roosevelt's Rough Riders in Cuba. Another Grand Canyon pioneer, Bucky O'Neill, was also a Rough Rider and was killed at San Juan Hill, but not in the famous charge up the hill. Just before the charge O'Neill was casually strolling around smoking a cigarette, though bullets from Spanish sharpshooters were flying down. An officer yelled at O'Neill to get down, but O'Neill puffed out a mushroom cloud and laughed and declared that "the Spanish bullet isn't made that can kill me."[21] A moment later a Spanish bullet struck him in the mouth and blew out his skull.

In the 1950s uranium was discovered in the abandoned Orphan mine and it reopened to become a labyrinth of shafts inside the canyon walls, from which a million tons of ore was removed. The ore was dumped into open trucks and hauled right through the tourist areas, spewing out uranium dust and occasionally chunks of ore, which local park kids picked up and took home. The mine site had remained private land and it held a motel with a swimming pool and bar, and the tourists just went right on lounging beside the pool, being bathed by uranium dust. Many of the ore truck drivers died of cancer. The ore was hauled one hundred miles to a mill in the Navajo town where Lori Piestewa would later live. Many of the Navajo mill workers died of cancer. The ore trucks raced down the highway spewing uranium dust, raced like America itself racing to use up its natural resources. The ore trucks raced past many Puebloan ruins. But the Puebloan's fate is not a historically valid predictor of our own fate. When the Puebloan's environment warmed up, they had only stone weapons with which to express the chaos of their societal collapse. When the modern world both runs out of resources and seriously degrades our environment, we will be heavily armed with nuclear weapons.

The media coverage of the Kerry visit to the canyon contained nothing like "Teresa Heinz Kerry, head of leading environmental foundation, contemplates world's greatest natural wonder." Instead it was mostly "Teresa looks grumpy: can America stand a First Lady without a smiley-face mask?"

I was given a good chance to watch the American press in action and consider the way events got reported. Over the next three months I would occasionally pitch in with the press detail at Kerry events, often herding the camera crews. I got to respect some journalists as individuals, but I had my doubts about the political culture that filtered their efforts. Some cameramen knew Victor, former CBS News cameraman turned Kanab, Utah, café owner, and I found I could start up a good conversation by offering Victor's opinion that the American political dialogue had degenerated noticeably. Some journalists firmly rejected this view, declaring that Victor was just indulging in nostalgia for a nonexistent good old days. Others agreed, but they placed the blame on political campaigns for always cynically manipulating the imagery.

At the canyon my main job was van-shuttling journalists around the rim. I took the CBS camera crew out to a spot where they could do a live shot with the canyon as backdrop. These guys had worked with Victor covering the 2000 New Hampshire primary in arctic cold. I asked them how they were enjoying the Southwest, and more specifically how they'd liked the Gallup pow wow. They said that at the Gallup pow wow some stupid Indians had started harassing them for no good reason.

I'd heard a very different version of events from Bubba McCloud the Cherokee Kerry bus driver. Bubba took Native spirituality seriously, and once when he drove the Kerry bus to some event in South Dakota he'd stopped at the sacred Black Hills and done his own ceremonial. Bubba said that at the Gallup dances one of the dancers had an eagle feather fall from his costume to the ground. For most tribes their relationship with eagles is sacred, and an eagle feather falling in a dance is a serious omen, requiring a special cleansing ceremony. But just when the dancers started their fallen eagle feather ceremony, some stupid white guys from CBS News tried to film it. Tourist-afflicted southwestern tribes are adamant about their ceremonials not being filmed. Officials told the CBS crew to turn off their cameras. The CBS crew said it was their job and their right to film it. The officials again ordered them to stop. The "negotiations" went on for several minutes, and Bubba suspected it included an implication of force against the cameras. The CBS crew didn't realize how close they'd come to setting off a riot.

We can presume that Victor in his many hikes through red rock canyons often came upon Native ruins but learned not to see them with the arrogance of a nation with superior technology.

When it was nearly time for the train to leave I shuttled the CBS crew back to the train. They told me that the Secret Service had set up a check-in spot for the press at the first crossing of the track and the road.

"The first crossing?" I asked.

"Don't you know where that is?" they asked, afraid they'd gotten stuck with someone who didn't know what he was doing.

"Yes, but it doesn't make any sense." In fact, the Secret Service didn't know what it was doing. It was disconcerting how chaotic these events could be behind the scenes. After I got to the first crossing and it was deserted, I found the right spot and dropped off CBS and headed back to the rim to pick up the CNN crew. I had to loop around the train station, but just as I was approaching the station an officer stepped into the road and announced that it was now closed since the Kerry motorcade was ready to come to the train.

"But," I explained, waving my security pass, "CNN is waiting for me at the rim and this train isn't leaving without them, or if it does a lot of people are going to be very unhappy".

Sorry, Secret Service orders.

"But the Secret Service is waiting for me on the other side of the train."

Sorry, back up you van to the curb and park it, now!

"See Charles over there? He's running this show for the park and he'll vouch for me."

"I said park that van NOW!"

The Secret Service was nervous, for they preferred controlled-entry events with magnetic gates and body searches, and now they were seeing foreigners half-hidden by trees.

When I failed to show up to pick up CNN, someone must have panicked, for another campaign van suddenly disappeared, except that no one told us, so when we discovered it missing we supposed it had been stolen. The law officers radioed back and forth to be on the look-out for a stolen white van, so when I finally walked back to my parked white van an officer declared: There's the thief! Grab him!

9: The Theater of the Ages

The locomotive fired up; the black smoke puffed out; the whistle sounded. The train pulled out and disappeared into a forest filled with Puebloan ruins. Tomorrow the Kerrys would be in a different world, Las Vegas, where everyone is a winner. Maybe other people are losers. The Puebloans were losers. But not us. America is a winner and there's always a jackpot just waiting for us.

When the newspapers came out the next day, the Kerry campaign was bummed out. There were indeed photos of John Kerry and Teresa and Vanessa on the canyon rim, but the stories were mostly about Iraq and not the canyon or Kerry's environmental positions. After all that trouble.

But in fact the stories really were about the Grand Canyon. This is exactly the way it happens. It's a story told over and over again in the canyon rocks. It's a story told by the Puebloan ruins and by the fossils within the stones the Puebloans picked up to make their houses. It's been happening like this for hundreds of millions of years. A new species arises with a unique advantage and expands its population rapidly. But then the environment changes, or the species uses up its resources. Perhaps some individuals realize that resources are dwindling, or perhaps not. Individuals and species end up fighting over the dwindling resources. Then the population crashes. It's a story told not just by the canyon rocks but by the gooey black corpses of ancient life buried deep but rapidly dwindling beneath the Middle Eastern desert.

7

The Bookie of Virtues

For hundreds of miles the Kerry train had been following Route 66 westward, just like the Joads. In the Joad's day there was no reason not to continue following Rt. 66 right into Los Angeles. But now in the hot dusty August night wind of Kingman, Arizona, the train ride was ending, and everyone piled into buses for the jog north, pulled by a new gravity that had arisen on the American map, a planet that pulled millions of Americans irresistibly to it every year. If the Joads were making their trek today would they keep going to California to pick fruit for low wages, or would they veer north and head for Las Vegas?

I was driving myself. For entertainment I fished out my supply of books-on-tape and rejected several, and then—aha, perfect! I slipped in cassette number-one of William J. Bennett's *The Book of Virtues*. I headed for Vegas.

Self-discipline. "In self-discipline," said Bennett, "one makes a disciple of one-self. One is one's own teacher, trainer, coach, and disciplinarian. It is an odd sort of relationship, paradoxical in its own way, and many of us don't handle it very well. There's much unhappiness and personal distress in the world because of failures to control tempers, appetites, passions, and impulses. 'Oh if only I had stopped myself' is an all too familiar refrain."[22]

The goose that laid the golden egg. "Here," said Bennett, "is Aesop's classic fable about plenty not being enough, about what happens when having it all becomes the motto of the day."[23] A narrator then told the tale of the man and wife who weren't satisfied with one golden egg a day and killed the goose to get all the gold at once, only to end up with nothing but a dead goose.

So far, so good. Who would object to Aesop or Hans Christian Andersen or Robert Frost offering tales of building character and avoiding disaster? But I seemed to recall that some critics had slighted *The Book of Virtues*. Perhaps liberal critics assumed that since Bennett was a leading conservative voice in the culture wars, *The Book of Virtues* must be up to no good. But who could object to virtues like responsibility, compassion, courage, honesty, friendship, persistence, and hard work? And the tales Bennett had selected to illustrate these virtues were fitting and often charming.

I drove onto Hoover dam, named of course for President Herbert Hoover. In his 1922 book *American Individualism* Hoover declared that in America economic success was an accurate measure of personal virtue. In old Europe personal success and religious life were blocked by hierarchies, but in Protestant America divinity dwelled within everyone and this empowerment of individuals had enabled Americans to conquer the frontier and prosper. Let European priests tell the poor that virtue would be rewarded in the next world; in America virtue brought worldly success. Hoover seems to have written *American Individualism* as an answer to progressives who were complaining that the rise of industrial monopolies had left our pioneer virtues an inadequate blueprint for society. Hoover answered that American individualism offered all the cures we needed. There was no need to regulate corporations because now that virtuous and thus prosperous citizens were buying lots of stocks, corporations would be forced to behave virtuously. There was no need for government to help the destitute because virtuous and thus prosperous citizens would do the virtuous thing on their own. Government intervention was actually a destructive thing, for it threatened to dam the bountiful river of American individualism and virtue.

Yet there may have been a flaw in Hoover's logic. Hoover may have underestimated the role that sheer greed played in American life. It wasn't virtue that sent prospectors combing the West for gold and jumping each other's claims and murdering each other. Often it wasn't a desire for religious freedom or political rights that lured the huddled masses across the Atlantic, but the desire to strike it rich. It was the craving to strike it rich that tempted millions to pour their savings into the stock market in the 1920s. When the stock market mania stalled, people were panicked by greed to get out with as much as possible and leave others holding the bag, and thus the market crashed and Herbert Hoover was left holding the bag. Yet Hoover refused to admit that anything was wrong with his faith in virtuous individualism, and he became a harsh critic of the New Deal: "The New Deal repudiation of democracy has left the Republican Party alone the guardian of the Ark of the Covenant with its charter of freedom."[24]

When I emerged from the valley of Hoover Dam I faced a huge bright dome of light on the horizon. There are places a hundred miles or more from Las Vegas, places on the rim of the Grand Canyon or in Utah red rock country, where you can see a faint glow on the horizon like a distant galaxy, and it is hard to believe that people live inside that glow as if it is the only reality. But now as I drove onto the Strip, that reality was massive and compelling. Lights glared everywhere, tens of millions of light bulbs in towers and banners, lights rolling and flashing, a Grand Canyon of lights colorful and hypnotic, lights promising money and glamour and fun and more money.

I passed Mandallay Bay, then Luxor, the black thirty-story hollow Egyptian pyramid, then Excalibur, the Arthurian castle. All three casinos were developed by William G. Bennett. No, not William Bennett of *The Book of Virtues*. William G. Bennett was the longtime president of the Circus Circus group of casinos, and in the 1980s he revolutionized Las Vegas by aiming for working-class and middle-class customers. Previously casinos had aimed for wealthy high-rollers and left slot machines as an afterthought to entertain the unskilled wives of the high-rollers. At Circus Circus William G. Bennett threw out the table games and the high-rollers and packed the casino with slot machines, then he dropped his hotel room rates to giveaway prices and opened mega-buffets with giveaway prices, and then he offered non-stop circus acts and amusement rides to draw families. The other casino owners thought Bennett was nuts, but soon Circus Circus was swarming with guests and profits. This set off a trend in designing and marketing Las Vegas as a family vacation destination. But by 2004 this trend had passed and Las Vegas was back to being sin city: "What happens in Vegas, stays in Vegas."

To avoid confusion between the two William Bennetts, try remembering that *The Book of Virtues* William Bennett is William *J*. Bennett, while the casino William Bennett is William *G*. Bennett. G as in gambling. But I would be surprised if William G. Bennett actually gambled. Few casino owners or employees throw away their money on gambling. They know their business too well, they know the math, they see the endless parade of losers, of pathetic suckers, pathetic delusional egotistical greedy suckers who are so sure they are the one out of 100 who will walk away with a jackpot. Or is it one out of 500? Only the casino insiders know the numbers for sure, right down to the decimal point, and that's why they don't gamble, because they don't want to look like pathetic suckers, and besides, they are getting rich off of the endless parade of suckers. William G. Bennett was regularly in the Fortune 400 of America's richest, with $250 million in 1986 and $630 million in 1997. G as in gold mine.

To expand on his success William G. Bennett turned to Michael Milken, who had invented the idea of junk bonds to finance another Vegas casino. Since money from the Mafia and the Teamsters had slowed down, Las Vegas needed a new cash cow. Milken sold his first $160 million batch of junk bonds to Utah Mormon bankers, whose religion might forbid gambling but not investing in gambling. Milken ended up in prison, his name synonymous with the financial piracies of the Reagan years. During the Reagan years Las Vegas marketed itself as "The American way to play."

Now William Bennett, J that is, the one who served as secretary of education under Ronald Reagan, was introducing the timeless story of Odysseus and his wife Penelope. Penelope's loyalty to Odysseus made her the ultimate example of female virtue.

One thing that William G. Bennett (the one who knew the decimal points to which gamblers are pathetic suckers) didn't really think about when he built Luxor was that its atrium, the world's largest, with row above row of hotel corridors, would become a magnet for suicides. The first suicide happened soon after Luxor's grand opening. A man jumped from the fifteenth floor and shattered his bones on the casino floor, though fortunately it was 3 AM and the floor was largely empty. Soon afterward a young woman jumped from the twenty-sixth floor at lunchtime, landing right next to the line of people going into the buffet, spraying blood and body fluids all over the place. Luxor had to replace the carpet. Luckily Las Vegas has a company devoted entirely to cleaning up bio-messes resulting from suicides and murders. Luxor recognized that it had a problem and discussed enclosing the hotel corridors with wire screens but rejected them as incompatible with the classy look of the place. An occasional body smashing down onto the slot machines was just the price Bennett would have to pay for running a classy joint.

Las Vegas has the highest suicide rate in America. Even if you subtract the casino visitors who lose their life savings and kill themselves and you count only residents, Las Vegas still leads the nation in suicides. Las Vegas also has far-above-average and often nation-leading rates of murder, theft, assault, rape, alcoholism, drug abuse, spousal abuse, child abuse, child neglect, homelessness, unwed pregnancies, auto accidents, (local) divorce, lung cancer, gambling addiction, and mental illness. Las Vegas is the national capital of pornography, prostitution, drug dealing, and scam artists. And we haven't even mentioned organized crime. Behind the glittering façade is a mass of desperation, a dark broken society whose moral values are failing.

According to William J. Bennett (the one who was clueless about the decimal points) the modern moral and social breakdown typified by Las Vegas was largely the fault of liberalism, of academic elites who refused to believe in God and America, of bohemians who scorned Puritan and pioneer virtues, of social engineers who violated the correlation between virtue and economic rewards by taking rewards from those who had earned them and diverting them to those who hadn't. Echoing William J. Bennett were dozens of prominent voices from the pulpit, talk radio, and the White House, angrily blaming liberalism for the moral decline of American society.

But here's a curious thought. Las Vegas is just about as far away as you can get from the center of American liberalism. The liberal intelligentsia of Las Vegas could probably fit into a small coffee house, and not necessarily a coffee house near UNLV, a lightweight in the academic world, with buildings and scholarships paid for by mobsters and an engineering school named for world-famous nutcase Howard Hughes. Maybe in Berkeley you could find a community college offering a course criticizing Puritan and pioneer virtues, but the community college in Las Vegas offers a massive room full of casino tables where kids train to be professional dealers. It's also very hard to find liberal social engineering schemes in Las Vegas, or even the most minimal social services like crisis hotlines. Las Vegas and Nevada are the epitome of the low-tax and low-services conservative philosophy, sometimes beating out Mississippi for the bottom rung on rankings of social spending and quality.

If the most morally and socially degraded city in America offers no correlation at all with the influence of liberalism, then what are the social values that rule over Las Vegas? What does Las Vegas worship above all else? Oh…could it possibly be money? Not just money, but an outright deification of get-rich-quick greed, a deification that built a pyramid worthy of the Pharaohs, inside which the unworthy could sacrifice themselves by throwing themselves down onto the altar of money.

Now here was a disturbing thought. What happens to Christian moral values in a society that makes its ultimate god out of money and greed? What happens when a society tries to live with a schizoid contradiction between the values it preaches in church and the values it worships in the marketplace and in society? But really, such worries were just too much for me to grapple with this late at night, especially with such amazing distractions all around me. Look, there's the Statue of Liberty and the Brooklyn Bridge at New York New York casino. Did anyone try to sell this Brooklyn Bridge to suckers? New York New York contained a replica of the New York stock exchange.

Odysseus sailed off to the Trojan War, which was not fought out of greed for wealth but over the honor of a woman, noble Helen. When the war ended, Odysseus set sail for home and his noble Penelope, only to meet one misadventure after another, but still Penelope waited loyally for him.

I saw lots of signs flashing "Loose Slots!" This was another tribute to William G. Bennett (the one who probably knew the odds of a suicide jumper landing on you as you played the slots at Luxor). Back when many casinos had pocketed

20% or more of the money put into slot machines, Bennett programmed the slots at Circus Circus to pay back 97.4%, by far the loosest slots in town. Again the other casino owners thought Bennett was crazy. Now he was giving away all his casino profits. But Bennett knew that very little of the slot jackpots actually went out the door. He put his trust in the power of greed. When people won a jackpot they felt lucky, they felt special—actually they'd felt special when they'd walked in the door and now their egos were validated and they were sure they could win even bigger so they plowed their jackpots back into the slots. The crowds flocked to Circus Circus, and the other casinos were forced to copy it.

When Odysseus failed to return, everyone else assumed he had died at sea, but Penelope refused to lose faith. Every day she set his place at the table. But now suitors greedy for his estate were showing up at her home and refusing to leave until she married one of them. They just lounged in his home and drank up his wine and ate his food.

Wow—look at the MGM Grand all aglow in emerald green. It was meant to invoke the emerald city of MGM's *The Wizard of Oz*. Pay no attention to the man behind the curtain.

There was Bally's, formerly the original MGM Grand, which was closed by a fire that killed eighty-four people. Some of the charred bodies were found still sitting at slot machines, as if they'd been too obsessed with their lucky machine to try to flee.

There was Ceasars Palace, which had launched the themed casino idea. Why wasn't there a Greek-themed casino? You could call it The Odyssey, with Penelope's Restaurant and the Lotus Bar and the Siren's gambling hall.

Relentlessly besieged by her suitors, Penelope finally agreed to choose a husband, but only after she finished weaving a shroud. Every day she worked on it, but every night she secretly unwove that day's work.

Can you believe all the traffic this late at night, all the crowds on the sidewalks? Across from Ceasars was the Flamingo, built by mobster Bugsy Siegel, the start of Mafia Las Vegas.

Just when Penelope's unweaving trick was discovered and her suitors demanded she marry, Odysseus returned. Odysseus slew the greedy suitors, and Penelope was rewarded for her virtue, and they lived happily ever after. Click. End of tape.

Just in time too, for I too was home, at least at my hotel, the New Frontier, which I liked for its Kennedyesque name, although I'd chosen it for its cheap rates. But the New Frontier seemed like good luck for John Kerry's visit to Las Vegas. Not that I believed in luck.

It turned out that the New Frontier had a bad luck story behind it. When I checked in, the desk clerk was sour and unhelpful, leaving me to find my room in a confusing layout of hotel towers and similar-sounding room numbers. I carried my stuff up and down and around and around. When I found my room I found that it had cheap rates because it was rather shabby. The next day while waiting for the Kerry rally to start I got into a long conversation with a professional poker player and he punctured my illusions about the Kennedyesque New Frontier. He knew all about labor issues in Las Vegas because he'd worked for the most virulently anti-union casino corporation in Las Vegas and had been drilled in anti-union tactics. The New Frontier too was notoriously anti-union. Back in 1991 the Culinary Workers Union, the main union in Las Vegas, had called a strike against the Frontier, as it was then called, when it tried to cut pay and health and other benefits. Picketers had marched twenty-four hours a day for the next six years, making it the longest strike in American history. The sour desk clerk probably hated working there. The Frontier was just down the street from Circus Circus, and William G. Bennett (the one who was not virtuous), who was greatly respected by his employees for treating them right and for numerous charitable donations, sent the Circus Circus catering truck down to the Frontier to feed the strikers three meals a day for five years, enraging the Frontier owners. Adding "New" to the Frontier was a feeble attempt at image makeover. My room was shabby because the owner had announced plans to blow up the New Frontier and replace it with a San Francisco-themed super casino.

There I'd been wandering around the New Frontier with my Kennedyesque illusions, when all the time the New Frontier was a legacy of the Mafia 1960s, probably built, like much of Mafia Vegas, with Teamster's pension money funneled, for kickbacks, by Kennedy-hating Jimmy Hoffa, and then the Frontier was bought by the world-famous nutcase Howard Hughes, and then it was bought by union-haters to host the longest strike in American history. Going further back in history, the Frontier was a replacement for the Last Frontier, one of Las Vegas' first casinos. In 1954, his movie career dead, a desperate Ronald Reagan tried to headline a stage show at the Last Frontier, a show with trained monkeys, dancing girls with two-foot-high plumed headdresses, and Reagan in clown pants and telling jokes and racing around hitting other performers with a rolled-up newspaper. The show bombed. "But leaving Las Vegas," wrote Roger Morris and Sally Denton in their study of Las Vegas, *The Money and the Power,* "he plans a new career in which he would take up politics after all and preside over policies that would make a national credo of the Las Vegas ethic of greed and exploitation."[25]

With all their contradictions it seemed there had to be more than two William Bennetts, so let me pause to do a William Bennett summary: William J. Bennett is the one who preaches Christian moral virtues even as he loyally serves a president who re-sanctified the creed of greed for the ever-more and launched an era of financial piracy and aggressive union breaking. William G. Bennett is the one who turns the greed of all the suckers in his casinos into five years of free food for strikers.

I was confused enough just wondering about the contradictions of William J. Bennett alone. I sure wished William J. Bennett was here so I could talk with him. He'd probably have a good answer. All I wanted to ask him was this: what is the meaning and fate of Christian moral values in a society that makes a greater god out of money?

The next morning I had time to walk around exploring the Strip, since the Kerry rally wasn't until afternoon. I started by looking around the New Frontier. Just inside the main entrance was a statue of a prospector holding a gold pan, his chest consisting of a slot machine. Some of the slot machines also had prospector themes, such as 'Yukon Gold' and 'Eureka!' The general décor continued the Wild West theme. The "saloon" featured a bull riding machine, and out front the big cowboy-figure marquee advertised 'Bikini Bull Riding.'

Most of the early Las Vegas casinos had Wild West themes—the Golden Nugget, the Horseshoe, the Pioneer Club. The obvious symbolism was that the Wild West was all about striking it rich quick, and Las Vegas was the present-day embodiment of that spirit. This symbolism must have resonated with Americans for Las Vegas to become our number-one tourist destination. But today's new casinos invoked not cowboy dreams but the wealth and power of old-world kings and aristocrats. What did this say about American values today? And how did Christian moral values fit into this picture? I sure wished William J. Bennett was here so I could ask him.

As I headed out onto the Strip I told myself that even though it would be a wildly unlikely stroke of luck, I would keep an eye out for William J. Bennett. After all, luck was what Las Vegas was all about.

The Wild West theme continued up the street at the Westward Ho. Their slot machines included 'Uncle Sam,' with a big American flag banner; the goal was to match up patriotic icons, including Mt. Rushmore, the Statue of Liberty, the Declaration of Independence, the Liberty Bell, George Washington, and honest Abe Lincoln, who was so virtuous he walked for miles to return a few coins. Other slot machines had various other patriotic themes, such as 'Red, White, and Blue'. There was a whole set of Beverly Hillbillies-themed slot machines, including 'Bubblin Crude' and 'Moonshine Money.' Even more than a 49er gold prospector, who at least worked hard to strike it rich, Jed Clampett embodied the Vegas ideal of getting rich quick through sheer dumb luck, with zero correlation between virtue and financial success.

On my way to the Westward Ho I had passed the Stardust with its iconic 188-foot-tall sign with 26,000 light bulbs. The Stardust was the star of the movie *Casino*, about the Mafia era in Vegas, in which even huge legal profits weren't enough and the Mafia took to illegal skimming and gangland murders. No virtue here. The Mafia was aided by Jimmy Hoffa, for whom organized labor wasn't about social justice but just another form of greed. Liberals and conservatives may not agree on much but here at least, since liberals claim corporations are driven by greed and conservatives claim unions are driven by greed, everyone is agreed that America is driven by greed. Americans have validated greed not just by flocking to Las Vegas but by legalizing gambling everywhere on the grounds that people refuse to pay for schools and hospitals through taxes but they will through lotteries. Is there any point in further considering the claim that wealth in America is an accurate gauge of virtue? Let's get back to considering how moral values work out in a society where the first virtue is greed.

I headed down to Treasure Island with its huge pirate ship; reportedly the pirate show was the favorite place in town for pickpockets. The pirate theme was continued inside; people didn't seem to hesitate about pouring money into slot machines with grinning pirate faces. They had a Ben and Jerry's ice cream shop, but considering Ben and Jerry's liberal politics, this was the one place where you'd never catch William J. Bennett; can you imagine the public embarrassment if Bennett was spotted munching on Cherry Garcia?

I looked into the gaming tables area. At the busy poker tables several players wore cowboy hats. Later on as I waited for the Kerry rally and talked with the professional poker player he said that he was often summoned by casinos to fill out high-roller games and he loved to see the Texans in cowboy hats. It was a sure sign that they had bought into the Wild West mystique in which poker loomed large as a paper shoot-out, that they had major fantasies about proving their manhood. The cowboy hats got slaughtered spectacularly. A pro played strictly by the math; if the math said fold, then you folded no matter how much you lost. But once the cowboy hats got their egos engaged in a game they were doomed, for they couldn't bear to look like losers to other guys, and a pro could bait and play the cowboy hats for all they were worth. It seemed to me that a similar disaster syndrome happens in foreign policy.

I went back out onto the Strip. Where would I be most likely to find William J. Bennett? I knew it was unlikely, but I was feeling lucky today, feeling like a winner. I'll bet I could find him.

One thing I wanted to ask him was whether some Christian churches had compromised their moral authority by enlisting in the creed of greed. I'm not talking about bingo. The old log-church promise that virtue would be rewarded with worldly success had turned into mammoth nationally televised services that were largely pep rallies for financial success. Christ was the ultimate salesman with a winning attitude and Christianity was the ultimate Dale Carnegie course, at least in suburban congregations where most members had business careers. In poor churches, white and black alike, they often dispensed with the career ladders and went straight to the miracles. If you simply had faith you would be rewarded financially. Some preachers made a naked connection between sending money to their church and being rewarded, telling stories of the woman who'd sent in $500 she couldn't afford and soon she got a great job, was cured of cancer, or won the lottery. There were probably gamblers in Vegas who were sure that this was how God would finally pay them back, and they knelt and prayed in their rooms before heading down to the casinos to be preyed upon.

I headed across the street to the Venetian. The Venetian was huge, with faithful recreations of Venetian towers and plazas and bridges over canals. The canals went on for a long way inside, lined by very fancy shops and restaurants. We had left the Wild West for the world of European class. Rooms here cost $200 or more, meals easily $100. In between Wild West Las Vegas and imperial Las Vegas there'd been another phase, the cool swinger Las Vegas, personified by Frank Sinatra and the Rat Pack, who hung out at the Sands, which was blown up to make way for the Venetian. Perhaps Americans weren't content with being cool swingers, with the era of James Bond and JFK and Viva Las Vegas Elvis, and they wanted to be social elites, which was actually facilitated by the policies of Ronald Reagan and George W. Bush, who ironically were still doing the Wild West thing in their cowboy hats. Now Bush was denouncing Kerry for belonging to the social elite even though Kerry was talking about helping ordinary workers, who would love to be social elites and stay at the Venetian but who wouldn't vote for Kerry if he really was a social elite. I was getting confused again. I was keeping an eye out for William J. Bennett so I could ask him about cowboy-hat presidents who preached pioneer virtues even as they were erecting in America the social structure the pioneers had fled Europe to escape.

The Venetian canals, like all the extravagant fountains and swimming pools in Las Vegas, came from pumping irreplaceable ground water; behind the façade of

European class, Las Vegas was still the Wild West in action, grabbing treasure for today with no thought of tomorrow.

Another thing I wanted to ask Bennett was why religion in America was so unique, with nothing like our evangelicalism in Europe. This was nothing new. Back in the 1830s Tocqueville observed that Americans were much more fervent about religion. Historians have suggested that since America was first settled in the heat of the Protestant Reformation and remained distant from intellectual trends of secularism, we retained more religious fervor. Yet as I walked around Las Vegas and studied the faces of Americans yearning to be Venetians, I was favoring a more sociological theory. Right from the start of our history Americans suffered from a severe lack of roots, immigrants having cut themselves off from the families, friends, communities, churches, and other institutions that support human sanity and survival. This cutting off of roots may have been beneficial when it cut off European hierarchies and allowed us to establish democracy and open up personal opportunities, but still we paid a psychological price for it. A nation of immigrants stripped of identities has gone fervently questing for identity. In a nation where family name and history officially meant nothing, the only way to prove your social worth was by conspicuously displaying your wealth. Thus Americans have plunged into a frantic contest for status symbols, which runs straight from the gold prospectors to Las Vegas. But the contest for status symbols seems to have left a deep spiritual void, even more so among those coming up short in the contest. To both the social void of support systems and the spiritual void of the status contest, religion offered an answer, which Americans embraced with a special hunger. If there was cognitive dissonance between the creed of greed and the Christian creed of doing unto others and doing without material things for the sake of the spiritual, Americans tried to rationalize it away by equating wealth with Christian virtue, and many churches embraced the status contest. People who were losing the status contest, who were bombarded with ads and interpersonal behaviors telling them they were worthless, were especially eager to hear about their spiritual worth. Those who were most fervent about Christianity also felt most threatened by anything opposed to Christianity, and thus when a preacher or a president declared that liberalism was opposed to Christianity, Christians angrily rejected liberalism, even if it was the Democrats who were offering to help economic losers. Thus America ended up with a strange coalition of poor and rich, of working-class Christians fervently supporting the erection of a European hierarchy that would permanently shut them out. The bond between poor and rich was reinforced by a shared faith in the American Dream. The rich believed in the American Dream because they were the living proof of it. The poor might have a harder time believing they would be the next Sam Walton but they had a more urgent need to believe in the American Dream. Ronald Reagan and George W. Bush assured the poor that the American Dream was real and combined this faith with Christianity. If evidence for the American Dream was getting harder to find on the loading dock, then you had to believe even harder in the lottery or Las Vegas.

I headed for Ceasars Palace. That's Ceasers without an apostrophe mark, meaning that it doesn't belong to Ceasar but that everyone who goes there is a Ceasar. I walked down another grand hallway full of opulent shops. The crowds were mostly window-shopping because few could afford to buy $1,000 dresses. People were also glancing up at the high arched ceiling painted with a blue sky and white puffy clouds. Decades ago Las Vegas crowds stared up at white mushroom clouds on the horizon from atomic testing, explosions that were advertised as a tourist attraction. Casinos offered rooms with the best view and served "atomic cocktails," and showgirls danced in skimpy mushroom-cloud costumes.

I went into the gigantic sports book. I knew that William J. Bennett had to be around here somewhere. I just knew it. I could feel it I my bones. Heads were glued to huge TV screens filled with racing horses, racing cars, racing baseball players. I wandered through the table games, and since the slots were William J. Bennett's favorite game (just like William G. Bennett), I paid special attention to the faces at the slots, faces absolutely hypnotized, not many smiling either, just faces pouring money into slots. No Bennett. But I knew he had to be here. Just one more casino and my luck would change, I could feel it. Just one more casino and then I'd give it up, I swear.

I entered the Bellagio, the ultimate Euro-aristocratic casino, with rows of the same shops you found on Rodeo Drive in Beverly Hills. At Tiffany's people were staring in the window.

This was where John Kerry and the campaign staff had stayed last night. From a public image viewpoint it might have been better for Kerry to stay at the MGM Grand with its imagery of Dorothy and Toto and Scarlet O'Hara. But from a Secret Service viewpoint the Bellagio was hard to beat. Most casinos were designed to force hotel guests to walk through the casino action and crowds, but the Bellagio had private entrances and private elevators for elite guests. Maybe this was why the Bellagio was William J. Bennett's favorite casino.

I strolled among the slot machines. It was a big mystery to me how someone could actually manage to lose eight million dollars on slot machines. It did seem that the Bellagio slot machines had classier themes than the slots at other casinos, which had more Wild West and TV sitcom themes. Come to think of it, speaking of Beverly Hills, I wasn't seeing Beverly Hillbillies slot machines here. It seemed like I had seen plenty elsewhere. I started looking specifically for the Beverly Hillbillies. This seemed like a fair test case in casino sociology, in the increasingly aristocratic values of American society. Even when rich, the Beverly Hillbillies remained hopelessly low-class, but they remained the epitome of the American Dream, of a common man striking it rich—surely the Bellagio wouldn't banish the American Dream? But the Beverly Hillbillies were nowhere to be seen. Presumably the Beverly Hillbillies were just too low-class for the Bellagio.

Presumably William J. Bennett loved the Bellagio, for reportedly it was mostly here that he lost eight million dollars, the profits from *The Book of Virtues*, playing slot machines. I finally figured out how he did it, for off to one side was a little Slot High Limit Room with a few dozen very pricy slot machines. There was a 'Red, White, and Blue' slot machine that took a token worth $1,000. It would have taken Bennett 8,000 pulls at this machine to lose eight million dollars, and more if he occasionally won, and a minimum of 80,000 pulls at the $100 machines. The room was nearly empty, only one aristocratic man playing. There was an attendant at a counter and I asked her if she had seen William J. Bennett, but of course there are company policies against discussing clients. Maybe this just wasn't my lucky day.

When Bennett was caught losing the profits from *The Book of Virtues* down slot machines he answered that it didn't do anyone any harm since he hadn't been betting the milk money. In fact right outside the Slot High Limit Room was a slot machine called 'Milk Money: Cows with Attitude.' But maybe this wasn't what Bennett was referring to. Naturally liberals refused to pass judgment on Bennett because that wouldn't be the liberal thing to do since moral values are all relative and no one has the right to impose judgment on anyone else and South Seas bone-nosed head-hunting cannibals are just practicing their religion and all that, and besides it's all society's fault. But in listening to *The Book of Virtues* I had been converted to William J. Bennett's viewpoint and now I was a firm believer in personal responsibility, so when I'd seen guys wearing gold chains with shark's teeth and rabbit's feet and horseshoes and stuffing money into slot machines I hadn't thought: innocent victims of society; I'd thought: losers, pathetic losers.

Seriously, I wouldn't have minded running into Bennett—or anyone who could shed some light on the fate of moral values in a society addicted to greed. This question wasn't just a challenge for Bennett or Christianity, it was a problem for American liberalism too. A big problem. It was an even bigger problem for liberals than for conservatives, for conservatives were primarily worried about moral values in personal behavior, and when it came to the moral values of American society, the greed of the marketplace and the casino ruled. But liberals wanted to go beyond personal morality and build a moral society which actually practiced doing unto others. Liberals held that morality had to be public, that a good example had to be set at the top, incorporated into society's rules. But it was very difficult to build a moral society on a foundation of greed. A moral society in liberal terms also required a foundation of personal virtue, first of all the virtue of people caring about one another. It was here that liberals and William J. Bennett and friends had much more in common than they usually recognized amidst their disagreements over private morals. Liberals and conservatives might have very different definitions of it, but both aspired to The City on a Hill, liberals in civic terms and conservatives in religious terms, but for centuries The City on a Hill had been competing against the greedy side of the American Dream and often losing, often losing in a rout. William J. Bennett's fall to the culture of greed might be amusing to liberals but it could also be taken as a bad omen for liberalism, for liberalism too was facing the almighty power of the United States of Bellagio.

It didn't look like I was going to run into Bennett, and anyway it was time to head for the Kerry rally. I'd see what the Democrats had to say about the prospects of moral values in a culture of greed.

It turned out to be the hottest day of the year, 112 degrees, and a long line of people were cooking on the pavement outside the UNLV basketball arena. UNLV was only a few long blocks from the Strip, so as a professor tries to explain moral philosophy the students are gazing out the window at the Bellagio.

A local radio station was circulating through the crowd with a microphone, gathering responses to the question: "Did you know that everyone who votes for John Kerry will receive a free bottle of Heinz ketchup?"

"Really? A jumbo bottle or one of those skinny bottles?"

"I don't want ketchup. I want the Heinz steak sauce."

This was, after all, Las Vegas. The radio DJs were also seriously discussing the topic: Is John Kerry's hair real?

Inside the arena there was a large presence of labor unions, including the Teamsters, whose pension fund had enabled the Mafia to build the casinos now run by union-busters. A few weeks from now I would work the crowd for volunteers at the St. Louis Labor Day parade, where by far the longest display came from the Teamsters, who were driving every variety of vehicle they drove at work, and there right behind two cement mixers came three black hearses, and I heard the Jimmy Hoffa jokes rippling through the crowd: "Look—it's the Teamster's tribute to Jimmy Hoffa: but is Hoffa in the cement mixer or the hearse?" "Look, it's Jimmy Hoffa on his way to the new stadium."

The arena was now packed with an overflow crowd of 12,000. To entertain themselves while they waited the crowd started doing "the wave," the roulette wheel of people standing up and raising up their arms that went round and round with much energy. This was, after all, a basketball arena, and it was, after all, Las Vegas.

At last the master of ceremonies came out, Mayor Oscar Goodman, and the crowd roared approval. Goodman came to Las Vegas in the Mafia 1960s and became a famous Mafia lawyer. He worked for godfather Meyer Lansky, and for savage hit-man Tony Spiloto, who was portrayed by Joe Pesci in the movie *Casino*. Goodman also appeared in *Casino*, playing himself. Goodman repeatedly got Spiloto off the hook for his twenty-plus murders. After the leader of the Culinary Workers Union was found naked and dead under a pile of rocks in the desert, Spiloto asserted even more Mafia control over the already corrupt and violent union, with Goodman's help. Goodman didn't apologize for his Mafia ties. One of his pet projects as mayor was to open a Mafia museum. He was a boisterous cheerleader for Las Vegas and the city loved him for it, recently re-electing him with 87% of the vote. Now Goodman was tossing John Kerry t-shirts to the crowd.

What does American liberalism say to Bellagio America about a moral society?

American liberalism used to be pretty good at grounding its agenda in a moral—often Christian—worldview. William Jennings Bryan never doubted that the God who created the world in seven days was also very angry with Gilded Age Republicans for crucifying America on a cross of gold. Teddy Roosevelt was sure that both God and evolution were on the side of American progress, including progress as in progressive. Woodrow Wilson's moral righteousness annoyed the hell out of the senate. Franklin Roosevelt justified the New Deal as "throwing the money changers out of the temple." Martin Luther King would have been powerless without the moral power of the black church. Yet as the twentieth century wore on and secularism became a more common language and toleration became the watchword, liberals became shyer about proclaiming their purpose to be building a moral society. Social gospel liberalism was harder to energize when it lost even a secular gospel and floated in philosophical limbo.

One option was to justify liberalism in terms of self-interest. Conservatives were looking out for corporate self-interest so liberals would look out for the self-interest of labor and other groups. The big loss here was that liberalism surrendered much of its claim to a greater moral vision and agreed that America was nothing more than a greed game where Enron, the Mafia, and Jimmy Hoffa agreed on the rules. Conservatives had always been irked at the claim of liberalism to represent a greater moral vision and they worked hard to discredit it by portraying Democratic constituencies as just more "special interests." By losing their moral vision, liberals risked playing right in to that anti-image.

By the start of the twenty-first century perhaps the strongest argument for liberalism, and indeed a moral argument, was socio-historical. For decades now, largely unnoticed by Americans, America and Europe had been trading places on the stage of history. Tens of millions of Europeans had fled hierarchical Europe for the American Dream, but driven by a hunger for social status that turned insane, Americans were frantically building the United States of Bellagio where wealth was more concentrated in the top one percent of society than it had been since the Gilded Age, if even then. Meanwhile, Europeans had gotten a long scary look into the abyss of feudalism, not just in how class polarization corroded their own societies but in how Russian feudalism collapsed into revolution and terror. Americans never had to worry seriously about a communist revolution, but for Europeans revolutions and gulags were a real threat that had to be addressed democratically before democracy failed. The result has been a social democratic Europe that has worked diligently to iron out centuries of feudalism. By many measures of class inequality and social well-being, the trajectories of America and Europe crossed some time ago. America is now more economically stratified than the Britain we once rebelled against. For now the Bellagioization of America is sustained by the power of the American Dream, which assured everyone that they would be winners. But eventually Americas would realize that most of those who walked into the Bellagio, even those sure of God's ordainment, walked out losers, and that the American Dream included an awful lot of suckers.

Finally the Mafia showman mayor made John Kerry an offer he couldn't refuse: get out there, Johnny baby, and put on a good show.

The crowd roared with joy as John Kerry strode onto the stage and waved and turned and waved to acknowledge the whole 12,000. The crowd stood and clapped and waved their hands and waved their signs and roared. Mothers lifted up their kids. People were actually wiping away tears—could you believe it? Faces were recognizably full of longing and hope. People were dancing their signs back and forth to the music, dancing themselves. The cameras flashed like the Vegas night. The crowd roared out of a long unfed hunger, a hunger that might actually be deeper here than anywhere else in America. Twelve thousand people—ahh look at all the lonely people—roared out of a hunger for something that was essential to human life but which Las Vegas was not providing, which America was not providing. Here more than anywhere else they felt that something was wrong in the land; even addicts knew when something was wrong with them. For a moment at least, 12,000 people weren't competing ruthlessly against one another, weren't just losers or winners, but were joined in some sort of community, and that in itself was a novelty worth cheering about. How could they hold onto such a feeling? By roaring on and on.

Yet this crowd was not so different from Kerry crowds all across America, who felt the same void and the same hunger and who cheered not specifically for John Kerry but out of the long-starved hope that America could change. Kerry crowds all across America had the same experience of realizing, the moment Kerry opened his mouth, no matter what he said, that they had attached all that hunger and hope onto what was, after all, just a man, and their hope paused for a moment, worrying if it was hoping for too much, but then Kerry started talking about how "we are all in the same boat" and the crowd recognized that this was indeed food for their hunger. By the standards of European social democracy Kerry's rhetoric and policy proposals were fairly mild, but where people were accustomed to being left to drown in Lake Bellagio it was refreshing to hear that we were all in the same boat. The crowd roared and roared.

After the rally I stepped outside into the heat, which was stunning. Heat boiled off the pavement and made the Strip towers shimmer like a dream. And they were a dream, the American Dream given manifest form in concrete and marble, the very dream that had lured the pioneers across the sea and across the Cumberland Gap and across the prairies and across the Rockies to here, where at last the dream revealed itself to have become a hellish desert mirage.

Over two months later I was freezing in a bitterly cold night as we waited for the Kerry campaign plane to arrive from Las Vegas. We were waiting in a place that as a cultural symbol was about as far away as you could get from Las Vegas, the Iowa state fairground.

The podium was set up to frame John Kerry against the dome of the agriculture building, a dome that was the iconic image of the state fair. Agriculture of course was what the fair was all about, to celebrate the honest hard work of farmers and the bountiful land of America. From all over the state farm families brought their pies and pickles and sheep. Their idea of exotic entertainment was a full-sized cow carved out of butter. It was a celebration of small-town virtues where neighbors looked out for one another. Like most states Iowa had established a state lottery, but Iowa was the only state to designate a portion of lottery proceeds to help out anyone with a gambling problem. The Iowa state fair was so much the measure of state fairs that three *State Fair* movies had been made about it, and as with Las Vegas casinos, these movies tracked the changing social values of America. The first *State Fair* starred New Deal populist Will Rogers; the second was a more sophisticated musical by Rogers and Hammerstein; and the third was cool-swingers-era version starring Bobby Darin and Ann-Margaret. We are still eagerly awaiting the Bush-era remake of *State Fair*, but maybe they are having trouble coming up with a script in which greed and aristocratic luxury conquer the Iowa state fair.

As in Las Vegas I was manning the press area, but unlike in Las Vegas I didn't have to fend off a steady stream of greedy infiltrators trying to grab the best spot; Iowans showed neighborly respect for the rules.

At long last Kerry arrived, and the national press stampeded into the press area, frantically setting up their cameras.

At a lull between speakers I climbed onto the press stand to talk with Jim the NBC cameraman. At a campaign stop at the Underground Railroad Museum in Cincinnati Jim had bought a stuffed Gandhi doll with big cute eyes, and ever since Jim had been entertaining himself by posing and photographing Gandhi on the campaign trail. Gandhi on the Kerry plane. Gandhi on the press bus. Gandhi peering through the NBC camera. Since Gandhi was hanging out with hard-bitten journalists, he sometimes indulged in their bad habits too. Gandhi smoking a cigar. Gandhi with a glass of Scotch. Every time I crossed Jim's path I asked him about Gandhi's latest adventures, and he would show me his growing album of photos. Of course I had to ask Jim about Gandhi in Las Vegas last night, since it seemed rich in possibilities. Gandhi playing a slot machine. Gandhi at the poker table. Gandhi with gaudy show girls. Gandhi with an Elvis impersonator. But all Jim said was: "Gandhi went to sleep." I asked him if Gandhi had avoided the casino because it might compromise his authority as an advocate of moral virtues, but Jim said "No. Gandhi was tired. Gandhi went to bed."

When Jim got busy I quietly asked Gandhi, who rode in the camera bag to see all the action, about missing out on all that action in Las Vegas. I never told Jim about this conversation since, being a hard-bitten journalist, he would probably say I just made it up.

"In fact," said Gandhi, "it was Jim who was tired and as soon as he went to sleep I slipped out to check out the casino. You see, I was a famous advocate of the spinning wheel. Being forced to buy textiles from Britain helped chain India to the British Empire, so if every Indian made their own clothes at home, it would help free us, as well as teach the virtue of simplicity. That's why there's a spinning wheel on the Indian flag. I'd heard that Las Vegas casinos were also famous for their spinning wheels. But they were really different, with numbers and pegs that go clickity-clack and balls that fall into slots. I couldn't figure them out. Then there were machines with wheels that spun round. But some guy explained them to me. I was watching him put $1,000 tokens into a machine called 'Red, White, and Blue' and he looked at me and said "Say, aren't you Gandhi? What a stroke of luck that I ran into you. I've been wanting to talk with someone with some experience at being an advocate of moral virtues. Didn't you find it hard to live up to that role in a world full of greed?" Not really, I answered. Then he said, "Well I'm having trouble figuring out how to implement moral virtues in a nation addicted to greed. Some guy was trying to ask me about this a couple of months ago, and he was even following me from casino to casino, but every time I'd spot him coming I'd flee, since I simply didn't have an answer. So maybe you have some answers." Oh boy, I thought. And I'd thought I'd had my hands full with India. Now this guy wants me to save America. My head started to spin with problems and confusion. If I'd had a better chance to think about it I might have come up with something that at least sounded wise, such as: you need different spinning wheels. But it was late at night, and all that noise, all those flashing lights, all those moral distractions. So I just told him: "I'm feeling very tired. I'm going to bed."

But the Iowa crowd wouldn't go to bed. They'd waited through several hours of bitter cold for Kerry to arrive from Las Vegas, and waited through an even longer hunger. The crowd roared and roared.

8

The Stations of the Cross

How could anyone doubt after yesterday's rally, a rally that set a new record for Bush rallies, with some 30,000 people (twice the population of the town) cheering the president, that democratic values in America are very healthy? This health was partly in how the rally came about. An average citizen of Poplar Bluff, Missouri, simply got tired of his town being off the beaten path of presidential politics and started a petition inviting the president to come to town. The Bush campaign recognized a good opportunity when it saw one and thus the president did indeed come to Poplar Bluff, and the national press liked the story and gave it a bonanza of publicity. This is indeed the way democracy is supposed to work: the people express their will, and the president enacts their will.

I've got some time to spare today, so I'm going to take a few hours to explore the health of democratic values in America. More specifically, I'm going to explore a town near the big rally, Cape Girardeau, Missouri, the hometown of Rush Limbaugh. At tourist brochure racks all over the area you can find a brochure called "Rush Limbaugh Hometown Tour," published by the Chamber of Commerce, with a map and guide to all the sites of importance in the early life of Rush Limbaugh. The existence of such a tour implied that quite a few pilgrims came to Cape Girardeau to seek out something important.

The tour brochure begins: "This self-driving tour will take you past the hospital where Rush was born and his childhood home. You will see where he attended high school and cruised Broadway, traditional during Rush's high school days." Here we are only two sentences into the tour guide and already there's a puzzle. Cruising Broadway was traditional all over America, and it still is, so why did the guide author feel obligated to insert this justification for why Rush was cruising Broadway? Was the author afraid we might take Rush for some kind of idle punk? The author assures us that cruising Broadway was traditional, and this seems to be all we need to know about it. It's traditional, therefore it's good. Perhaps this is a clue about the place that formed Rush Limbaugh: traditional.

To do even fuller justice to Rush's story, maybe we should start with the origins of the town itself.

Cape Girardeau was founded as an act of hatred for democratic values and the government of the United States. It was founded by Louis Lorimier, who fled here to escape Americans. According to the town history:

> During the American Revolution Louis Lorimier was a violent and loyal Tory and widely known as a hater of Americans. This political preference was not at all unusual since many of the merchant class were not in sympathy with the revolting colonies. Lorimier's place was often the base for supplying and equipping Indian expeditions against the American frontier outposts. According to tradition he paid his Indians for American scalps with British gold. Apparently Lorimier planned and even led some of these raids. On one occasion in 1778...Lorimier...led a raid into Kentucky and attacked Boonesborough. They either captured Daniel Boone, or persuaded him to come along...[26]

Patrick Henry, as governor of Virginia, sent General George Rogers Clark to the Ohio valley to clean out old British and French loyalists, and Clark burned down Lorimier's outpost. Lorimier fled across the Mississippi River to what was then Spanish territory, where in exchange for his loyal service to Spain, including organizing Indians against the encroaching Americans, he was granted a huge tract of land, the future downtown of Cape Girardeau. When the Louisiana Purchase placed Cape Girardeau into American hands the U. S. government hauled Lorimier into court on trumped-up charges designed to punish him for his disloyalties, but the case didn't hold up. But when the U. S. refused to honor Spanish land grants Lorimier couldn't sell his land, so new settlers avoided Cape Girardeau and old settlers left and the town nearly faded away. Finally the county court relocated itself to nearby Jackson; the first justices on that court included Louis Lorimier and Frederick Limbaugh. Sixty years later Lorimier's grandson would wear a Confederate uniform in the battle of Cape Girardeau and carry on his family's hatred of the United States. Two hundred years later the Limbaughs, still prominent lawyers in Cape Girardeau, would be reminded every day they had to commute to Jackson of how a tyrannical federal government had smothered property rights and economic growth.

The timing is perfect for my tour. I turn on the radio and hear Rush talking about President Bush "at a campaign rally in Poplar Bluff, Missouri, last night." Rush plays President Bush attacking John Kerry, who believes in federal government, and we hear a big crowd laughing with scorn at John Kerry, and then Rush adds: "at Poplar Bluff, Missouri, just south of my hometown of Cape Girardeau." And here I am in Cape Girardeau listening to Rush talking about Cape Girardeau. Cool! I head for the hospital where Rush was born.

The Limbaughs were typical of the first settlers of the Cape Girardeau area and of all of Missouri in that they were Southerners. Settlement in Missouri spread along the Mississippi and Missouri Rivers, for the rivers were the easiest transportation route and the river valleys offered incredibly rich topsoil. The Southerners brought with them all the traits of Southern culture, including slavery. The first American settler near Cape Girardeau came from Harper's Ferry, Virginia, and set up a plantation. Missouri's plantation culture was most concentrated in central Missouri along the Missouri river, a region still known as Little Dixie, where slaves accounted for at least a quarter of the population. It was here that I was born and grew up, surrounded by emblems of Southern culture. Quite a few plantation mansions still stood, and in fact one of the liberal activists who got me involved in politics lived in a mansion called Confederate Hill. One local Confederate family of the 1860s was the Todds, as in Mary Todd Lincoln. At the other extreme I saw black slums so decrepit that people called them slave shacks. My hometown held a school and street named for Robert E. Lee, and right in the middle of the University of Missouri campus was a monument to the Confederate dead. I am telling you where I came from because the goal of our tour is to figure out where Rush Limbaugh is coming from, and the best tour guides are the natives.

I pulled over below the Southeast Missouri Hospital, where Rush was born on January 12, 1951. His eyes were hazel. The brochure didn't mention that Cape Girardeau was world famous for the problem of babies getting mixed up at birth and sent home with the wrong families. Mark Twain wrote an entire novel about Cape Girardeau babies getting switched at birth, a novel whose purpose was to assess the health of democratic values in America and assess the damage America had suffered from being born with its southern half loyal to the values of feudal aristocracy.

In the opening paragraphs of *Pudd'nhead Wilson* Mark Twain makes it clear, at least to anyone familiar with Missouri geography and history, that his fictional town of Dawson's Landing is actually Cape Girardeau. Twain describes the town's river distance from St. Louis and its physical setting and its history and describes the layout and appearance of the town, all a good fit for the Cape Girardeau of Twain's time. Twain talks about the high hills in town, which is the most striking thing about Cape Girardeau for a river traveler, for Cape Girardeau is the last high ground before the Mississippi River rolls into the flatlands of the

Missouri boot heel, a transition not just geological but sociological, for these flat-lands allowed cotton planting just like in the deep South, whereas the rest of Missouri slave country was more like Dawson's Landing, "a slaveholding town, with a rich slave-worked grain and pork country back of it."[27] Twain also quickly introduces the sociological landscape of Dawson's Landing, whose leading families are descended from the noblest families of old Virginia and proud of it, ever upholding the code of honor of Southern gentlemen, including the readiness to fight a duel "if any act or word...had seemed doubtful or suspicious to you."[28] The leading citizen is York Driscoll, judge of the county court, the same county court on which Frederick Limbaugh had been judge in real life some twenty years before the time of this story.

Judge Driscoll's brother Perry has a slave named Roxy, who is only one-six-teenth black and often taken for a white woman, but who under law is still a black and a slave. One day she bears a son who is only one-thirty-second black, but by law he too is still a black and a slave. Roxy decides that there is something unfair in this, so she switches her child with that of Percy Driscoll's son, born on the same day. No one ever notices the difference. Roxy's son is raised to be a Southern aristocrat and sent to Yale and comes home full of arrogance. Percy Driscoll's son lives the life of a slave.

Now, I know it doesn't happen all the time that babies get switched at birth, but considering Cape Girardeau's fame in this matter it is not entirely unreasonable to wonder if this might have also happened to baby Rush. Perhaps the real Rush, son of one of the town's leading families, was mixed up with the son of some guy who worked at the International Shoe Company factory. If Rush planned to grow up to work at the shoe factory he was out of luck when it closed, so Rush was forced to work as a clerk at Wal-Mart, at least until he was caught trying to organize a union and was fired. Or perhaps Rush was switched with a black baby who looked white, so in the 1950s the real Rush had to stand for-lornly outside Woolworth's and stare in the window at the black Rush sitting at the lunch counter and stuffing himself with a hot fudge sundae and glaring with-out sympathy at the face in the window. Perhaps all this time it's been a black Rush Limbaugh on the radio railing against Jesse Jackson and worthless black quarterbacks who usurp the rightful jobs of white quarterbacks only because of bleeding-heart white liberals.

Anyway, it's a curious thing that out of all the towns Mark Twain could have chosen to frame his attack against feudalism in America, he chose the future birthplace of Rush Limbaugh.

I headed for Rush's childhood home.

There were actually some famous reasons why Mark Twain might have focused on Cape Girardeau.

In 1839 Pope Gregory XVI issued an encyclical regarding slavery, which caused quite a stir in America. Some Catholics interpreted the encyclical as a condemnation of slavery, but the bishops in the American South insisted that the Pope hadn't condemned slavery, only the slave trade, and only certain aspects of it. In particular the Pope ruled that Catholic institutions should not be involved in the slave trade. According to the version of events that took root in Cape Girardeau, this papal bull was issued in direct response to a famous case involving St. Vincent's College in Cape Girardeau. In 1838 a baby, Jane Renfro, was born to a slave owned by St. Vincent's, and the college decided to sell the baby down the river. The phrase "sold down the river" bore such grim meaning for Midwestern slaves that it entered the American lexicon to mean a severe betrayal and condemnation. This phrase was nowhere grimmer than in Cape Girardeau, for here a slave sold down the river would end up in the grueling life of a cotton plantation field hand for a whip-cracking overseer in the Southern heat. It was the prospect of her baby being sold down the river that inspired Roxy to switch her baby with Driscoll's baby, whom Mark Twain conspicuously named Thomas a Beckett Driscoll after the Catholic saint who was murdered at the altar of Canterbury Cathedral by knights of feudalism. The prospect of Catholic priests selling a baby down the river would have troubled many who otherwise had little moral concern over slavery. (Actually it's difficult to verify whether the Jane Renfro case really inspired the papal bull, as the facts have become quite vague. But at least it's plausible that Mark Twain heard this version of events in which a Cape Girardeau slave baby sparked a world controversy).

The condemnation of the Pope himself didn't seem to shake the Southern loyalties of the priests of St. Vincent's College, for after the Civil War they refused to take an oath of loyalty to the United States and were hauled off to the county jail. But the most famous St. Vincent's faculty member was no longer around, for he had resigned early in the war and gone off to become a Confederate chaplain. Father Abram J. Ryan would win lasting fame as "the poet laureate of the South," and was one of the main architects of Lost Cause mythology. Ryan would put in an appearance in *Gone with the Wind*, where his poetry "never failed to make the ladies cry." [29] Ryan portrayed the South as a noble and superior society that was unjustly attacked by a tyrannical U. S. government. Ryan celebrated the martial glories of the Confederacy and mourned its ruins and vowed that the South would never forget and would rise again. One of his most famous poems was "The Sword of Robert Lee."

> Forth from its scabbard, pure and bright,
> Flashed the Sword of Lee!
> Far in the front of the deadly fight,
> High o'er the brave in the cause of right,
> Its stainless sheen, like a beacon light,
> Led us to victory!

> …Shielding the feeble, smiting the strong,
> Guarding the right, avenging the wrong,
> Gleamed the sword of Lee!

> …Out of its scabbard! Never hand
> Waved sword from stain as free,
> Nor Purer sword led braver band,
> Nor braver bled for a brighter land,
> Nor brighter land had a cause so grand,
> Nor cause a chief like Lee!

And so on. Ryan epitomized the hyper-romantic view of the South that made Mark Twain nauseous, and which he attacked in book after book. In *Life on the Mississippi* Twain took a direct shot at St. Vincent's College and Cape Girardeau:

> Cape Girardeau is situated on a hillside, and makes a handsome appearance. There is a great Jesuit school for boys at the foot of the town by the river. Uncle Mumford said it had as high a reputation for thoroughness as any similar institution in Missouri…He directed my attention to what he called the "strong and pervasive religious look of the town," but I could not see that it looked more religious than the other hill towns with the same slope and built of the same kind of bricks. Partialities often make people see more than really exists.[30]

This was a very mild swipe compared to the scathing attacks Twain launched later in the book as he explored the deep South and met Ryan-like glorifications of it.

In "The Prayer of the South" Ryan compared the defeat of the South to the crucifixion of Christ:

> And while they climb their Calvary with their cross
> Oh! Help them, Father, to endure its weight.

...Forgive my foes—they know not what they do—
Forgive them all the tears they made me shed;
Forgive them, though my noblest sons they slew,
And bless them, though they curse my poor, dear dead.

On further thought, to hell with forgiveness. Ryan cultivated an implacable Southern grievance against the North, a rage for resistance and revenge. In "A Land Without Ruins" he hoped:

And the graves of the dead with grass overgrown
May yet form the footstool of liberty's throne,
And each single wreck in the war path of might
Shall yet be a rock in the temple of right.

Boy, Rush is really going after John Kerry today. Kerry has come up with a new slogan, "W stands for wrong," and yesterday Kerry declared that Iraq was "the wrong war at the wrong place at the wrong time," as if it wasn't even about liberty's throne and the temple of right but just a disaster started by a foolish Southern hothead.

I pulled onto Sunset, Rush's home street, which is not, maybe, the same as Hollywood's Sunset Boulevard, the ultimate address of people gone mad from trying to live in the past. I paused in front of 412, a modest white frame house. The brochure said: "Now a private residence, it is rumored that Rush's room was directly above the porch and he threw water balloons at trick-or-treaters from his room."

The main thing that Northerners often fail to understand about the South is that Southern political values contain a solid democratic core. The South was settled in the Jefferson-Jackson era and it absorbed the Jeffersonian-Jacksonian worldview with its agrarian ideal, its faith in the common man, its emphasis on self-reliance, its distrust of central government authority and big city elites and capitalist power. The South continued living in the Jeffersonian-Jacksonian universe long after the North, grappling with the problems of industrial capitalism, realized that an agrarian ideal was an inadequate blueprint for a modern democratic society. Nevertheless, the Jeffersonian-Jacksonian values of the South could have been an enduring source of strength for American democracy. But the disaster of Southern history was that the Jeffersonian-Jacksonian impulse with its powerful distrust of northeastern elites and strong government became yoked to a society that was deeply undemocratic. Even as Southern farmers were naming their towns Jefferson and Jackson, Southern aristocrats were transplanting to

Southern soil a full-blown recreation of feudal Europe, with its values of hierarchy, martial glory, a hair-trigger code of honor, and a ferocious discipline needed to keep the serfs in line. There were plenty of Southern small farmers who disliked slavery for its unfair competition, but soon they were trapped allies of Southern feudalism, for they realized that if the slaves were ever freed, poor whites would face massive competition for jobs, land, and political power, and they were also trapped in a system where a few hundred families dominated the economic and political power. But the citizens of Jefferson and Jackson were not unwilling captives of the love of martial glory or the code of honor; they fervently embraced many of the social codes of feudalism and combined them with Jeffersonian-Jacksonian impulses inside a wrapper of sectional pride and patriotism, all of which proved fatal to the South, for now the farmers of Jefferson and Jackson would gloriously march off to defend the sacred honor of the South against the Boston tyrants. Southern apologists often point out that the average Confederate soldier didn't own slaves, therefore, they claim, the Civil War wasn't about slavery. Likewise, the South didn't resist the civil rights movement because of racism, only to defend state's rights. The Northern version is that since Southerners were fighting against racial equality they were motivated by nothing but racism. Neither version does full justice to the tragedy of Southern history and indeed American history, the tragedy that the full force of American democracy, with its centuries of brash momentum and its pantheon of heroes and its rallying cries like "Liberty!" threw itself willingly and fervently into a catastrophic betrayal of democracy and embrace of feudalism.

When Mark Twain reached Baton Rouge in *Life on the Mississippi* he contemplated the Louisiana state capitol in the form of a medieval castle, and he unleashed his wrath against Walter Scott, whom he blamed for making the South fall in love with feudalism:

> Sir Walter Scott is probably responsible for the capitol building; for it is not conceivable that this little sham castle would ever have been built if he had not run the people mad, a couple of generations ago, with his medieval romances. The south has not yet recovered from the debilitating influence of his books. Admiration of his fantastic heroes and their grotesque "chivalry" doings and romantic juvenilities still survives here.[31]

In New Orleans Twain defends the French Revolution for removing the *ancient régime,* but

Then comes Sir Walter Scott with his enchantments, and…checks this wave
of progress, and even sets it back; sets the world in love with dreams and phantoms; with decayed and swinish forms of religion; with the sillinesses and
emptinesses, sham grandeurs, sham gauds, and sham chivalries of a brainless
and worthless long-vanished society…[In the South] the genuine and whole-
some civilization of the nineteenth century is curiously confused and commin-
gled with the Walter Scott middle age sham civilization and so you have
practical, common-sense, progressive ideas, and progressive works, mixed up
with the duel, the inflated speech, and the jejune romanticism of an absurd
past that is dead, and out of charity ought to be buried. But for the Sir Walter
Scott disease, the character of the southerner…would be wholly modern, in
place of modern and medieval mixed…It was Sir Walter Scott who made
every gentleman in the south a major or a colonel or a judge, before the war;
and it was he, also, who made these gentlemen value these bogus decorations.
For it was he who created rank and caste down there, and also reverence for
rank and caste, and pride and pleasure in them…[32]

I drove past Kentucky Fried Chicken with its smiling face of Colonel Sanders,
who was not a real colonel but a governor-appointed member of Kentucky's most
elite Honorable Order of Kentucky Colonels. I drove past the five-story tall
Union Planter's Bank, a bank widespread in the South, whose name implied
pride in the South's plantation heritage. I knew people in my hometown who
would let you know they were descended from planters, not mere farmers, but
planters.

I pulled up at the Bank of America, the former site of Wimpy's Hamburgers.
According to the brochure "Wimpy's was where Rush and his friends would
often hang out for lunch when he was in high school. Encountering a closed door
one day, an over-eager Rush pushed on the glass door only to break it, earning
him several stitches on both arms."

Hmmm. Do I detect a pattern emerging here? First Rush was smashing water
balloons onto little kids, and now he's smashing through glass doors. You'd
almost think that Rush had always been some sort of pushy bully.

Now Rush is diagnosing John Kerry's character defect. "There's something in
his makeup. He wants flexibility and nuance on everything. He just doesn't have
the fortitude, guts, I don't know what it would be to take a position and stick to
it…There's clearly a lack of confidence on Kerry's part."

In *Huckleberry Finn* Mark Twain has a steamboat named the *Walter Scott*
wreck on a rock in the dark, and Huck and Jim come along and salvage some
great loot from it, including some books about kings and castles and knights and

all, which Huck reads to Jim, but Jim can't make sense of any of this glorious king business, and finally Huck gives up in disgust.

By contrast, the people of Dawson's Landing are thrilled when two real Italian counts show up in town, so thrilled that they press the counts to run for office and rule them. But the counts offend Driscoll family honor, and now the town is thrilled at the prospect of a real duel. Everyone has accepted the Southern code of honor, including the poor white farmers and even the slaves, even Roxy, who is utterly ashamed that her son Tom doesn't want to fight the duel. When the duel proves inconclusive the Driscolls turn to politics to defend their honor, running against the Italians in full Rush style.

> The summer dragged by, and then the political campaign opened—opened in pretty warm fashion, and waxed hotter and hotter daily…The closing speech of the campaign was made by Judge Driscoll, and…it was disastrously effective. He poured out rivers of ridicule upon them, and forced the big mass-meeting to laugh and applaud. He scoffed at them as adventurers, mountebanks…He assailed their showy titles with measureless derision; he said they were back-alley barbers disguised as nobilities, pea-nut peddlers masquerading as gentlemen, organ-grinders bereft of their brother-monkey.[33]

I got out at Esicar's Old Hickory Smokehouse, where "the owner is a childhood friend. Inside you will find photos and other memorabilia of Rush Limbaugh." Unfortunately the owner was out. The photos included Rush in a baseball team.

Because the Southerners arrived in Missouri first they obtained the best lands, and many leading families became wealthy and thus politically powerful, so powerful that they very nearly took Missouri out of the Union. If Missouri had joined the Confederacy it would have enormously complicated the North's military strategy, and perhaps made it impossible, for the North would have lost control of the Mississippi River and perhaps have had to defend Illinois from invasion.

Missouri was saved from the Confederacy because the original Southern settlers were followed by waves of immigrants, primarily Germans and Irish, who settled in St. Louis and in farmlands farther from the rivers. The Irish were mostly peasants while the Germans included many who had been cultural and political leaders back home but who had fled the failed democratic revolutions of 1848. The Irish thought they were escaping feudalism, and the Germans were Enlightenment democrats and sometimes socialists, and both were disturbed to find feudalism reigning in Missouri. Whereas for the Irish who settled in Boston and the Germans who settled in Milwaukee slavery was an impersonal idea, those who settled in St. Louis saw slavery at work every day. Booming St. Louis had already attracted a core of Yankee leading families, such as the Eliots, who came out from Massachusetts and preached against slavery and founded Washington University—site of the 2004 presidential debates—and later gave birth to T. S. Eliot. The influx of Germans, who had names like Gephardt, brewed up not just Budweiser but a political culture that was eager to civilize Missouri and the rest of frontier America. For instance, it was in St. Louis that Germans introduced the kindergarten to America. Quite a few Germans settled in the Mississippi and Missouri river valleys, whose rich soil allowed them to continue their old trade of wine making. But this meant that Catholic, wine-making, slavery-hating socialist Germans were living next door to Baptist, alcohol-hating, slave plantation Southerners. The Germans who settled in Cape Girardeau set up their own Methodist Church apart from the pro-Southern Methodists, but it was shut down at the start of the war.

The Civil War in Missouri was especially personal and brutal, for it was fought less by armies than by neighbors, neighbors torching each other's barns, confiscating each other's property, evicting each other, ambushing each other in the fields and roads. The war in Missouri actually started well before Ft. Sumter, with guerilla raids between Missourians and anti-slavery Kansans like John Brown. When Confederate forces failed to take over Missouri at the start of the war Southerners were left to carry on a guerilla war, roaming out of Southern strongholds. In Cape Girardeau hundreds of Southerners formed a cavalry called the Swamp Rangers but when the Union army occupied the town they withdrew into the countryside and carried on guerilla raids for years, and some of them didn't stop when the rest of the war stopped at Appomattox. Such wars leave deep and lasting grievances.

My next stop was supposed to be the Limbaugh family law office, but maybe I missed it since this map didn't have much detail. I'd try again later. The law office was an important part of the Limbaugh story, for the Limbaughs were a leading legal family not just in town but in Missouri. For years Rush had been the black sheep of the family for not following in the family profession. The law office was now run by Rush's brother David, who after years of looking down on Rush as a loser now had the nerve to cash in on Rush's success by becoming a political commentator himself. Last year David had a national bestseller, *Persecution: How Liberals are Waging War Against Christianity*. At least Missouri was in safe hands: the chief justice of the Missouri Supreme Court was Stephen Limbaugh, cousin of Rush and David, appointed by Governor John Ashcroft.

I did find the Varsity Barber Shop, "where Rush worked shining shoes. It was rumored that Rush enjoyed conversing with adults on political issues while shining shoes. The shoeshine chair that Rush used is still there." And there it was in the back of the shop: the very chair at which Rush had knelt! I explained to the barber that I was doing the Rush tour and I asked him if many Rush pilgrims came in. He said that a fair number did, all from out of town, never locals. The guy in the barber chair said that he'd been a customer here for decades and remembered "the fat little kid shining shoes." He said "fat little kid" without any fondness. Was it true that Rush "enjoyed conversing with adults on political issues while shining shoes"? Well, he said, "conversing" might be a polite way of putting it; even as a fat little kid Rush was pretty opinionated. I asked if the Limbaughs were well-regarded in town. A guy sitting in a waiting chair had been looking me over, probably assessing if I was a Rush lover, and now he said: "If you don't agree with their religion, then to both Rush and David you are *dirt.*"

The deep South knew it had been beaten. They watched Sherman's armies clog their roads and torch their mansions. They watched impotently for years as the armies of Reconstruction ruled the South. But in Missouri few Southerners ever saw a Northern army, and since Missouri had never seceded it was never reconstructed. The anti-federal grievances that found no outlets in the deep South (except, of course, against the freed slaves) were free to go on raging in Missouri, for the neighbor who had torched your barn was still right there and no one else was going to punish him, or defend him.

The most famous instrument of Dixie vengeance got his most famous initiation in blood in my home county. Jesse James began his career riding with Bloody Bill Anderson, the most vicious of Missouri guerilla leaders, infamous for torturing, mutilating, and scalping his almost random victims. In September of 1864 Anderson's band rode into Centralia and looted it. When a train arrived they robbed the passengers and shot two of them for not yielding their money readily enough, and then they lined up two dozen Union soldiers, who were unarmed and even wounded, and shot them and slit the throats and clubbed the heads of those who didn't die quickly enough.

Because of the Centralia massacre I grew up learning that Jesse James was a vicious bloodthirsty punk who refused to give up at the end of the war and just went on killing and robbing, and not randomly, but targeting Northern sympathizers. The strange thing was that there were books in which Jesse James was a romantic hero of the Wild West, a Robin Hood robbing from the rich and giving to the poor. The contrast in these two images tells a story about the power of journalism placed at the service of a ferocious grievance.

Like Abram J. Ryan, John Newman Edwards refused to give up on the Confederacy and set about building a myth of the glorious Lost Cause. In his Kansas City newspaper Edwards loved romanticizing rebel exploits, and one day he was thrilled to discover that rebel exploits weren't just history. A man had walked into an area bank, pointed his gun at a banker who supposedly had killed Bloody Bill Anderson, blown him away, and robbed the bank. Two years previously a gang had shot up another town where the dead body of Bloody Bill Anderson had been mockingly displayed and photographed, and they robbed the bank too. When the James gang robbed their first train they were wearing Ku Klux Klan masks. Edwards publicized these robberies and in an editorial called "The Chivalry of Crime" compared the robbers to Lancelot and the knights of the round table. For years Edwards went on glorifying Jesse James. The result is that nearly a century and a half later Americans still accept Jesse James as a romantic hero resisting some kind of oppression. A single obsessed Missouri journalist had left a large warp on America's sense of history.

Rush was speaking "with talent on loan from God." Or rather "Goawd," like an uptown god echoing from venerable stone walls rather than a plain wooden-wall Baptist god. And sure enough, the Centenary United Methodist Church was an elegant stone building. "Rush attended this church while growing up." It took generations for the Methodists to become United, for they were bitterly divided by slavery and broke up into a pro-North church and a pro-South church. The Limbaugh's church was the pro-South church. In the 1960s a young director of the Wesley Foundation led some foolish young people south to work for civil rights, but church leaders forced him to resign. Church leaders debated what to do if blacks showed up and tried to attend services, and they hoped that if the blacks were politely ignored they would go away and not return.

I drove past the Confederate soldier's monument, which was built by the local chapter of the United Daughters of the Confederacy. According to the town history: "For a long period the annual UDC ball was one of the social highlights in the community. A large children's chapter was active for many years." TheUDC's mission is "to present a true history of the War between the States."[34]

Like Jesse James, Mark Twain was a product of Missouri's river country Southern culture. Like Jesse James, Twain's family had moved west from Kentucky and Virginia and owned slaves. Like Jesse James, Mark Twain joined a band of Confederate guerillas. Twain's band was small and amateurish and didn't last long, but they did succeed in killing a man, who turned out to be an innocent stranger.

Several books have been written defending Mark Twain in the Huckleberry Finn controversy, and they entirely omit mentioning that Twain joined a Confederate guerilla band, as if this was just too incriminating. Twain's liberal-minded biographers often skim over this episode and ritually insert a disclaimer that Twain's account of it, "The Private History of a Campaign that Failed," was "fictionalized" and satirical. Yet Twain scholars need not have been so embarrassed to acknowledge where Twain was coming from, and indeed it could have been cited as proof that Twain knew exactly what he was talking about. Growing up in Missouri's river-country culture might have been the best vantage point in America for understanding the schism in the American soul, a schism in which the values of both democracy and feudalism had been planted deeply and incompatibly. Elsewhere in America people absorbed more of one value than the other, but in Missouri both were powerfully alive and constantly contending against one another, and not just contending between individuals but within individuals. In Mark Twain the full contradictory powers of American history wrestled for an answer and a voice. "Out west," he wrote in "The Private History," "there was a good deal of confusion in men's minds during the first months of the great trouble—a good deal of unsettledness, of leaning first this way, then that, then the other way. It was hard for us to get our bearings."[35] The result of Twain's confusion was America's most significant literary lifework exploring democratic values in America, especially how those values were fractured and cancelled by feudalistic values. It wasn't just in *Pudd'nhead Wilson* and *Huckleberry Finn*, where feudalism was defined by race, that Twain attacked feudalism, but also in his works set in Europe, *The Prince and the Pauper, A Connecticut Yankee in King Arthur's Court*, and *The Innocents Abroad*. It was all the same story. Some critics have regarded Twain's European books as expressions of nineteenth-century American confidence in the superiority of our democratic way of life, yet Twain was far from confident that democracy actually had triumphed in America. The Civil War hadn't settled it. He understood the intractable roots of un-democracy in the South, and that America's racial problems were rooted in something that went even deeper than race, in a worldview in which severe inequality was the natural order of society. Even white masters were victims of Southern feudalism, such as the Grangerfords and Sheapherdsons in *Huckleberry Finn*, who were locked in a mindless and destructive feud, a feud modeled on a real Missouri feud that went on downriver from Cape Girardeau. As the nineteenth century progressed and America became an industrial power and then an imperial power, Twain worried and raged over the signs that feudalism and not democracy was driving American capitalism and foreign policy. The South's readiness to accept severe inequality as natural was a rotten foundation for American capitalism, and the South's martial spirit and code of honor were dangerous engines for American imperialism. In *A Connecticut Yankee in King Arthur's Court* Twain discoursed on how feudalism manifested itself in economic terms, and he said that economic feudalism needed to be cured by an infusion of democratic values that he called "a new deal." Franklin Roosevelt was fond of this book and would remember Twain's phrase "A New Deal."

Now Rush was "playing with half of my brain tied behind my back to make it fair." My next stop was Houck Stadium "where Rush played high school football." In an earlier edition of the Rush tour guide it said "where Rush played high school football and scored a winning touchdown." They had taken away Rush's winning touchdown. Could it be that Rush was an egomaniacal bullshiter who had invented a legend about scoring a winning touchdown?

Like Jesse James and Mark Twain, Harry Truman was a product of Missouri's river-country culture. Like Jesse James and Mark Twain, Truman's family had moved west from Kentucky and Virginia and owned slaves. Like Jesse James and Mark Twain, Truman's uncle—actually named Jim Crow—joined not just a band of Confederate guerillas but Bloody Bill Anderson himself, and after the war Jim Crow too refused to accept the peace and terrorized Independence, Harry's future hometown, and reportedly killed two blacks in cold blood. As a young man seeking his first political office Truman thought it prudent to join the Ku Klux Klan, but they rejected him as insufficiently anti-Catholic.

At age twenty-six Truman shelled out a small fortune for a twenty-three volume complete works of Mark Twain. Like Twain, Truman got a long hard look at the schism in the American soul, understanding American racism from the inside. Twain and Truman understood first of all that American racism was embedded in and empowered by a feudal worldview and social order even more serious than racism, and they had no illusions about how easily racism could be changed.

Truman must have seen the iron weight of American history as he sat in Fulton, Missouri, in the heart of Little Dixie, and heard Winston Churchill declare that an iron curtain had descended across Europe and eclipsed human freedom; Truman must have seen the iron curtain still dividing Missouri and America. Truman knew that this iron curtain would never budge for moral exhortations but it might just yield to the power of the federal government to change the fundamental rules of Southern society. Truman did what he could by signing executive orders banning discrimination in the military and in federal employment, and then he pushed legislation to address lynching and the poll tax and much more, the most ambitious civil rights program since Reconstruction. Yet Truman knew that this iron curtain would remain a curse upon America for generations to come.

The theme music for Rush's show came on, a hard-pounding bass riff. Now here was a curiosity. This was the music of the Pretender's Chrissie Hynde, the epitome of the rock and roll strong woman. Hynde was an ardent environmentalist, and this very song, "My City was Gone," condemned mindless development. Yet Rush used this riff to fire up his bashing of strong women and environmentalists, to defend private property rights even as he pirated Chrissie Hynde's song without ever paying her royalties. In an even stranger parallel, Sean Hannity had adopted as his theme song Martina McBride's "Independence Day," a notorious feminist anthem which celebrated an abused wife avenging herself on her husband by setting fire to her house with him asleep inside it. This song had scandalized the world of country music, with numerous stations refusing to play it. But Hannity must have liked the song's refrain of "let freedom ring" and he used it to fire up his bashing of "feel-good feminism."

I headed for Southeast Missouri State University, where "Rush attended one year" before dropping out. I had an insider's knowledge of Southeast Missouri State because I'd once gone out with a woman who taught there before quitting in disgust at the archaic social world on campus, which only reflected Cape Girardeau's traditional Dixie values regarding women. I heard a long, full report on how women faculty members were not just seriously undervalued but egregiously abused, including things like male department chairs lecherously following female professors into the bathroom. The status of women in Cape Girardeau and environs actually became a statewide controversy. The business school building at Southeast Missouri State was named for Robert Dempster, who in 1977 was appointed to the University of Missouri board of curators. A reporter went to interview Dempster and Dempster invited the reporter to glance around his place of business and notice that there were no plain or ugly women there, as Dempster only hired pretty women. The women attending the University of Missouri to become business executives, teachers, doctors, or lawyers were not amused that their fate was in the hands of someone who thought that the only function of women in the workplace was to look pretty. Women students organized a drive to get Dempster off the board of curators, but he remained there for many years.

Ten years later when Rush Limbaugh burst onto the national scene raging against "feminazis" and declaring that feminism was just neurotic resentment from plain and ugly women, women nationwide wondered where Limbaugh was coming from, but some of us in Missouri simply thought: Cape Girardeau.

I'm sorry to pick on poor Cape Girardeau, for it is simply typical of Missouri river-country culture. I'm actually fond of river towns like Cape Girardeau. They have the beauty of a powerful river going right through town, and they have architectural beauty, for when the steamboat era ended, many river towns ceased growing or changing, so entire downtowns and residential zones of stately nineteenth century architecture are still intact, if often sagging. The problem is that this architectural stasis can be echoed by a social stagnation that has left towns trying to live in the world of Tara.

I'm going to give Cape Girardeau a break for a moment and look one hundred miles north to St. Louis, the birthplace of Phyllis Schlafly. Schlafly was the deadliest opponent of the Equal Rights Amendment and never let up attacking feminism. It's probably fair to say that the two most vociferous longtime critics of feminism are Phyllis Schlafly and Rush Limbaugh, and I submit it's no coincidence that both were born in Missouri's river-country culture. As with questions of race, the weather fronts of gender tradition and change mixed more violently in Missouri than elsewhere. A belle growing up in the South in the 1930s wasn't confronted by many stirrings of feminism, and a Chicago girl wasn't tempted to become a Southern belle. But in St. Louis tradition and change clashed as strongly as the swirls in the Mississippi River, clashed not just between individuals but within individuals. In a previous generation Kate Chopin was born in St. Louis and raised as a proper Southern belle by her slave-owning family, and at age thirteen she was even arrested by Union soldiers for tearing down an American flag, for which Kate's family proudly nicknamed her St. Louis' "littlest rebel." But as an adult Chopin grew restless in traditional female roles and rebelled in her feminist novel *The Awakening*, which caused a national scandal. Confronted by such forces, traditionalists like Schlafly and Limbaugh are more likely to feel besieged and thus become more militant in defense of tradition.

The most important mentor of Southeast Missouri State University was a president named Dearmont, who turned it into a full-fledged university and built many buildings, but when he turned out to be a supporter of Wilson's League of Nations, outraged townspeople drove him out of office. In the 1960s a group of instructors opposed the Vietnam War, and they were forced to leave.

Recently a history department member had published an interview-biography of Rush Limbaugh's grandfather, also named Rush. I went looking for someone who could shed more light on this book and I ran into Bonnie, a scholar of social reform. As soon as I mentioned Rush Limbaugh she felt obligated to defend the honor of Cape Girardeau, saying that not everyone was a mean-spirited windbag. As for the Limbaughs, Rush #3 the radio star had definitely inherited his political interests and conservatism from his family. Rush #1 recalled how at age five in 1896 his father had taken him to the courthouse to listen to political speeches, presumably regarding that liberal wacko William Jennings Bryan. Rush #1 served in the Missouri state legislature where he prosecuted the impeachment of the State Treasurer; Rush #3 was just following family tradition in prosecuting Bill Clinton.

One curious thing about the biography was that Rush #1 made no mention at all of Rush #3. The truth was that Rush #3 had long been an embarrassment to the Limbaugh family. At first he was an embarrassment for not going into the law, then for making a mess of his disc jockey career, getting fired four times, mainly because of his big ego, once because he insisted on playing the Rolling Stones' distinctly un-feminist "Under my Thumb" all the time against the orders of the station manager. Even after Rush #3 became a huge success he remained an embarrassment, not for his political philosophy but for having the demeanor of a loud bigot, a far cry from the demeanor expected of lawyers and judges. Missouri Supreme Court Chief Justice Stephen Limbaugh would probably prefer to be respected for his legal scholarship and he didn't want people, especially black and female attorneys, coming into his courtroom expecting to find someone ranting against feminazis and doing mocking imitations of Jesse Jackson.

The book contained one surprise, perhaps the biggest scandal in Limbaugh family history, although almost no one would recognize it as such. Rush #1 coyly mentioned that while he was studying law at the University of Missouri he was interested in the writings of an unnamed economics professor and enrolled in his class. Since I knew the history of the University of Missouri I could match up the few years that Rush #1 was there with the few years that Thorstein Veblen was there, and the truth comes out that Rush #1 studied economics under one of the greatest icons of American liberalism.

Thorstein Veblen was the epitome of American egalitarianism. He grew up in a Norwegian town in Minnesota and absorbed the Scandinavian social code in which it's a major sin to assert your own superiority or anyone else's inferiority, for this disrupted the social bond that was essential for cooperation and survival in an overpowering northern environment. Yet Veblen grew up in the heyday of the Gilded Age, when the rich were flaunting their superiority. For Veblen the Gilded Age was a horrifying violation of the basic code of human decency. If the South had its feudal code then the North too had forces powering inequality, not just capitalism but immigrants desperately trying to establish their social status by displaying their success very publicly, which Veblen labeled "conspicuous consumption" in his 1899 bestseller *The Theory of the Leisure Class*. Veblen portrayed

America as a society gone mad with a craving not for just survival or comfort or success but status, never enough status, which was also unavoidably a craving for inequality, a craving that was jeopardizing America's democratic values and mission.

Then Thorstein Veblen came to teach in Little Dixie and one day into his classroom walked Rush Limbaugh, who carried in his intellectual genes all the past and future weight of American inequality. If only Rush #1 had paid more attention, Rush #3 might be raging against inequality and not against unwanted social obligations.

In his anti-government invective Rush reminded me of Pap Finn. Though Mark Twain could be a sharp critic of government, it's noteworthy that Twain placed his most caustic attack on government in the mouth of the drunken, loafer, abusive, racist father of Huck Finn. "Whenever his liquor begun to work," said Huck, "he most always went for the govment."[36] Pap Finn rages on and on against Judge Thatcher for taking away his son on grounds of child abuse and placing him with a guardian, and then he rages on and on against a government that allows a black man to be a professor at a college and wear fancy clothes and even vote when he should have been seized and sold into his proper place as a slave. "Pap was agoing on so, he never noticed where his old limber legs was taking him to, so he went head over heels over the tub of salt pork and barked both shins, and the rest of his speech was all the hottest kind of language—mostly hove at the nigger and the govment."[37]

It starts with the Jeffersonian-Jacksonian distrust of central government, including a distrust of taxes, which King George levied for the sake of empire. Right from the start Missouri had a strong anti-tax philosophy, and it still has one of the lowest gasoline taxes in the country—which means that Missouri also has the worst mess of crumbling highways and bridges in the country. The New Deal built tons of roads and bridges in Missouri but many have been neglected ever since, meaning that hundreds of rural bridges are now designated one-lane, requiring trucks to stop and wait for one another, a poor incentive for economic development in rural areas. If the dislike of taxes was so strong that Missouri farmers refused to vote taxes to repair their own bridges, then just wait for government to try to build bridges between disparate social groups.

To the Jeffersonian-Jacksonian distrust of government, add the ferocious grievances of a whole section of the country that had its sons killed and its homes burned and its economy wrecked and its society reconstructed by the soldiers of the federal government. Just when the Klan and friends had spent decades getting things back in order, along came Harry Truman and Lyndon Johnson, betraying their own people, imposing another round of Reconstruction. But at least Truman and Johnson knew who and what they were dealing with. They recognized that poor white Southerners too were victims of feudalism, certainly not on the bottom segregated rung but still trapped for life in bad jobs, bad trailers, bad educations, and bad pickup trucks waiting for each other on crumbling bridges. At least Truman and Johnson were building concrete bridges as well as human bridges. But when Northern liberals started calling poor Southern whites trailer trash and using their taxes to help blacks and women leapfrog right over them, two centuries of resentment was powerfully stirred up, and gratitude for FDR's concrete bridges didn't count for much.

Now I saw why I'd driven right past the Limbaugh law office. It was inside a big colonial-style bank building. I told the secretary I was a Rush pilgrim and asked if many pilgrims stopped here, and she said no, it was easy to miss; I was the first in months. I was disappointed that the waiting room held no Rush memorabilia. There was one framed newspaper article about the Limbaugh family, in which Rush #1 said he was proud of four of his grandsons and their career success. There was no mention of Rush #3. I asked the secretary about this and said I'd heard a rumor that the Limbaugh family was embarrassed by Rush, and she showed no sign of surprise and only shrugged her shoulders.

I headed for KGMO Radio, "where Rush made his debut in broadcasting as disc jockey Rusty Sharpe."

It's not hard to figure out why radio broadcasting has long been taken so seriously in the Midwest. The Midwest contains lots of empty spaces and lots of towns too small to have a movie theater or bowling alley. It can get pretty lonely and boring out there. Even in the days of wagons and dirt roads farmers went into town just to sit at the café and hear voices other than the crazy wind. So when the age of radio arrived, it was a godsend. Now you could stay at home and be entertained by the Lone Ranger or Jack Benny or best of all the St. Louis Cardinals. For decades the Cardinals were the only baseball team west of the Mississippi River and their fan territory was enormous, from North Dakota to Arkansas. Thus the Cardinals took their radio broadcasting network very seriously, and it would spawn Hall of Fame sports broadcasters like Harry Caray, Jack Buck, Joe Garagiola, Bob Costas, and Tim McCarver. Doing baseball announcing is different from doing basketball, which is so fast-paced that announcers are left breathless. Baseball is as full of empty spaces as the prairie, and to fill those spaces you have to know how to talk, to talk on and on for maybe three hours. The Cardinals network developed three hours of talking into an art form, the announcer introducing news items and issues of baseball philosophy and discussing them.

Thus it was hardly a leap when in 1960 the Cardinals flagship radio station in St. Louis replaced its afternoon music programming with four hours of talk shows, including one hosted by Jack Buck. Some historians of broadcasting designate this as the birth of talk radio.

And a hundred miles away a young Rush Limbaugh was taking it all in. He'd listen to Harry Caray doing the Cardinals broadcasts, and when the Cardinals were on TV he'd turn down the sound and do his own narration for three hours.

Sometimes the geographical logic to something new coming out of a particular place is so strong that it almost seems like destiny. There was a logic to Memphis—a boiling pot of musical influences from up and down the Mississippi River—being the place where generations of ingrown or forbidden black music suddenly mutated into a white body and voice and swept the nation like a new strain of flu. There was a logic to Hannibal, Missouri—the northernmost tip of Southern culture and a busy port swarming with social influences from New Orleans to Minneapolis—being the origin of America's most searching examination of the mix-up of Northern and Southern values. And there was a logic to Cape Girardeau, for it lay in the relatively thin overlap of two huge powerful empires, the empire of Cardinals radio broadcasting and the empire of the South's implacable grievances, newly stirred back into rage. For a century the South had grumbled mainly to itself, for Northerners didn't read Southern newspapers or allow Southern politicians to have a soapbox in Northern newspapers. But now a mutation occurred, and suddenly Southern grievances took hold of a powerful new nationwide medium. Most importantly, just as Elvis didn't have a black accent, Rush didn't have a Southern accent.

After KGMO I headed downtown to KZIM, "which currently airs Rush's syndicated talk show." From a loudspeaker KZIM broadcast Rush's voice onto the sidewalk. I went inside and told the black lady at the reception desk that I was a Rush pilgrim, but she didn't know what I was talking about. I explained the Rush tour and she looked at me like this was a big joke.

You also have to factor in Rush's personality. Not long after Rush hit the national airwaves in 1988 I was listening to a broadcast of a Kansas City Royals game. Rush had worked for the Royals, not as a broadcaster this time but as an office guy handling promotional events, and this was one of the four jobs he'd been fired from. The Royals' announcers, trying to fill some of that empty baseball space, started talking about Rush's newfound success, and clearly they were incredulous that a radio audience would actually choose to inflict Rush's blow-hard ego upon themselves.

It turned out that there was a large audience ready to hear their grievances expressed with unwavering confidence, even belligerence. From hundreds of radio stations all over the country people heard a very cross man, and some wondered why he was so cross, where he was coming from. Some of us who had grown up in Missouri river country knew exactly where he was coming from, and we were dismayed. It was as if the Confederate statues had begun to speak, as if Jesse James had been reincarnated with a mike instead of a pistol.

The most significant thing about it was that it wasn't just Southerners who were listening. They were listening in their John Deere tractors in Kansas, in their cattle trucks in Wyoming, in the lumber towns of Oregon, and on the loading docks in Pittsburg where the muscles a guy had built up at the steel mill still came in handy. A grievance coming out of Cape Girardeau seemed to fit the cross mood of the country. It seemed that poor whites all over America were feeling resentful. They knew that all of their hard work was getting them nowhere. The American Dream guaranteed that if you worked hard and believed in America, you'd get ahead. What the hell was wrong? Rush was saying that nothing was wrong with the American Dream, except for liberals and government crippling the American Dream with regulations and promoting blacks and women over poor white males. The irony was that in their resentment and their yearning for the American Dream, the Joads were now ready to vote for the landlords who throw Joads off their land.

Meanwhile, while an entire gang of right-wing blowhards was taking over the American air, what were American liberals doing? For one thing, they were banning Mark Twain from the classroom on the grounds that since his slave owners didn't address their slaves with "Please, Mr. African American, sir," Twain must be a racist. They were making sure that when TV showed the movie *Blazing Saddles*, a satire of racism on the Gilded Age frontier written by Mel Brooks and Richard Pryor, Brooks and Pryor couldn't use the word "nigger" to satirize racism. Some liberals also demonized Harry Truman. Howard Zinn in his *A People's History of the United States* makes no mention of a famous story in which Truman was outraged when a black World War Two veteran was pulled off a truck in the South and beaten and blinded, making Truman decide that enough was enough. Zinn maneuvers to evade any possibility that Truman was motivated by humane and democratic values. Yet Truman gets off easier than Lincoln. Zinn denies that the Civil War had anything to do with slavery or democracy and asserts it was all started by a tyrannical Lincoln to impose capitalist domination on the South, leaving Zinn virtually indistinguishable from Abram Ryan and the most obsessed champions of the Lost Cause.

In a nation with a South crippled by feudalism and a North full of immigrants gone mad trying to prove their superior status, the forces of equality are already too weak. Instead of drawing upon the resources we do have, such as a writer who spent decades exploring the strengths and weaknesses of American democratic values or a president who tried to build not just concrete bridges but bridges of national health insurance and bridges of racial compassion, many liberals have been burning their bridges, or rather deconstructing their bridges, cutting themselves off from mutual sympathy with the Joads, cutting themselves off from the strengths of the American story, leaving them with a demonized American story that was only gasoline to conservative rage.

The final stop on my tour was a long mural on the floodwall protecting the downtown, like an iron curtain, from being invaded by the north. The mural was a Missouri Wall of Fame, featuring the portraits of forty-six famous Missourians. It was quite an assortment of people, a diverse, contradictory, almost crazy assortment. Indeed, this wall could illustrate why Missouri was the political bellwether of America, choosing the winner of every presidential election in the twentieth century but one. Missouri was a representative mixture of North and South, East and West, black and white, urban and rural, Baptist and Catholic, union member and farmer, the traditional and the modern. Even the subcategories in the mural held quite a mix-up. The media category included Joseph Pulitzer, Rush Limbaugh, Walter Cronkite, Jack Buck, and Marlin Perkins. If you were an African American looking for a role model you could choose from Dred Scott, George Washington Carver, Scott Joplin, Lou Brock, Josephine Baker, and Langston Hughes.

Langston Hughes had written a line that John Kerry had taken up in his campaign speeches: "Let America be America again." It was a fine line, a nice cadence to it, a summons to some kind of idealism. Yet it seemed to suppose that we had ever known what America was or was supposed to be. Looking at this mural with its sweep of history and all its contradictions, I wasn't so sure. America seemed pretty confused. At one end were Jesse and Frank James, and at the other end was Tennessee Williams, evoking Blanche Dubois and her pathetic clinging to the glories of Tara. Right next to Jesse James was Calamity Jane, who rode with General Custer's 7th cavalry against the Indians, but as a female role model she was competing with Kate Chopin and Laura Ingalls Wilder and Ginger Rogers. There was Thomas Hart Benton, not the senator and champion of Manifest Destiny but his namesake, the artist of the New Deal Common Man. There was

Dred Scott, and there was John J. Pershing, a racist put in charge of making the world safe for democracy. There was Mark Twain and Rush Limbaugh together. If all this seems too paradoxical, the mural offers you Yogi Berra.

This confusion was still in my mind when I stopped at a gas station to fill up. I watched the price-dial spinning and smelled the odor of gas. If it wasn't clear what or who was in the driver's seat of American history, it was clear what was in the gas tank. This was probably Saudi oil, brought to you by the Saudi royal family, the living and ludicrous embodiments of feudalism, given the full protection of the U. S. military. It was clear what was in the driver's seat of the tanks that rolled out of Saudi Arabia to "liberate" Kuwait for the Kuwaiti feudal lords, and it certainly wasn't democracy. If this was the sole evidence by which to judge, you might conclude that the South had won the Civil War and even conquered the North. It made you worry, with Mark Twain, how much else in American life was being driven by feudalism and not democracy. Certainly it was liquid feudalism, it was Saudi gas that was splashed all over the wooden crosses in the night, wooden crosses that burned in the center of midnight Klan rallies and were raised in the front yards of Mississippi hovels or churches to glow in the terrified eyes of black children peering from the windows. Yet these weren't the most visible crosses America had to bear. It wasn't just white-hooded hands but mainly white-collar hands that had splashed Saudi oil onto larger pillars for years until they were drenched, and when those pillars were finally set afire, it wasn't just a few families on a Mississippi back road who watched with terror, but the entire nation. It was white stockbrokers and black janitors and immigrant cabbies who watched in terror as the flames raged and the smoke roiled into the sky and who fled in terror down the street; it was the entire nation that would long be haunted by this specter. Yet if anyone dared to suggest that the burning crosses reigning over New York City had been set burning not just by barbarians but by our own betrayal of democracy, then from a thousand radio stations they were denounced for betraying America.

A couple of evenings later I was sitting in a hotel lobby in downtown St. Louis and contemplating the state of American journalism. Journalism was on my mind partly because I was there to shepherd the national press coming in on the Kerry campaign plane, to pass out room keys and messages and schedules and help them find their gear. I was also contemplating the state of journalism because my Rush pilgrimage had left me discouraged and now I was sitting a few blocks from the home base of Joseph Pulitzer, who had done more than anyone to raise journalism into being a real profession with high standards by establishing the Pulitzer Prizes and the Columbia University School of Journalism. I was wondering to what degree the Pulitzer Prizes might represent the social-improvement mania of St. Louis Germans confronted by a rough frontier society. Actually Pulitzer was an Austrian Jew but he was welcomed into the German community, and he threw himself into journalistic crusading for social improvements. Years later, after Pulitzer's bitter rivalry with William Randolph Hearst reminded him of how easy it was to lower your standards, Pulitzer began campaigning for some university to establish a school of journalism. The University of Missouri was paying attention and beat Columbia University to founding the world's first school of journalism. For many years I lived two blocks from the University of Missouri School of Journalism and I had many J-friends who went on to major careers, proudly wearing the word "Missouri" as proof of their journalistic excellence. And then there's Rush.

After the motorcade arrived and I had checked in the press, I noticed Candy Crowley of CNN wandering around the lobby waiting for her gear to arrive. Since Candy was born and raised in St. Louis I thought she'd be a sympathetic ear regarding the steep downward trajectory of Missouri's contribution to American journalism. I started telling her about my Rush pilgrimage, and she looked at me incredulously, as if the idea was too absurd to be true. Now, before anyone thinks 'Aha, we always knew those network people were liberals,' I should establish that our conversation never touched on politics but was entirely a matter of two Missourians nursing our hurt pride in journalistic professionalism. Every time I told Candy about a stop on my Rush tour she looked at me with new incredulity. I told her how the Chamber of Commerce was selling Rush souvenirs like t-shirts and refrigerator magnets. She shook her head and said she couldn't believe that anyone would want to see Rush's shoe shine chair.

Then I asked Candy if she knew that there was a Walter Cronkite exhibit in a museum in St. Joseph, Missouri, Cronkite's hometown. Actually the exhibit consisted of a reconstruction of the dentist office of Walter's father. Candy was delighted to hear this. She said she had relatives in St. Joseph whom she hadn't seen in ages, so she could stay with them. Now it was my turn to be incredulous. Do you mean you'd go all the way to St. Joseph just to see Walter Cronkite's father's dentist chair? Now Candy was asking if there was a tour guide to all the Walter Cronkite sites in St. Joseph.

When Candy was done seeing Walter Cronkite's father's dentist chair, which was in an old hotel built by a Southerner but seized by the Union army for a headquarters, she could go next door to the house where Jesse James was shot to death. She could even see the bullet hole in the wall, except that now after

decades of advertising this as the bullet hole of Jesse's death, historians were saying this bullet hole actually had some other cause. Even in death Jesse James was
being blown into legend. Candy could read about the legends that Jesse James
really faked his own death and lived on secretly for decades in Texas, a legend
that got so out of hand that a few years ago a judge ordered Jesse exhumed, only
to be reburied with Confederate military honors.

It was all right there, encapsulated in one little spot, the gold standard of
American broadcast journalism right next door to the ultimate example of journalism's power to warp the American story against the service of democracy.

Candy and I were holding this conversation only two blocks from the courthouse where Dred Scott had been denied his humanity.

In the morning we headed down I-55 to a town hall meeting in the suburbs. If
we had gone just a few miles further down I-55 we'd be on the stretch of the Rosa
Parks Highway where the Adopt-a-Highway had been adopted by the Ku Klux
Klan.

The Klan was shrewd in selecting this stretch of highway, for down it inner-
city kids were being bused to suburban schools in a controversial court-ordered
school desegregation plan. The state of Missouri rejected the Klan's application
to adopt a highway, but the Klan complained that their civil rights were being
violated and they filed suit, and in court they were represented by the ACLU.
The Klan won thanks to a ruling by Judge Stephen Limbaugh, not the Stephen
Limbaugh on the Missouri Supreme Court but his father, a Reagan-appointed U.
S. district judge. The state of Missouri appealed all the way to the U. S. Supreme
Court but lost. Up went the highway signs reading: "Knights of the Ku Klux
Klan, Realm of Missouri." Notice that in spite of all of Mark Twain's railings
against Walter Scott, the Klan are still knights. The citizens of St. Louis waited
for the Klan to appear along the highway, wondering if they'd be wearing their
white robes, wondering if they'd be picking up all the trash, or just the white
trash. But no sooner had the signs appeared than someone tore them down,
much to the regret of the black citizens who had started eagerly saving up their
trash for a drive down I-55 to the Klan's realm. The signs went up again, down
again, up and down again. Refusing to be defeated, Governor Mel Carnahan
signed an order declaring this to be the Rosa Parks Highway. The Klan
denounced this as a "betrayal of white Christians." Later that year Governor Carnahan was killed in a plane crash but Missouri voters preferred a dead Carnahan
over a live John Ashcroft in the U. S. senate. The Klan never did show up to clean
up the highway and thus officially forfeited their adoption rights.

I confess that I am telling this story in my own self-defense, to establish that race relations in America are so crazily messed up that there was nothing I could really do about it. You see, my assignment for this morning was to solve centuries of racial problems in America.

For decades now, ever since television became the dominant medium of American politics, just about every presidential campaign event has been carefully stage-managed to give the public the right image. In particular you don't want the words a candidate is sending out to be contradicted by the image he is sending out. Thus if President Bush is delivering a speech on farm issues, you don't want him to be surrounded by bankers in business suits. You line up a bunch of farmers in overalls behind him, and maybe throw in a few hay bales. The press is so accustomed to such stagecraft that they hardly notice it, although if a campaign messed up and put up a background of white faces for a speech on civil rights, the press would take mischievous notice. Usually these staged backgrounds are arranged well in advance, but today it seems that someone has suddenly realized that there may be a problem, so at the last moment I have been appointed the stage manager. Or maybe it wasn't a mess-up but just a concession to sensitivities. It was easy enough to call up veterans or firefighters and invite them to come stand behind John Kerry so the TV cameras would see vets or firefighters. But in the confusing etiquette of race in America, were you really allowed to call up African Americans and invite them to come stand behind John Kerry so the TV cameras would see some black faces? Ordinarily this wouldn't be an issue in St. Louis, where the city proper has a black majority, but we are way out in the suburbs, for this event was meant to honor Richard Gephardt and we needed to be in his suburban congressional district, and it soon becomes obvious that only a modest number of African Americans have driven out from the city. We are about to broadcast a backdrop of white faces to a black city. I am appointed the gatekeeper to steer whites away from the backdrop even if they have the VIP tickets for that section and steer African Americans towards it. Fortunately these really are the best seats in the house so I don't have to feel like the bus driver sending Rosa Parks to the rear of the bus. I am much too busy to contemplate the value or philosophical ramifications of my actions, but when Jesse Jackson gets up and starts talking about race in America, I start to worry. Jesse Jackson has seen every game that white politicians play with African Americans, and it probably took Jesse Jackson about two seconds to notice the disproportionate concentration of black faces behind the podium. It wasn't hard for Jackson to look around and spot the stage manager, especially since I was still directing straggler traffic. When Jackson finished and sat down and looked around he did indeed look right at me, and I averted my eyes, fearful that in the next moment I would hear his voice saying: "Hey, you. You know who I'm talking to. The white guy who is rearranging the African Americans on the deck of the Titanic while Rush Limbaugh and crew are steering the ship of state into the icebergs of cold indifference to social injustice."

It was all right here, encapsulated in one little spot: the whole centuries-long mess of inequality in America. Here was the iron curtain of wealth and opportunity separating inner city from suburb. Here were the descendants of slaves who had probably worked alongside Dred Scott, quite a few of them named Jackson to honor their master's favorite president. Here was Richard Gephardt of the St. Louis Germans who had saved Missouri from joining the Confederacy. Here were reporters from Joseph Pulitzer's newspaper, *The St. Louis Post Dispatch*, still owned and run by Pulitzers, and substituting for Rush was Fox News. The ghost of Harry Truman was here in the form of John Kerry invoking him on national health insurance. This whole town meeting was supposed to be on the subject of health care for seniors, but the ghost of American violence past and future was here too, for most of the national press coverage of this event would go to Kerry's comments on the assault weapons ban, set to expire in three days. In such a room my little exercise in affirmative action seemed not just feeble but pathetic.

I was reminded again of Mark Twain and *Pudd'nhead Wilson*. In his original version, a story called "Those Extraordinary Twins," Twain made the Italian Nobles Siamese twins who constantly fought for control over one body. Luigi and Angelo had seriously different values. Luigi was a drunk, while Angelo was a teetotaler. Luigi was rude and selfish, while Angelo was considerate. Luigi loved gambling, while Angelo loved church. Luigi sang bawdy songs, while Angelo sang hymns. Luigi was pro-South and pro-slavery, while Angelo was pro-North and anti-slavery. They ended up running for office against one another. It was an ingenious metaphor for the two souls wrestling for mastery of America.

When the event was over and the print reporters were in the press tent writing their stories, the cameramen relaxed on the lawn, which included a playground. Jim the NBC cameraman photographed Gandhi on the swing. Gandhi in the crawling tunnel. Gandhi atop the ladder. I talked with a sad black man whose son, who was wheeling a portable respirator, had contacted some malady in the first Iraq war and now was diagnosed with one month to live. Then I spoke with an ABC cameraman who had recently come home from Iraq, where he had been embedded with combat units and thus been ambushed more than once, the bullets flying overhead. Did I mention that Luigi had gotten both himself and

Angelo into a duel that Angelo thought was pointless but couldn't escape from because for now Luigi had control of the arms and legs?

What was it Colin Powell had said about Iraq? The Pottery Barn rule: if you break it, you have to pay for it.

Perhaps inequality in America all came down to the Pottery Barn rule. America broke the promise of democracy right from the start, and we've been paying for it ever since, not just minorities, but the whole country.

Did I mention that today's date was September 10? Three years ago today Americans weren't worrying—only losers like Rosa Parks were worrying about it—about the price America had to pay for breaking the promise of democracy.

9

The Bridges Too Far of Madison County

Stagecoach

"Can't you even walk," shouted director John Ford at John Wayne, "instead of skipping like a goddamn fairy?"[38] In front of all the cast and crew Ford also called Wayne "a dumb bastard" and "a big oaf." It wasn't the first time John Wayne had been called a fairy. He had been given the name "John Wayne" because the studio head of his first western epic, *The Big Trail*, had decided that his real name, Marion Morrison, made him sound like a fairy. The director of *The Big Trail* had always admired the Revolutionary War hero "Mad" Anthony Wayne, a notorious womanizer who won the name "Mad" for his hot temper and reckless boldness as a war leader both in the revolution and fighting Indians afterwards. But "Anthony" sounded too Italian and the studio head and director wanted Wayne to sound all-American, so they decided that Marion would become "John Wayne."

As a kid growing up in Iowa Marion was often called a fairy because of his name. Boys trying to find an outlet for the eternal need of boys to prove their toughness picked on Marion, calling him a girl, teasing him about not wearing a dress, leaving him lastingly insecure about his masculinity. As a boy Marion devoured the novels of Zane Grey.

John Ford was yelling at Wayne because he was convinced that *Stagecoach* would lift the western out of the realm of hack melodrama and into the realm of national myth, but Wayne had learned too many bad acting habits in his series of B westerns, and Ford was hounding him into becoming a better actor.

In Wayne's famous opening shot in *Stagecoach* the stagecoach is heading across Monument Valley when suddenly Wayne appears standing in the road, rifle in hand, dusty but tough, and the camera zooms in on him and holds there for a long moment that says that this man is all man and all hero, the rugged individualist who won the frontier.

Perhaps it was growing up in a town whose legendary son had changed his name that gave Angela permission to change her name. It isn't normal for kids from small Iowa towns to change their names. But unlike all those Iowa kids who go off to Los Angeles and try not to admit they're from Iowa, Angela wasn't repudiating her roots; she was embracing her roots like corn roots embracing the prairie soil. When she went to live in Buenos Aires she found herself missing the American prairie, the wide open rolling expanses, the golden glow of the autumn corn, the rich scents of the soil, the sounds of the creeks echoing under the red covered bridges. Perhaps it was studying poetry at the University of Iowa that gave Angela (her real name) permission to take on the more poetic last name of "de Prairie," making her Angela of the Prairie, a deeper statement of belonging than the loud patriotism of Marion who repudiated his roots to hide behind the name of a blustering madman.

Growing up in the hometown of John Wayne, Winterset, made Angela especially aware of the dynamics of tough-guy blustering. At the University of Iowa Angela got degrees in women's studies and global studies, which further sharpened her focus on the negative consequences of tough-guy blustering as it worked in the larger world. That was why she was now on the staff of the Kerry campaign in Iowa.

Angela took a special interest in the campaign in Winterset and Madison County. She would love for John Kerry to beat John Wayne in Wayne's hometown. Angela kept the modest Winterset Democratic headquarters well supplied with materials. One time she had to re-supply the headquarters after someone had entered the headquarters at night and stolen half of the Kerry yard signs. This wasn't exactly breaking and entering since the key to the headquarters was always left sitting outside on top of the fence post in plain sight. This was, after all, small-town Iowa. But it was quite un-neighborly of someone to actually use this key and steal half of the Kerry yard signs. Of course he could have stolen all of the Kerry yard signs. He did put the key back on the fence post.

Another initiative Angela took for the Madison County campaign was to order a video copy of the film *Going Upriver* to show in Winterset. *Going Upriver* was made by longtime Kerry friend George Butler, who had won filmmaking fame for his documentary *Pumping Iron* about tough-guy Arnold Schwarzenegger. *Going Upriver* was about John Kerry's experiences in Vietnam, both as a tough-guy hero and as a conscientious young man realizing that America's tough-guy myths had helped get us into serious trouble. The film followed Kerry's activities in protesting the war, and it included interviews with several of his relatives and close friends. When Angela realized that I knew several of the people interviewed in *Going Upriver* she asked me to take the film down to Madison County and give it a personal introduction and discussion.

The Man Who Shot Liberty Valance

John Ford was giving John Wayne a hard time again, this time about Wayne never having served in the military. Ford was bragging about his own service in World War Two, and about co-star Jimmy Stewart interrupting his movie career to serve in the war, and about co-star Woody Strode not just serving in the war but playing in the NFL while Wayne was warming the bench at USC. Wayne had spent the war making movies, getting great heroic roles because the other male leads were risking their lives in the war, and now in 1961 John Wayne was the epitome of the American hero and much of the public was convinced that Wayne had been a real war hero. Now if Ford made a western without Wayne it flopped, and Ford was dependant on the hack actor he had turned into a star in *Stagecoach* twenty years ago, but in his pride Ford had to put Wayne in his place. Wayne was quietly furious, since his lack of military service was another chronic insecurity. As a kid he had dreamed of a Navy career, but the Naval Academy had rejected him. But he was too in awe of John Ford to fight back. According to one fellow actor "He'd bully John Wayne and make a quivering pulp out of him."[39]

They shot *The Man Who Shot Liberty Valance* in one of the toughest stretches of the Cold War, and it testified to the need for toughness. A naïve idealistic lawyer played by Jimmy Stewart is robbed and beaten unconscious by the desperado Liberty Valance, but still Stewart naively goes on and on about the need for people to respect the law and be nice. The John Wayne character declares that men like Liberty Valance will never be nice or respect the law; they'll only respect a gun. Stewart is shown as a wimp who wears an apron to cook in the saloon, and when Liberty Valance trips him and Wayne tries to stand up to Valance, Stewart can't comprehend the necessity of it and sabotages the showdown. Stewart again shows his feminine streak by teaching a classroom of kids about fancy words and about the U. S. Constitution, and then Wayne interrupts the class and declares that when villains hate the law you can't defend it through legal means. Finally Stewart gets mad enough to face down Liberty Valance in the street, but it's really Wayne who shoots Valance from an alley, leaving everyone—including Stewart—thinking Stewart was the hero, and they send him to congress to go on preaching his fancy ideals. Only later does John Wayne reveal that Stewart owes his life and career to the gunfighter code of the West.

It was a couple of hours before sunset when I rode into town. It was a tough-looking town, the kind of town where desperados would take a key right off a fence post and steal half the Kerry yard signs, so I kept my eyes out for tough characters with guns lurking in alleyways. I had come to tame the town by preaching the niceness of being nice. But first I had to rustle up some grub.

Actually the town square in Winterset was in much better shape than thousands of Midwestern downtowns that had been walmarted into ghost towns. Almost every storefront was filled, some very attractively. There were gift shops, a Ben Franklin variety store (where for one dollar you could buy a little plastic Navy PT/swift boat made in China), several cafes, and even a bookstore, now a rare thing in towns of only 5,000 people. The Iowa Theater was still going strong after fifty years of showing John Wayne movies. The courthouse looked well cared for. Angela had told me that Winterset hadn't been doing so well when the John Wayne home was its only attraction. The covered bridges were only a modest Sunday attraction for people from Des Moines. Then *The Bridges of Madison County* became a national bestseller, and then the movie version was filmed here, and now tourists were coming from far away. The draw wasn't just the romantic love story; it was that many people in urban America were already romantic about friendly little Mayberry town-square towns. Without even looking I saw signs that Mayberry was for real here. When I couldn't find a payphone on the square I went over to the grocery store and asked the bagger boy if they had a payphone, and he said no but he was sure no one would mind if I went into the manager's office and used his phone. The lost world of small-town Norman Rockwell America, which included white-hat heroes and black-hat villains in black and white movies, had a lot to do with the romantic appeal of John Wayne too.

I headed into the drug store, where the pharmacist and his kids were cleaning up the old-fashioned soda fountain, and he started a neighborly conversation with me. When I told him what I was doing in town he told Pat the owner and she came over and sat down at my table while I ate my complete hamburger steak dinner for only $4.95 including an old-fashioned phosphate soda. Pat had never voted for a Democrat until Bill Clinton came along. She had met Clinton this fall at Senator Tom Harkin's annual steak fry and told Bill it looked like he'd lost some weight, and Bill said he was sure trying. Pat still wasn't happy with the way the Republicans were doing things these days, especially their attacks on John Kerry's war heroism.

After awhile I asked Pat about the John Wayne imprint on Winterset. It was obvious she was a John Wayne fan. She told me proudly that John Wayne's daughter had been here recently for the Covered Bridges Festival, which drew 50,000 people. Wayne's daughter was eager to help the town build a proper museum next to the Wayne house, which was crammed with exhibits. I had to ask Pat if there might be a bit of a contradiction between being a John Wayne fan and a John Kerry fan, whether the John Wayne macho patriot mystique had actually helped get us into trouble in Vietnam and Iraq. Pat was thoughtfully quiet for a moment. I'm sure she knew what I meant. But she just wasn't going to go there. She did give me a free dessert of banana crème custard. If I had known my John Wayne history better I could have asked her if this was the pharmacy where John Wayne's father was working when John was born.

Some of the town-square shops and cafes had been spruced up for filming *The Bridges of Madison County*. When I asked Angela de Prairie about *The Bridges of Madison County* she seemed still incredulous that one quiet little town in Iowa could draw so much bad macho karma. It was hard enough trying to grow up as a feminist in John Wayne's hometown, but why of all the guys they could have chosen for *Bridges* did they have to pick Clint Eastwood? From a marketing angle it was obvious enough: the readership of the *Bridges* novel was mainly female, and it's hard to have a Hollywood hit if you eliminate half the audience before you started, so Clint Eastwood was there to make it safe for guys to go see a sappy love story. Go ahead, Francesca, make my day. Angela thought that Eastwood played the part too much like Dirty Harry, a remote tough guy unskilled at human intimacy or honest, heartfelt conversation, speaking in clichés. Angela had met the author of the novel and found him and the book the same way.

As a girl growing up in Winterset Angela tended to blame the John Wayne influence for all the absurd macho posturing she saw on the playground and on the Saturday night teen scene. Later when she got a wider perspective on it she realized that this went on everywhere, no doubt a biological flaw. But still she could see the difference it made when cultures either glorified this flaw or tried to curtail it. She regretted that her own little town had provided America with the fullest mythic power for glorifying national machismo. It was only during the first Gulf War that Angela saw Winterset's John Wayne culture fully express itself on a national issue, the town being militantly for the war, and it made her finally realize how out of place she was there. Her mother had been a peace protester in the 1960s and now Angela was using virtually the same phrases against this war, and for some of her conservative relatives it was just too creepy, like the return of a ghost. Some of her cousins lived on farms and were *real* cowboys—she emphasized *real* as opposed to George W. Bush. Her cowboy cousins insisted proudly that we needed a cowboy in the White House. Angela said that part of the cowboy code was relying not on law or even a posse but on do-it-yourself force, and this was certainly what Bush had done in charging into Iraq like the U. S. cavalry.

Fort Apache

Now this is the way to start a movie. Against the spires of Monument Valley a cavalryman on a horse stands in proud silhouette and sounds the bugle. As the credits roll, a band of Indians rides along to ominous music. Then the cavalry parades along to glorious martial music, their American flags flying. A stagecoach rolls through Monument Valley just like in *Stagecoach*, but this time it's bringing Henry Fonda to command Fort Apache. Fonda is appalled at being stationed in the middle of nowhere and determined to win glory at the expense of the scum Apaches. Captain John Wayne tries to warn Colonel Fonda not to underestimate the Apaches, and Wayne sympathizes with them for going on the warpath after the corrupt U.S. government broke its treaties with them and abused them—Cut! Cut! What the hell kind of John Wayne movie is this anyway? Someone named Fonda is giving jingoistic speeches about wiping out inferior colored people for the sake of national empire, while John Wayne is denouncing the U. S. government and defending its enemies? If Hanoi John won't support his country right or wrong then he ought to go—Oh—wait a minute. Fonda is supposed to be an egomaniacal General Custer heading for disaster. After Wayne gives his word to the Apaches, Fonda breaks Wayne's word and leads the cavalry out to attack the Apaches. Those crazy Fondas. Colonel Fonda ends up being massacred with most of his men. But Wayne survives, and in the end he proves his loyalty to America by spreading the myth that Fonda was a hero who died nobly at the hands of treacherous enemies. Wayne delivers a patriotic speech about how dead heroes will live forever, and the cavalry rides off to glorious music.

This was the second time Angela had dispatched me to Winterset. On my first visit I'd sat in the courtroom of the Madison County courthouse and watched a trial of a commander who had unrealistic expectations in sending U. S. troops to fight in a desert. Actually it was a political forum that used the courtroom as a meeting hall. Some of the audience sat in the jury box. From the wall Presidents Lincoln and Madison looked on. Two young soldiers were introduced as having recently returned from Iraq. They were now out campaigning for John Kerry. Jeff was a marine from Ohio, Patrick a bronze star army captain from Pennsylvania. Patrick had served five years with the 82nd Airborne Division, which had an illustrious history including parachuting into France on D-Day. In Iraq he had commanded a unit in a remote border town where things were more chaotic than in Baghdad. Patrick was also a West Point professor of military law and a prosecutor at Fort Bragg. Since we were in a courtroom with people sitting in the jury box Patrick seemed instinctively to take on the air of a lawyer making a case, a careful diplomatic air, yet I also sensed an urgency about him. He told me later that as an officer responsible for the morale of his troops he didn't feel it was proper to share with them his doubts about the war. But now he was free to speak, and he skillfully mapped out a soldier's case against the war and for "why we need a new commander in chief."

The jury listened carefully, and so did Presidents Lincoln and Madison, both of them war presidents, but Madison seemed to be taking Patrick's criticism personally. Madison had audaciously declared war against the world's greatest empire, an act many Americans thought foolish and unnecessary, and the war brought many disasters, including the British burning the White House, and it nearly cost America its independence. War advocates like Henry Clay had dreamed of annexing Canada but the U. S. was lucky to get out of the war alive. Even the war's famous phrases of triumph had a heavy ring of unlikely endurance: "Our flag was still there" and "Don't give up the ship." Madison's expression seemed to be saying something like: after 200 years you'd think presidents would have learned something about brash over-confidence.

When Jeff and Patrick had finished making their cases I went up to them and said they were just like John Kerry a third of a century ago, soldiers coming home to speak with special authority about a problematic war. They took this as a high compliment. I asked them if they had received any grief over this role, and both said yes. Jeff said that only this morning he'd been calling up veterans and one had called him a traitor for backing Kerry.

Then I asked them if they realized that Winterset was the birthplace of John Wayne and that the Wayne house was a few blocks away, and they got wide-eyed with pleasure. Patrick pointed to a pin he wore with the letters "AA" and explained that this was the insignia of the 82nd Airborne, the "AA" meaning "All American" since in World War Two the 82nd included soldiers from all fifty states. John Wayne had belonged to the 82nd Airborne in *The Longest Day*, so Wayne was a special icon to the 82nd. Soon we were merrily walking down John Wayne Drive to John Wayne's house, and I was thinking: wait a minute, are these the same guys who just delivered thoughtful critiques of John Wayne-style foreign policy?

Shhhh. Can you keep a secret? Several Winterset Democrats would tell me this with an obvious sense of mischief, but each made me swear not to tell who spilled the secret. It wasn't really much of a secret considering that Wayne biographies, including his own ghostwritten autobiography, make it clear that no one is really sure which house Wayne was born in. Wayne's autobiography includes a photo of a birth house long demolished. The doctor who delivered Wayne said it was in an upstairs apartment. But now the Winterset tourism business has a lot riding on the claim that Wayne was born in a little white house visited by tens of thousands of people a year. Isn't it just like liberals to go around debunking a patriotic myth and trying to undermine American capitalism?

We went into the little John Wayne gift shop next to the birth house, a shop packed with t-shirts and videos and posters. Patrick was delighted to see a poster of John Wayne from *The Longest Day*, his shoulder bearing the "AA" insignia of the 82nd Airborne. Patrick said that this poster was up on the barracks walls of the 82nd, both in the U.S. and in Iraq. Now he could buy one for himself. He would show it to all his buddies and tell them where he got it and they'd probably get tired of him telling them all about his visit to John Wayne's house.

The 82nd Airborne had also starred in another epic World War Two movie, based on a book by the same author who wrote *The Longest Day*, but John Wayne hadn't appeared in *A Bridge Too Far*.

A Bridge Too Far

John Wayne didn't appear in *A Bridge Too Far* or movies like it because after he established his movie persona as a patriotic hero, he refused to appear in any movie that reflected poorly on America. He also refused to play roles that showed any cowardice or weakness. He even publicly denounced movies like *All the King's Men* for showing American democracy as cynical and corrupt, and he denounced *High Noon* for showing a town of cowards and a marshal throwing his badge onto the ground in disgust—"the most un-American thing I've ever seen in my whole life," said Wayne.[40] In the 1960s Wayne became obsessed with making self-funded patriotic epics like *The Alamo* and *The Green Berets*, filled with patriotic speeches. Even the advertising for *The Alamo* in the middle of the 1960 presidential campaign took a swipe at John F. Kennedy. Referring to Kennedy's ghostwritten *Profiles in Courage*, the *Alamo* ads declared: "There were no ghostwriters at the Alamo." Later Wayne said that critics of *The Alamo* were commies.

A Bridge Too Far was unacceptable because it showed the American armed forces overreaching, parachuting 35,000 troops behind enemy lines to capture some key bridges but failing badly because of bad intelligence reports, bad logistics, and bad generals.

The three ladies staffing the gift shop noticed Patrick admiring *The Longest Day* poster, and he explained that he had been serving with the 82nd Airborne in Iraq until a few weeks ago. He diplomatically explained that he was touring Iowa because "We need a new commander in chief." If the defenders of the Winterset Alamo had any disagreements with this they kept it to themselves out of respect for Patrick's service. One of the women told Patrick how her nephew had served in Iraq and come home only to die in a truck accident at Fort Bragg, a muddy road sending the truck rolling over. She said it's been very hard on her sister. Patrick listened carefully and then expressed his sympathies and told her that he would tell his colleagues back at Fort Bragg that he had met her and expressed his condolences for them all.

Then one of the women took us to the Wayne house. Later on Angela told me that her grandmother was one of the tour guides, so maybe this was her. The guide said that this was where John Wayne was born, all thirteen pounds of him: he was larger than life even as a baby. The house was a mixture of period furnishings and Wayne family photos and movie memorabilia. Wow, there were some old suitcases that rode on the *Stagecoach*. There was the eye patch that Wayne wore in *True Grit*. The tour guide explained that the eye patch was thinned out in the middle so that Wayne could actually see through it, and as I bent down to look at it I saw that its middle threads were indeed spacious enough to see through. Cool! I looked around for something from *The Alamo*, such as Davy Crockett's rifle Ol' Betsy; I still remembered the cool way that John Wayne swung Ol' Betsy by the barrel and conked those Mexican devils. But I didn't see anything. How could a John Wayne museum not have any stuff from *The Alamo*? Patrick and Jeff, wearing their big 'Veterans for Kerry' buttons, were having a swell time too.

After we had visited the gift shop again and were carrying our cool souvenirs back up John Wayne Drive to the courthouse, I asked Jeff and Patrick if they didn't detect a bit of a contradiction here. Didn't they think that the Iraq policies they had critiqued so authoritatively owed something to the John Wayne code of force? Jeff and Patrick agreed that President Bush had at least one blind eye to the complexities of the world and was too quick to rely on force. But perhaps my question was poorly timed and we didn't pursue the subject any further.

The John Wayne house included a photo of President Ronald Reagan visiting there in 1984 in the midst of his re-election campaign, smiling with John Wayne blessing.

Not long after the 2004 election I found myself standing on the bridge of the *USS Ronald Reagan*, the navy's newest aircraft carrier. There are several layers of bridges on "the island" that sticks up from the flight deck, and I was standing in the flight control bridge, from which are directed all the aircraft operations. The flight control bridge offered a great view of the flight deck, all 1,092 feet and 4.5 acres of it. In combat the flight deck is an extremely busy place, and inside the flight control bridge was an array of computers and radars and check lists and phones for keeping all the action organized.

But the flight deck was quiet today, save for one guard patrolling with a rifle. The *Reagan* was docked at its base in San Diego, the same base that President George W. Bush had sailed into after landing on the *USS Abraham Lincoln* and giving a triumphant speech beneath a bridge banner declaring "Mission Accomplished." On the morning that Jeff and Patrick spoke in Winterset I'd met another vet touring Iowa for Kerry and he said he'd been serving on the *USS Lincoln* when Bush landed and at the time he was thrilled but later he'd felt ill-used.

In spite of my anti-war inclinations I took a family interest in warplanes. My uncle-in-law had been the president of McDonnell-Douglas and before that he'd been in charge of building the F-4 Phantom fighter used in Vietnam and the F-15 Eagle fighter used in the Gulf wars. On the morning in 2001 when the U. S. launched air strikes in Afghanistan in retaliation for September 11, I'd woken up in his St. Louis home and received a personal narration of the building and combat characteristics of his plane.

Out of the wild blue yonder I had been invited on a private tour of the *USS Reagan*, a tour that included areas usually well off-limits even to most *Reagan* officers, such as the flight control bridge and the war room that ran combat operations. The first thing you see when you step on board the *Reagan* is a bust of Ronald Reagan. Then you see a life-sized metal statue of a smiling Reagan, with whom sailors enjoy posing for photos. Off to the side was a small Ronald Reagan tribute room with displays about his life and careers. There was a poster for *Hellcats of the Navy*, the only movie starring both Ronald and Nancy Reagan. There was a video of Reagan's "win one for the gipper" speech. Reagan never made it into a John Wayne movie because Reagan just wasn't in the same league as Wayne. Another video showed Reagan giving his "Mr. Gorbachev, tear down this wall" speech. There was a small chunk of the Berlin wall. A panel listed President Reagan's accomplishments, including single-handedly defeating communism by talking like John Wayne and most importantly restoring "America's sense of destiny and optimism."

On the mess-hall floor right in front of the serving line was a "Walk of Fame" set of stars, voted on by the crew, including of course a star for John Wayne. Nearby was an elevator that came up from the ammunitions warehouse and from which bombs were carted out to go on their way, so as crew members were sitting there eating their cheeseburgers, bombs were wheeling by; it was possible that someday someone standing on the John Wayne star would watch nuclear warheads being wheeled off to be mounted on fighter jets to make someone sorry for messing with the U. S.

The war room was packed with computers for tracking everything moving in the air or on the water or underwater and for determining friend from foe and for dealing with foes. One computer system was called Isis, or Integrated Shipboard Information System. Isis was also the Egyptian god of the dead.

On the flagpole above the bridge flew the ship's flag of the *Reagan*, consisting of old frontier cavalry swords crossed. The cavalry sword flag flying over a nuclear-powered, nuclear-armed, jet-fighter-loaded aircraft carrier represented the severe discrepancy between American technology and American myth. The *Reagan* was one of the most sophisticated fighting machines in human history, yet it was at the service of a B movie plot in which good and evil was as simple as a white hat and a black hat, in which toughness was by far the preeminent virtue in human conflict and law and negotiation were synonymous with weakness and foolishness, in which loner heroes were much more reliable than posses, and in which violence could easily settle every issue.

Perhaps America's self-image was already a cavalry movie in 1776 long before we had a cavalry, a West, or movies, because from the start we envisioned ourselves heroically riding to the rescue of the world. In cavalry movies we finally found the perfect expression of that self-image, onto which we added the moral lessons of two centuries of pioneering the frontier. When America was defining its new role as world leader in the 1940s, 50s, and 60s we filled movie theaters and TV with westerns for guidance. With the Vietnam War westerns went into a sharp decline and were challenged by anti-westerns like *Little Big Man*. But a two-century-deep ethos doesn't disappear so readily, and it soon reappeared on city streets in the hands of Clint Eastwood, and then it reappeared in the White House. Ronald Reagan was the perfect personification and restoration of national myth because he knew all the images and all the lines and believed in them with untroubled certainty. He saw a simple choice between good and evil and a simple solution of talking tough and having the best weapons. And it worked, the Soviet Union collapsed, just like in a John Wayne movie.

In the wake of the Cold War a new myth has taken deep root among conservatives, the myth that after liberals showed a lack of faith in America and a lack of strength that allowed disgrace in Vietnam and beyond, Ronald Reagan restored "America's sense of destiny and optimism" and forced the Soviet Union to fail. There's no mention of the possibility, well illustrated by 150 years of failed utopian communes in America, that communism was doomed from the start and was lucky to last seventy years in the Soviet Union; there's no mention of Harry Truman setting up the framework of containment and calling for patience while others were calling for war. Instead, it's Reagan at high noon facing down the Soviets; Reagan wielding such superior guns that the Soviets surrendered; or Reagan fiscally drinking the Soviets under the table. The latter scenario of the Soviet Union bankrupting itself by building weapons while neglecting its societal needs may have more truth to it than liberals like to admit, but then conservatives don't seem to consider that this scenario also applies to the United States; we might have more margin for absorbing military spending, but we too are bankrupting ourselves socially. The best weapons in the world can't defend a society from internal imbalances. But the Reagan myth was hard to resist because it fit too many longstanding elements of American myth, including our pride in superior technology, our code of John Wayne toughness, and our sense of national destiny. The Reagan myth destined America for more trouble.

The Green Berets

The Pentagon was appalled when John Wayne came to them in 1966 and said he wanted to make a movie out of the bestselling novel *The Green Berets*. The novel depicted the Green Berets as ruthless and racist, as adventurers who were there more for the thrill of the hunt (including the hunt for women) than for the sake of democracy, and as having contempt for humanitarian acts like handing out chocolate bars or building schools. The novel showed the Green Berets making illicit missions into Laos. It showed our South Vietnamese allies as corrupt and cowardly, unwilling to fight for themselves, and as fiendish torturers of enemy prisoners. Since Wayne needed army equipment and facilities to make the movie, the Pentagon was able to force him to clean up the plot, not that he needed much encouragement to present the Americans as pure heroes and the communists as depraved savages. The movie was basically a western, yet without John Ford's occasional sympathy for Native Americans. In another mismatch between myth and reality the movie was filmed at Fort Benning where Georgia woods had to play Vietnamese jungles, at least until an early frost turned the woods yellow and the film crew retreated to Hollywood and built a million-dollar jungle set. Delays meant that *The Green Berets* came out in the summer of 1968, after the leaves had fallen from America's faith in the war.

Going Upriver was being shown at the Democratic headquarters, which included a John Kerry action doll in a blue suit; if you pressed his hand he danced and sang "God Bless the USA." I was told there was a George W. Bush action doll dressed in the flight suit he wore on the *USS Lincoln*.

The audience, mostly sympathetic, included a Vietnam vet named John who walked with crutches. When John was drafted in 1968 he hadn't known much about the war, and when he came home he "went into hiding" in the sense that he never talked about the war. John didn't have much use for John Wayne.

I explained why Angela had sent me, and then tried to explain something about John Kerry that many people had long found puzzling. How could someone go to Vietnam and be a gung-ho warrior and then come home and be a gung-ho war protestor? For many people this seemed too contradictory, and so it was tempting to believe that one of these John Kerrys had to be a phony. But Kerry wasn't so hard to figure out. Both his war heroism and his antiwar heroism were motivated by the same thing. He had been an earnest believer in the Kennedy summons to serve your country and change the world, and when he discovered that this wasn't actually what the war was all about he had felt a much deeper sense of betrayal than would a soldier who went over indifferently or for the thrill or the hunt, and this sense of betrayal and of being misused had fueled his antiwar passion, which was still guided by a Kennedyesque hope about changing the world.

Speaking of John Wayne, I said, in Vietnam Kerry had run up against the weakness of the John Wayne model of American power, but as an antiwar leader he had run up against the power of the John Wayne myth, drawing enormous hostility from those who didn't want to be told that this myth was flawed. They still didn't want to hear it, and this was why Kerry was drawing so much hostility today. Kerry was certainly wary of the power of the John Wayne myth, and he even tried to walk the John Wayne walk, wrapping himself in war hero imagery, but it was Bush doing the John Wayne talk, and Kerry with all his war hero status was having a hard time competing with it.

Going Upriver rolled, and the speed boats rolled up the river through the jungle. The helicopters circled, my uncle's Phantoms roared, the bombs and napalm fell, the fireballs rolled up out of the jungle. The swift boats sped past huts and sampans, and there standing on the deck was John Kerry, perhaps trying to look like John F. Kennedy in *PT-109*. Or was he trying to look like John Wayne in John Ford's PT boat movie?

They Were Expendable

John Ford gave John Wayne such a hard time while filming *They Were Expendable* that Wayne stalked off the set in a pouting rage. Once again the issue was Wayne's lack of military service. Ford was very proud of his own navy service in World War Two and meant for *They Were Expendable* to be a tribute to the navy. His main star Robert Montgomery had actually commanded a PT boat, and in the credits Ford listed the service record of every vet in his cast and crew. Wayne had a conspicuous blank by his name. Ford complained that Wayne wasn't even good at pretending he'd been in the service, couldn't even do a plausible salute.

They Were Expendable portrays the time right after Pearl Harbor when the navy was in retreat and had only spunky little PT boats to carry on the fight. Wayne leads a brave attack that destroys an enemy cruiser but in the end the PT boats and much of their crews are left behind in the retreat. The Pacific beach where they were left behind was actually in yet-undeveloped Key Biscayne, where Richard Nixon would later have his Florida White House and decide how many thousands of men were expendable for national honor in Vietnam.

If John Kerry was trying to look like John Wayne, he soon realized that his heroism too was expendable. But it was still a shock for Kerry to realize that John Kennedy's Vietnam crusade was a shipwreck from the start. *Going Upriver* followed Kerry home and into his antiwar leadership, focusing especially on the veteran's march on Washington, on Kerry's testimony before congress, and on the vets tossing their medals over the fence, a scene that riveted the nation.

As the credits rolled there were some photos of Kerry in the 1972 campaign, including his election-night concession speech. To me these shots still packed a punch, and they brought back a memory I hadn't visited in years.

On the morning after election night I'd walked down to the headquarters as early as usual, only to find that no one else had the heart to be there yet. The phones were ringing, so I started answering them. A voice with a thick accent said: "Hello, this is Otto Preminger." Seven years before, Otto Preminger had made a John Wayne movie, *In Harm's Way*, which was also about the navy in the wake of Pearl Harbor. Preminger had donated $1,000 to Kerry's campaign, and Kerry's opponent took out newspaper ads attacking "Otto Preminger of Hollywood," symbolic of the alien, un-American influences behind Kerry. Never mind that Preminger had made a John Wayne movie.

"I'm calling from California," said Preminger, "and I haven't heard any news about Kerry's election. Tell me, did he win?"

I hesitated. "No, I'm afraid he lost."

"He lost?" Preminger was surprised and hurt. "He lost? But what happened?"

I didn't know if Preminger knew that his name and contribution had been used against Kerry, and I certainly wasn't going to be the one to tell him. "He's been attacked for weeks by the newspaper and his opponents, attacked as being un-American. There are just too many people here whose sense of patriotism is…just too old-fashioned." Thank goodness I didn't say that their idea of patriotism came from John Wayne movies. I didn't realize at the time that Preminger had made a John Wayne movie. When I eventually did notice this it made me wonder what was going through Preminger's mind when I basically told him that John Kerry had lost to John Wayne.

When *Going Upriver* was done I tried to stir up a discussion by saying how the filmmaker, George Butler, had co-produced with Kerry a book about the veteran's march, and Butler's front-cover photo featured some long-haired vets flying an American flag upside down, a longstanding military signal for soldiers in distress. But Kerry's opponents in 1972 had asserted that this photo meant disrespect for the flag and proved that Kerry was un-American. Now in 2004 people were still bringing up the upside-down flag as treasonous. The whole of *Going Upriver* read like a justification for what Kerry had been trying to do. It was sad that after a third of a century this was still incomprehensible to so many.

The audience made various comments, and the veterans in particular agreed that it was a powerful film. Then I tied to stir up a discussion of the John Wayne model of patriotism, figuring that Winterset residents had to be experts on that subject, but they really didn't want to go there.

But they did want to go to the town sports bar for a Democrat's social hour. The first thing I saw on walking in the door was a mural with a big smiling John Wayne and a covered bridge.

As we ate and talked, another profane liberal said that John Wayne wasn't really born in the mythological John Wayne house. I could feel John Wayne's huge eyes taking aim at me. I knew exactly what he was thinking: "Okay partner, you've had your fun. You thought you were going to ride into my town like Jimmy Stewart and say a bunch of pretty words and clean up the town. Well, it didn't work. This is my town and the cowboy is going to win this county by 300 votes, or 55%. Now I'm giving you until sundown to get out of town."

"But," I looked at the darkness outside, "it's way past sundown."

"That just shows what a nice guy I am. But don't push me any further or you won't see the sun rise." Clint Eastwood, apparently hiding in the shadows in the covered bridge, said: "Read my lips: you won't make your day, punk." And wouldn't you know it, Ronald Reagan was there and said "You heard them, get out of Dodge."

"But we're not in Dodge."

"Don't try to use logic against myth."

"But three against one—that's not fair."

John Wayne laughed scornfully. "Typical liberal, complaining about fairness. Life isn't fair, and only toughness gets you through. In *True Grit* I charged right into four killers, and I only had one eye."

"But the eye patch was fake—you could see through it. I studied it in your birth home."

"Hell, I was never born in that fool house, and of course the eye patch was fake. But we're talking myth here. John Ford would never let me forget that he was the master mythmaker and I was only his tool, an actor who could never live up to the myths."

"But look at all the trouble America has gone to trying to live up to those myths. Look at Lyndon Johnson and Ronald Reagan and George W. Bush doing the whole cowboy act and thinking they have to live up to the cowboy myth in foreign policy. Maybe someone should tell them that America can never live up to the myths."

"I don't want to hear it, pilgrim. Now I'm going to count to minus 250 billion—we're talking deficit spending here to pay for the *USS Ronald Reagan* with the cavalry flag—and if you aren't gone by then, me and Clint and Ronald will be waiting for you in the dusty windswept street."

"But I'd planned to leave an hour ago."

"That's what they always say. Just keep telling yourself that as you run like a chicken back to Des Moines. If you had any guts you wouldn't let yourself be pushed around like this. You'd stay and fight."

"But there's no reason at all to fight. I was leaving anyway."

"Minus one. Minus two. Minus three…"

What more could I say? Honest, I really was leaving anyway.

I drove out John Wayne Drive and past a sign that pointed to one of the covered bridged and headed into the prairie night, and I thought of what it took for Angela de Prairie to grow up in John Wayne's hometown.

True Grit

When Angela said she had never been able to sit through an entire John Wayne movie I asked her, "Not even *True Grit?*" My tone implied that she had missed something worthwhile, and she answered a bit defensively that she had never seen *True Grit*. I'd once gotten a similar reaction from some staunch feminists who were discussing the lack of strong female roles in western movies, and I said "What about *True Grit?*" and they answered incredulously, "But isn't that a John Wayne movie?" Yes, I answered, but it's a John Wayne movie where John Wayne is led and bossed all over the landscape by a tough, determined fourteen-year-old girl. And unlike the usual larger-than-life John Wayne heroes, Wayne plays a flawed, lonely one-eyed drunk who falls off his horse.

True Grit was made in the middle of the Vietnam War when Wayne realized that the western was being rejected and he thought that maybe he should try playing a real, flawed human for a change, and he even won an Oscar for being a real, one-eyed drunk falling off his horse and being bossed all over the landscape by a tough little girl. "Wow!" he proclaimed at the podium as he took his Oscar "If I'd known what I know now, I'd have put a patch on my eye thirty-five years ago."[41] There was a lesson here about the costs of living in a world of myths and impossible-to-live-up-to cowboy heroes, and the value of living in the real, complicated, ambiguous world. Yet Wayne never applied this lesson to America. And America was far too lost in the glorious western sunset land of myths to want to leave it or even listen to anyone who suggested it was unreal.

By the way, in *True Grit* the girl was bossing John Wayne to pursue a bad guy named Cheney.

The last time I saw Angela de Prairie was late on election night, and she was still diligently on the phone, juggling reports and problems and solutions. Somewhere or other, she'd learned something about grit, and not the false grit that leads one-eyed nations astray.

10

The Waste Land and the Second Coming

When T. S. Eliot's grandfather, William Greenleaf Eliot, founded Washington University in St. Louis, site of the second 2004 presidential debate, he was pursuing Emerson's vision of America as the enlightener of the world. William Greenleaf Eliot was a great admirer of Emerson, and Emerson visited Eliot in St. Louis and hailed him as "the saint of the west."

When Eliot graduated from Harvard Divinity School in 1834 and moved to St. Louis, St. Louis was indeed "the west." It was only thirty years after Lewis and Clark left St. Louis to explore the "Nature" part of Jefferson's "Nature and Nature's God." Eliot too felt the sense of national destiny Jefferson had felt, but Eliot was more interested in the "Nature's God" part of it, in the moral adventure of America. Eliot could have been far more comfortable staying in New England where the Eliots were a prominent family, where in July of 1776 a sheriff Eliot had stood on the balcony of the state house in Boston and read out the Declaration of Independence and where an Eliot became president of Harvard, but the frontier was where America's soul was being forged. Like Emerson and the rest of the New England moral leadership in the era of the Missouri Compromise and expanding slavery, Eliot was aware that America's moral world mission was being compromised by the unfolding frontier and the temptations of worldly profits. Inspired by Emerson, Eliot became a Unitarian, viewing Christianity not as a ticket to heaven but as a duty to improve this world. He combined the Enlightenment's confidence in human progress with a religious faith that social progress was mandated by Christianity. Increasingly the Enlightenment social project was receiving support from liberal theology, which suggested that the Christian millennium would arrive through human effort, if divinely inspired; humans would create a just world and only then would Christ return to reign on Earth. Thus America was the instrument of the cosmic plan for justice.

Eliot pursued this goal in three ways: charitable works, education, and social reform. For the first, Eliot worked tirelessly to aid the sick and poor and orphans, and at the outbreak of the Civil War he founded the Western Sanitary Commission to give medical aid to the Union army. For the second, Eliot brought New England-style public education to St. Louis. When Protestants and Catholics started fighting over whose Bible should be used in public schools, Eliot used his presidency of the school board to establish non-sectarian schools. He also founded and later headed Washington University, which became one of the very few Midwestern universities to rank with the Ivy League schools, and in 1992 it became a regular host of the presidential debates. For the third, Eliot devoted himself to women's suffrage and especially abolitionism.

When Eliot arrived in St. Louis it was the home of the most outspoken abolitionist in America, Elijah Lovejoy, whose printing press was vandalized by angry mobs several times. When the Missouri state legislature passed a law forbidding Missourians from promoting anti-slavery views, Lovejoy moved across the river to Illinois, but there too a mob attacked him and finally killed him. In spite of the dangers Eliot took up the cause of emancipation, preaching passionately against slavery. Living in a slave state made Eliot more pessimistic than Northern abolitionists about the political prospects for quick abolition, and he also feared it would be a disaster of white persecution and black destitution unless the way was prepared by the moral uplifting of Southern whites and the educational uplifting of slaves. But Eliot's political pessimism didn't stop his moral passion, and when it came to the fugitive slave law he advocated open resistance. Eliot played a huge role in building a strong abolitionist culture in St. Louis, culminating in pushing the case of St. Louis slave Dred Scott to the U. S. Supreme Court. When Chief Justice Roger B. Taney ruled not only that slaves were strictly property without rights but that all congressional measures to limit slavery were invalid, it sparked the Civil War. It turned out that Emerson's moral vision for America would require far, far, far more blood than what he had sanctioned in the tidy verse of "The Concord Hymn"—the shot heard round the world.

I was heading from Iowa to St. Louis for the debate when I passed a unit of the Missouri National Guard on weekend maneuvers. There were jeeps, humvees, and troop trucks with arched canopies just like covered wagons, all painted in desert camouflage. Until a dozen years ago army vehicles had been painted green to hide in the forests and fields of Europe, to enact the American mission of saving the world from kings, to enact it with a reach and a power that would have been unimaginable to the Lexington minutemen who couldn't even evict the kings from their own village green. But now army vehicles no longer fit in with the American land and were actually a violation of it, inflicting a feudal desert upon our green democratic land.

In a few days John Kerry and George W. Bush would start a heated exchange over the National Guard, with Kerry complaining that the guard was severely overstressed and turned into "a back-door draft." Moderator Charles Gibson tried three times to get President Bush to address the "back-door draft," but three times Bush cut him off sharply in order to answer a further Kerry comment about the U. S. acting alone, which had made Bush visibly angry. Bush insisted that America was leading a great democratic coalition. Was Bush dreaming of the glories of D-Day and the Argonne? Kerry answered that Missouri alone had supplied more troops in Iraq than any nation besides Britain: "That's not a grand coalition."

Echoes of the Argonne. I saw a highway sign pointing to Laclede, the childhood hometown of John J. Pershing, the commander of U.S. forces in World War One. Over the years I had passed Laclede a few times without stopping, for I found World War One a dismal verdict on the sanity of the human race. Yet now I felt a reason to stop. General Pershing's grandson, Dick Pershing, had been one of John Kerry's best friends in prep school and college. I pulled up at the white, two-story gingerbread-frilled house and went inside to learn about the Pershings.

John J. Pershing's father had been a firm believer in America. During the Civil War he insisted on flying the Union flag above his house though his Tennessee-born wife was strongly pro-Southern. To pro-Southern neighbors who demanded he take down the flag, he swore he'd shoot anyone who touched it. When rebel commandos raided the town and shot two people and herded others into the town square, he took a shotgun-aim on the raiders until his wife pleaded for him to think of the safety of their son John, who was watching it all.

Yet it's hard to find any Emersonian vision of America in the early decades of John J. Pershing's military career. After West Point he lived the real Wild West in its closing years, riding a horse in the U. S. cavalry and chasing Geronimo and the Apaches through the Southwest, and then he went to South Dakota to quell the Sioux unrest caused by the ghost dance, a Native American version of the Christian Second Coming. A medicine man had a vision of the Christian God, who declared that whites would soon be annihilated, that the Native dead would return, and that Native lands and glories would be restored, and all you had to do was to perform the ghost dance, which also rendered the white man's bullets harmless. The ghost dance died at Wounded Knee, along with 200 Sioux. Pershing didn't arrive at Wounded Knee in time for the massacre, but he did patrol the still-scarred battlefield afterwards and he saw the Sioux standing there in despair. Pershing was proud of having helped finished off 250 years of Indian resistance.

Only fifty years before Wounded Knee Emerson had been enraged by Andrew Jackson's campaign to remove the Cherokees from their homelands. Emerson published an open letter to the president warning that America was jeopardizing its very reason for existing, its moral mission to redeem the world. The removal was "a crime that really deprives us as well as the Cherokees of a country; for how could we call the conspiracy that should crush these poor Indians our government, or the land that was cursed by their parting and dying imprecations our country, any more?...The name of this nation, hitherto the sweet omen of religion and liberty, will stink to the world."[42] Emerson had little doubt that the American people shared his moral vision: "Sir, does this government think that the people of the United States are become savage and mad? From their mind are the sentiments of love and good nature wiped clean out? The soul of man, the justice, the mercy that is the heart's heart in all men, from Maine to Georgia, does abhor this business."[43]

Pershing next saw combat in the Spanish American War, leading a cavalry unit up San Juan Hill right next to the Rough Riders, then helping command the brutal suppression of Philippine independence forces. Many American officers were veterans of the Indian wars and looked upon the Filipinos as just more Indians in the way of Manifest Destiny. Like Emerson over the Cherokees, Mark Twain railed that the Philippines war was a betrayal of American ideals, but after sixty years that included the Civil War, the Gilded Age, and Wounded Knee, Twain had notably less confidence than Emerson in America's moral mission. But it was still alive: just ask William Randolph Hearst, astute national psychologist, who knew that Americans might not go to war for nationalism alone but would rally to the old iconography of America's world mission. In 1916 Pershing spent nearly a year wandering around Mexico with horse cavalry and covered wagons, trying to catch Pancho Villa. The Mexican people hated to see the Americans coming and helped Pancho Villa always get away.

At long last Pershing finally found someone who was actually happy to see the Americans coming. Or at least, the British and French were willing to put up with America's annoying sense of moral superiority in exchange for more bodies to fill the trenches. Woodrow Wilson invoked the full iconography of America's mission of redeeming the decrepit old world, and this time it came powerfully to life with American soldiers actually advancing on European soil. Just from the viewpoint of national pride it was a heady experience for us to be testing our power against the great empires. One hundred and forty years of optimism sent Pershing's troops to Europe. Far less optimism came home.

Americans found more redeeming value in the war than did Europeans, yet Americans shared in the deep disillusionment after the war, and in some ways our disillusionment was worse, for we'd had more illusions to lose. The technological progress that had dramatically encouraged the idea of human progress had ended up as an assembly line of death amidst which millions of men ran back and forth madly, futilely, knowing they were going to die for nothing but powerless to stop. The long Western idea of human dignity ended up as hundreds of miles of muddy stinking trenches in which millions of men lived like rats and died like rats. The war was a deep trauma for the Enlightenment faith in human reason and human progress, a trauma from which the West has never recovered.

This lost confidence soon showed up in the art and literature of the Lost Generation, including the novels of Ernest Hemingway and most famously the poetry of T. S. Eliot. Eliot's *The Waste Land*, with its images of desolation so suggestive of the barren no-man's-lands of the trenches and of more spiritual desolations, became a religious text for the Lost Generation. Eliot's disjointed poetic style and disjointed images were a long way from the free verse with which Walt Whitman had tried to ennoble the blood of the Civil War, and a very long way from the neat rhymes of Emerson's "Concord Hymn." The anti-hymn *Waste Land* was a very long way from the democratic optimism of T. S. Eliot's grandfather, and *The Waste Land* was only the start of Eliot's withdrawal from it. Eliot left America, became a British citizen, affected a British accent, dressed like an English gentleman, ridiculed the lameness of Unitarianism and joined the Anglican Church, denounced democracy and embraced royalism, and promoted the idea that civilization could be saved only if it was ruled by a Christian elite.

The publication of *The Waste Land* marked eighty years since Emerson's hopes for America had been outraged by the Cherokee removal, which he called the worst injustice "since the earth was made." Confidence in America's humane world-renewing mission faced another eighty years of traumas and disappointments, and it had many more miles to withdraw.

Meanwhile, as the liberal vision of America was waning, another force was rising in America through the twentieth century. This force also had a strong faith in American destiny, but a faith of a very different kind.

I could almost summarize this whole story by offering a simple contrast between Washington University and another college in the opposite corner of Missouri, not just a geographically opposite corner but a culturally opposite corner too. Still, both colleges were located right off of old Rt. 66. While Washington University has a stately Ivy League-look, a campus with gothic architecture, statues, and other signs of abundant financial resources, Evangel University in Springfield still uses a maze of dilapidated World War Two army barracks as classrooms, with creaking hallways, leaking roofs, warped windows, and broken, rusty overhead heaters. While Washington University has huge research facilities that have won seventeen Nobel Prizes for medicine, Evangel University teaches faith healing. While Washington University teaches a dozen foreign languages, Evangel University teaches speaking in tongues. Washington University's openness to the world is symbolized by the fact that some of its facilities were built to welcome the world to the 1904 St. Louis Olympics and world's fair. Evangel University's relationship with the world is symbolized by the fact that its parent church—the Assemblies of God—not only bought surplus army barracks for sending onward its Christian soldiers but a B-17 bomber and a C-46 military cargo plane to carry missionaries around the world. The athletic field house at Washington University, built for the Olympics, was the site of the presidential debate, in which John Kerry will several times criticize John Ashcroft's rough handling of civil liberties. The athletic field house at Evangel University is called the Ashcroft Center, named for a former president of Evangel University and the father of John Ashcroft. The Washington University athletic team name is—very conventionally—the Bears. The Evangel University athletic team name is—talk about symbols—the Crusaders. Yes, the medieval knights who invaded the Middle East to reclaim the Holy Land from the devil Muslims. The name of the Evangel University campus newspaper is *The Lance*, with a masthead illustration of a knight's lance. Back and forth, back and forth the Crusaders basketball team runs, and the Ashcroft Center rings with yells: "Go Crusaders! Go Crusaders!" After a Bears game Bears fans head to the many coffee houses near campus and talk about the St. Louis Symphony or a new film at the local art house. After a Crusaders game Crusaders fans can go to Hemingway's, which is located on the very same street as the world headquarters of the Assemblies of God, not of course the Hemingway of Lost Generation doubt but the gun-loving Hemingway for whom the photo of George W. Bush is smiling, and they talk about going fishing on Lake Taneycomo, Taneycomo being short for Taney County, Missouri, the only county in America proudly named for Chief Justice Roger B. Taney, who with the Dred Scott decision smashed the hopes of William Greenleaf Eliot.

It was inconceivable that the 2004 presidential debate could be held at Evangel University, for it lacked the facilities and prestige of Washington University.

Yet it was much more of an open question whether America in 2004 was being schooled by Washington University or Evangel University, whether America was following the vision of William Greenleaf Eliot or the vision of the Ashcrofts. Perhaps this was ultimately what the 2004 election was all about.

In 2004 Evangel University finally managed, after years of saving, to replace some of its decrepit army barracks with a new building of real bricks and all. In the lobby is a plaque listing all the donors. If this was any other Christian college in the Ozarks region the name at the top of the donor list would be the Waltons. Walton money has transformed some hardscrabble Ozarks Baptist colleges, which now boast elegant buildings named for the Waltons. But at Evangel University the Walton name is conspicuously missing. Right here, in both the poverty of the Evangel campus and in the lack of affinity felt by other Christian sects for Pentecostalism, you have a symbolic summary of much of the history of the Pentecostal Church. When Pentecostalism arose at the start of the twentieth century even other evangelicals loathed it and denounced it as, at least, a religion for demented hillbillies, and at worst, the work of Satan. Yet by the end of the twentieth century Pentecostals were sitting in the cabinet and directing national policy on the environment, the law, and national security. Did Pentecostalism change dramatically and thus become more acceptable, or did the whole center of gravity of American life shift towards the Pentecostals? The Pentecostals offer a case study that might summarize the gravity shifts in the rise of the evangelicals in the twentieth century, for the Pentecostals started out on the fringe, indeed the lunatic fringe, of the evangelical community.

The early Pentecostals were subjected to not just angry denunciations from Baptist pulpits, but mob violence. In 1902 a mob of North Carolina Baptists torched a Pentecostal church. Not to be outdone by the Baptists, a North Carolina Methodist minister burned down a Pentecostal church. Arsonists burned down a Pentecostal revival tent in Kansas and a school in Mississippi. From coast to coast, Pentecostal services were interrupted by violence. In Ohio thirty men invaded a service and threw sulfuric acid on the worshipers. In Houston in 1906 the weapons were just rotten eggs. In San Antonio it was rocks. In Illinois it was so much cayenne pepper that the worshipers gasped for breath. In Tennessee it was a stink bomb. In Santa Barbara it was flying whiskey bottles. Pentecostal preachers found they weren't even safe at home. In Tennessee a preacher had bullets fly through his window. In Georgia a preacher who had already found dynamite under his church was clubbed on a neighborhood street.

At the same time that the Pentecostals were being attacked by other evangelicals, they were also being denounced by liberal theologians, though for quite different reasons. The liberals were attacking the idea of premillennialism, which was now spread across many evangelical sects, but the Pentecostals stood out as the most fervent advocates of premillennialism. The liberal attack was led by the University of Chicago Divinity School, which was committed to social progress and the theology that America was God's instrument for building the millennium on Earth. By contrast premillennialism held that the millennium would begin only at Christ's return, which the Pentecostals said was very imminent, and thus it was completely pointless to worry about social progress or anything else worldly, not only because the end was near but because humans are inherently sinful, incapable of utopia on Earth, and the only job for society was to hold the line against sin until Christ returned. The Chicago theologians declared that premillennialism was a dangerous denial of America's purpose of leading world progress. According to Dr. Shirley Jackson Chase, premillennnialism "strikes at the very heart of all democratic ideals..."[44] "In the name of religion we are told that the world cannot appreciably be improved by human efforts."[45] More specifically, as World War One raged, liberal theologians were appalled that the premillennialists were preaching that the war was pointless since the Second Coming was imminent. "The American nation," said Chase, "is engaged in a gigantic effort to make the world safe for democracy." Thus "It would be almost traitorous negligence to ignore the detrimental character of premillennial propaganda." Then Chase went further and suggested that the premillennialists were indeed traitors being secretly funded by the Germans to undermine America's war effort.

As the war raged, Pentecostals studied newspaper accounts and found perfect fits for Biblical prophecies of the Second Coming. Pentecostal preachers advised young men not to serve in the war because it was a waste of energy in the face of the Second Coming. One leading evangelical newspaper even quoted Bertrand Russell against the war. Some Pentecostals also decided that the South's racial policies were a waste of energy in the face of the Second Coming, and they started holding integrated services. Leading Pentecostals declared that the whole idea of patriotism was a foolish waste of time. (But it wasn't the Pentecostal's pacifism or integration that made other evangelicals hate them).

From today's perspectives this all seems wildly scrambled. The forebears of John Ashcroft were denouncing American patriotism, preaching draft dodging, quoting a British atheist against the capitalist warlords, and practicing integration in the South long before Martin Luther King was born, while the liberals were beating the drums for war and accusing evangelicals of being not just unpatriotic but traitors serving an evil foreign power, deserving some sort of Patriot Act to bring them under control. What has changed?

The first thing that happened was World War One, and its wasteland.

The Pershing museum included an old poster for a Hollywood movie called *Pershing's Crusader's*. The poster featured a heroic image of Pershing on a horse, leading a long parade of troops who blur off into the distance. Riding a horse alongside Pershing is a ghostly image of a heroic knight, a medieval crusader, wearing armor and holding a sword.

In the disillusionment following World War One, American liberals were much less willing to embrace such symbolism, and by 2004 it was unthinkable. But this symbolism was a perfect fit for "Ashcroft's crusaders."

I looked over the museum photos of early family life and Pershing in various stages of his career, the displays of medals and other honors, and Pershing's sword from the final era when swords weren't decorations but a real weapon of cavalrymen. The museum also included a model of the Pershing missile, which I guessed could carry nuclear warheads.

I asked the interpreter about Pershing's descendants, and she said that in fact some Pershings had been there this morning, visiting from Iowa. But they weren't direct descendants. Pershing's wife and daughters were killed in a tragic fire. His son had survived the fire, but this son's two sons had died without leaving offspring. One of Pershing's grandsons, Richard, had served as a lieutenant in the 101st Airborne in Vietnam, but he had been killed in combat and was buried in Arlington next to his grandfather. I asked her if she knew that Richard Pershing had been a close friend of John Kerry, and she said no.

Outside was a monument of a dozen cement slabs arranged Stonehenge-like around a statue of General Pershing. The slabs held the chiseled names of war dead, arranged by war. I looked over the Vietnam list, and two names popped out at me: Richard W. Pershing, and John D. Disney.

I asked the interpreter about John D. Disney. Walt Disney grew up in a town twenty miles from here. The interpreter led me to the office and she looked through the file on all the names on the memorial. John D. Disney was indeed from Marceline, Walt Disney's hometown. Disney was a rare name and Marceline was a small town. It seemed that some relative of Walt Disney had died in Vietnam. To me this whole idea seemed incongruous, for the name "Disney" had long ago ceased referring to a mere man and had become a symbol of innocence, mainly childhood innocence, but American innocence too. Walt Disney's TV show had regularly celebrated American history and heroes, most famously Davy

Crockett, and the Disney theme parks continued doing so. The idea that "Disney" could die in Vietnam held the same sad incongruity as if the Pershing monument had listed Mickey Mouse dying in Vietnam.

The long painful withdrawal of liberalism's innocence and confidence in America left a void, a void ready to be filled. But I am getting way ahead of the story here. There are several other voids that need to be filled in first before we can discuss how William Greenleaf Eliot's crusaders turned into Ashcroft's crusaders.

The first void was a sociological void. Foreign observers have long puzzled over why the world's most worldly, most technological, most economically successful, most comfortable nation should also be the nation that most eagerly hoped for the end of the world. It was understandable for the Sioux to plunge into the ghost dance after their people and lifestyle had been devastated. But why were white Americans plunging into their own version of the ghost dance? A large part of the answer was that Americans were far more emotionally rootless than other peoples, having abandoned old-world roots, home, family, community, history, and churches to plunge into a whirlwind of grasping for success. For many of those who succeeded, comfort and social status took the bite out of America's rootlessness, but for some parts of America economic success wasn't much of an option. The South had been devastated by the Civil War, devastated by the same soldiers who would go on to devastate the Sioux and set them ghost dancing. Other regions, such as the Ozarks, didn't require a war to limit the opportunities for success. For people who were feeling the full spiritual void of American rootlessness, the ready answer was religion.

But then came the religious void. For a long time after the pilgrims, Americans practiced the faith of their fathers. But as Americans became more enthralled with the idea of human progress, mainline Protestant churches increasingly enlisted in the theology of social progress, talking less and less about heaven and hell. Many churches were also accommodating themselves to the news from science, abandoning everything in the Bible that didn't fit in with science, such as the Genesis story and the miracles of Christ. Christ became a Super Emerson who came to Earth to teach the social gospel. But the Ozarks wasn't seeing much social progress, and the South gagged at the notion that God was a Yankee dogooder. If mainline Protestant churches weren't going to fill America's spiritual hunger, Americans would invent faiths that would. One result was fundamentalism, which reacted strongly against modernism by insisting on the literal truth of every word of the Bible. But prolonged studying of Biblical texts wasn't everyone's idea of religious worship, so another response was more experiential, the seeking of religious ecstasies. The experiential approach had the added advantage that at the start of the twentieth century many rural Americans were illiterate, incapable of reading the Bible even if they wanted to, and their preachers were too poorly educated to sustain coherent discourses on Biblical texts. Thus it was probably no coincidence that one of America's largest pockets of illiteracy, the Ozarks, became the epicenter of Pentecostalism, the foremost expression of religious ecstasy. Thus the headquarters of the Assemblies of God, the leading Pentecostal church, sits on the Missouri edge of the Ozarks. It's in same town as the Bass Pro Shop because they represent the same culture of rural isolation and self-sufficiency. On the Oklahoma edge of the Ozarks sits Oral Roberts University; Oral Roberts used TV to push the Pentecostal belief in faith healing to major new national prominence. Ozarks folks relied on faith healing for the same reason they relied on hunting and fishing to eat, because they couldn't afford modern medicine.

The first thing that Bible-preoccupied fundamentalists disliked about Pentecostalism was that Pentecostals happily ignored the Bible to pursue ecstasy. Faith healing was one form of ecstasy, and on the whole fundamentalists disdained faith healing. The ultimate form of Pentecostal ecstasy was speaking in tongues, in which the holy spirit manifested its visitation in your body by allowing you to speak previously unlearned foreign languages. A Pentecostal service might turn into a room full of people shouting in two dozen "languages," although to outsiders it sounded more like meaningless gibberish. There are stories of Pentecostals being convinced that they now spoke Brazilian or "the African tongue" and flying off to Brazil or Africa as missionaries only to find that no one could comprehend a word of them or vice versa. Speaking in tongues was often accompanied by a frantic jerking of limbs. The fundamentalists denounced it all as Satanic possession, or delusion. Speaking in tongues did occur in the Bible, but then this was the heyday of spiritualism and the Pentecostals were disconcertingly like the mediums in séances. The Pentecostals crowned their theology with the insistence that speaking in tongues was essential for salvation itself. Thus at the rapture George W. Bush would not only be left behind while John Ashcroft was raptured, George W. Bush was going to burn in hell.

In spite of the enormous hostility heaped upon Pentecostalism, it exerted a huge gravity on the rest of the evangelical movement. It made faith healing much more acceptable. It helped make "spirit-filled worship" very mainstream, if without tongues. Yet Pentecostalism also accommodated itself to fundamentalism. Even though the Pentecostal churches had prudently avoided setting any official date for the Second Coming, Pentecostals had made numerous predictions any-way, all of which had failed, and so the Pentecostals became much quieter about the Second Coming. But they also did what other sects have done when dates set for the climax of the warfare of God and Satan passed without incident; they decided that they would finally involve themselves in the spiritual warfare on Earth. Eventually the Pentecostals and fundamentalists agreed that their differ-ences weren't as important as their mutual duty to wage spiritual warfare on Earth. Thus James Watt and John Ashcroft were allowed to sit at the president's side. It was no coincidence that whereas the Assemblies of God makes up less than one percent of the American population, they supplied the two most con-troversial cabinet members in several decades, loathed by liberals who were clue-less about the differences between Pentecostals and fundamentalists but who still recognized that there was something different about Watt and Ashcroft.

At the very moment the Pentecostals were taking up spiritual warfare on Earth and the fundamentalists were marshalling for an all-out war against modernism, William Greenleaf Eliot's grandson was filling *The Waste Land* full of voids. Even more problematic for liberalism, the Russian revolution had seized the language and theology of social progress and was declaring that it and not America was the instrument of the cosmic plan for human history. For evangelicals who had seen even the local tavern as Satan's lair, there was now no doubt that Satan and his armies were on the march on Earth. Whereas before World War One evangelicals had talked a lot about charitable works as their own form of the social gospel, they now dropped social concerns to focus on saving souls and helping God beat back Satan's advance in history. The liberalism that had long seemed like a differ-ent Christian culture now seemed more like an outright enemy, talking suspi-ciously like Moscow. The irony was that both fundamentalism and liberalism derived some of their energy from the same source, the gnawing spiritual hunger left by a rootless predatory whirlwind society. When fundamentalism and liberal-ism clashed and drew lasting battle lines in the high theater of the Scopes trial in 1925, the truth was that both fundamentalism and liberalism were side shows in American life, both acutely frustrated by the 1920s religion of the stock market. It took a void as big as the Great Depression to let liberalism take charge, but the New Deal talked mostly about fixing a national emergency. Now it was only the evangelicals who were talking about a looming millennium.

I asked the interpreter about Richard W. Pershing, and she looked into his file, but all it indicated was that the association in charge of this monument had placed his name on it, though he had never lived locally.

John Kerry met Dick Pershing at age thirteen and they struck up an energetic friendship. If Dick Pershing took his pedigree seriously he didn't show it, as he had a genius for humor and high spirits. Pershing and Kerry played sports together and went to Yale together and finally went off to Vietnam, though not together. One day in February of 1968 Kerry heard that Pershing had been killed in combat, quite violently. Kerry was devastated. This was the time of the Tet offensive, a huge shock to America's confidence in the war, forcing Americans to finally measure the human cost of the war against the results. Kerry started measuring the war against the loss of Dick Pershing. Kerry had gone to Vietnam to serve Camelot but instead he was finding a wasteland of bomb craters and defoliated jungles. The death of Dick Pershing became more than just the death of a friend, for just as the death of "Disney" in Vietnam suggested the death of innocence, the death of "Pershing" suggested the death of America's heroic crusading self-image.

But cultural symbols like "Pershing's Crusaders" are not so easily killed off. Two centuries had charged this image with a great deal of energy. If liberals were no longer happy with the crusader idea, this left it up for grabs. It was like someone walking away from a powerful and attractive car and leaving the door unlocked and the engine running. The religious right, now committed to making America the instrument of spiritual warfare, came upon the unattended imagery of "Pershing's Crusaders" and they've been joy riding in it ever since.

The void left by Lost Generation disillusionment was captured by W. B. Yeats in his most famous poem:

> The best lack all conviction, while the worst
> Are full of passionate intensity.

The poem was "The Second Coming," and the next lines were:

> Surely some revelation is at hand.
> Surely the Second Coming is at hand.
> The Second Coming!

Given Missouri's well-known role as the most accurate bellwether of presidential elections, it's worth taking a more detailed look at the rise of John Ashcroft, for Missouri's internal politics too has been an accurate bellwether of national political and cultural trends. The tension of cultural forces in Missouri is nowhere better illustrated than by the fact that at the same time Missourians elected John Ashcroft governor—in 1984—they elected a lieutenant governor who was a Democrat, a woman, a Jew, a resident of the Washington University neighborhood, a liberal and feminist activist, and a future president of the National Women's Political caucus. (If you even need to ask if Ashcroft got along with Lt. Governor Harriet Woods, the answer is no). For the last third of a century the leading story of Missouri politics has basically been Washington University versus Evangel University, or more specifically, the efforts of St. Louis liberals to hold back the rising power of the religious right.

Of course, Evangel University might have its own way of telling this story:

God left numerous signs that John Ashcroft fulfills Biblical prophecies of the Second Coming. God planned it so that when Satan struck America on September 11, America's national security would be safely in the hands of "Ashcroft's crusaders." John Ashcroft owed his cabinet post to a miraculous resurrection—the rising from the grave of Mel Carnahan. On the day that George W. Bush and Al Gore were in St. Louis preparing to debate at the ungodly Washington University, God sent a very clear message. As Mel Carnahan's plane was leaving St. Louis in his campaign to unseat John Ashcroft from the senate, God seized Carnahan's plane and slammed it to the ground. This should have given pause to Al Gore in his obstruction of God's servant George W. Bush. God summoned Carnahan from the dead so that Missourians could elect a dead man to the U. S. senate and John Ashcroft would be freed to serve in Bush's cabinet. By now Ashcroft had figured out, as he said in his autobiography, that his political defeats, his lost races for congress and state auditor, were all part of God's plan for him. Long before September 11 God had signaled this plan. Ashcroft got into the senate due to another plane crash back in 1976, which killed the Democratic senate nominee Jerry Litton and allowed Republican John Danforth to win the seat, clearing the future path for Ashcroft. God's plan was spelled out in the math: Litton's plane crashed on August 3, Carnahan's on October 17. Look at those two dates. What date lies precisely in between? September 11! Since we all know how Satan schemes to undermine our faith in prophecy, right now Satan is trying to plant this thought in you: if God knew about September 11 decades ago and has the power to seize planes and smash them down, then why didn't he seize the jetliners on September 11? This question is the devil's work. All the arrows of human history and all the forces of God and Satan are relentlessly converging upon Armageddon and it is absolutely essential that American armies be there for the final battle. Perhaps September 11 was even a warning, a final vision of hell, to a city full of unbelievers.

Let's face it. It's tough for conventional Washington University-style history stories to compete with this.

Before John Ashcroft's senate seat was held by moderate Republican John Danforth it was held by liberal Democrat Stuart Symington. This trajectory tells a story of changing cultural forces.

When John Kerry finished his 1971 testimony before the Senate Foreign Relations Committee, Senator Symington quietly looked at Kerry's combat decorations and announced them for all to hear, so no one would question Kerry's credentials.

When Stuart Symington turned against the war in Vietnam he carried more credentials than most senators. Symington had been the first secretary of the Air Force, appointed by his friend Harry Truman, and before that he'd been president of Emerson Electric in St. Louis, a huge armaments maker in World War Two. Symington's credentials had let him stand up to and help crush Joe McCarthy. Symington headed up a procession of St. Louis liberals, most notably Tom Eagleton, Richard Gephardt, Harriet Woods, and Mel Carnahan. But they faced a long retreat before a Republican advance led by John Danforth, who came from a completely different world than John Ashcroft.

Danforth had a degree from the Yale School of Divinity and was an ordained Episcopal priest, but he was very quiet about this, so quiet that decades later when Danforth showed up in clerical clothes and presided over the funeral of Ronald Reagan, many Missourians were dumbfounded. But if you prompted Danforth he could talk quite thoughtfully about the role of religion in American life and the dangers of mixing religion and politics, of senators claiming they had special moral authority from God.

In 1970 Danforth challenged Symington for his senate seat. At a big kickoff dinner for the Symington campaign I stood up, representing the idealistic youth of Missouri, and presented Symington with a token of our support, a jack-in-the-box. Jack Danforth was the scion of the Ralston Purina fortune, and recently Ralston Purina had acquired the fast-food franchise Jack-in-the-Box. Symington stood there turning the crank on the jack-in-the-box, but for a long, embarrassing time Jack refused to come out. It would turn out that little Jack had a better sense of timing than big Jack, for Danforth would lose that race and wait six years to win Symington's seat. It also turned out that little Jack had a better sense of timing than John Ashcroft. After hiding his light for the start of his career, Ashcroft finally decided it was safe to pop out as a full-blown champion of the religious right, but Missouri voters were not amused.

Just as Missourians were dumbfounded to see John Danforth in clerical clothes, many were dumbfounded to see John Ashcroft wearing the war paint of the religious right, and perhaps the most appalled of all were the moderate, mainline Protestant Republicans who had appreciated the smart-and-moderate image John Danforth had given Missouri Republicans. Ashcroft owed his career to this smart-and-moderate image opening the door for other Republicans, and he knew it: as state attorney general Ashcroft was mainly memorable as a consumer advocate, and when Ashcroft ran for governor he ran as a Nader-style consumer crusader. Governor Ashcroft turned out to be very conservative, so much so that Judge Stephen Limbaugh officially rebuked Ashcroft for obstructionist tactics of a St. Louis school desegregation plan, accusing Ashcroft of abusing the court system for political ends. As Ashcroft's career progressed the religious right was becoming increasingly vocal and powerful in national politics, and when Ashcroft reached the senate he seemed to think it was safe to emerge as an unapologetic hellfire evangelical, and he became one of the loudest critics of the Clinton moral apocalypse and started cultivating the religious right to be its candidate for president in 2000. Ashcroft had been elected to the senate with 60% of the vote, and he probably thought he had a safe seat, but a 1998 poll showed that only 34% of Missourians thought he'd make a good president. Ashcroft abandoned his presidential ambitions.

The shifting moral and political geography can be illustrated by the issue of capital punishment. In John Danforth's moral reasoning, to be morally consistent one had to oppose both capital punishment and abortion, leaving him one of few senators with this stance, and leaving the religious right with a grudging respect. In 1999 the Pope visited St. Louis and made a public appeal to Governor Carnahan to commute the imminent death sentence of an inmate on Missouri's death row. Carnahan was the son of a St. Louis-area congressman but was born in the rural Ozarks and was a Baptist and believed in capital punishment and had already allowed several executions. The day after the Pope left, Carnahan commuted the death sentence. Evangelicals flew into a rage, accusing Carnahan of being un-American, taking orders from the papacy, and Ashcroft pounced on the incident for all it was worth. Perhaps Ashcroft got so absorbed in playing to the evangelicals that he didn't notice that Missouri Catholics, who were very proud that the Pope had visited their state, resented Ashcroft turning the Pope into a political football. Ashcroft had crossed a line that was dangerous to cross even in a Bible-belt state, or perhaps especially in a Bible-belt state where for a long time the majority had been keeping a concerned watch on the boundary between religion and politics, and where even anti-abortion Catholics would travel only so far with Pentecostals. Ashcroft had crossed the line between religion and civic life not just in constitutional terms, but in terms of whether our vision of America should be religious or civic.

It's a rare thing for a senator who gets elected with 60% of the vote to be rejected in the next election, but Ashcroft's fall wasn't any last laugh for Missouri liberals. Ashcroft's career had opened the door to others from the religious right, most notably Roy Blunt, who had been president of a Baptist university just up the highway from Evangel University, and who was soon majority whip in the U. S. house.

In 2004 Roy Blunt's son Matt was running for governor, and this race forced me to see how far the cultural dynamic in Missouri and America had shifted since I represented the idealistic youth of 1970. Matt Blunt's Democratic opponent was Claire McCaskill; it had been Claire's mother Betty who did more than anyone to get me involved in politics as a kid. I sat around the McCaskill dinner table with Claire and stuffed envelopes. If you had told me then that two familiar faces of my idealistic youth would be running on the same ticket for president and governor in 2004, I would have assumed this marked the triumph of that youthful idealism. And yet the real America of 2004 was a very different place. Who would have guessed that America would be run by two evangelicals from the Ozarks? I was taking the rise of the religious right pretty personally this fall, since it looked like Missouri could turn out to be crucial for a Kerry victory and it also looked like having a strong Kerry campaign in Missouri could turn out to be crucial for a McCaskill victory. But unlike other Midwestern toss-up states like Ohio or Iowa, Missouri had a hardcore Southern-style Bible belt, and the Kerry campaign couldn't penetrate this wall, leaving the math for the rest of the electorate too discouraging. Soon after the debate the Kerry campaign abandoned Missouri, and Claire would end up losing narrowly.

About an hour after leaving Pershing's house I drove through a little town where General Omar Bradley was born. Bradley commanded U. S. armies on D-Day and across Europe in World War Two. By 2004 Americans had become very nostalgic about World War Two, a war where they didn't have to argue over what was right or wrong. Bradley was the perfect embodiment of the democratic purposes of that war, for he was unassuming and full or respect and concern for the average soldier. But then people were comparing him with the other leading general of the European front, George Patton. Patton was a megalomaniac who believed God had chosen him for glory. This wasn't the first coming of George Patton, or even the second coming, for in his personal religion he had been reincarnated many times and found glory in the most famous battles of history. Bradley found Patton "the strangest duck I have ever known. He appeared to be motivated by some deep, inexplicable martial spirit. He devoured military history and poetry and imagined—in the spirit of reincarnation—that he had fought with Alexander the Great, Genghis Khan, Caesar, Napoleon...He was unmercifully hard on his men...most of them respected but despised him...I sometimes wonder if [his] macho profanity was unconscious compensation for his most serious personal flaw: a voice that was almost comically squeaky and high-pitched, altogether lacking in command authority. Like Douglas MacArthur, Patton was a born publicity hound, a glory seeker."[46]

In the middle of the Vietnam War I walked into a theater in my hometown thirty miles from the birthplace of Omar Bradley to see the movie *Patton*. A whole platoon of ROTC cadets walked in and sat down right in front of me. The movie began with Patton standing in front of a giant American flag and delivering a maniacal pep talk to an unseen audience of soldiers, and the cadets in front of me took it as if Patton himself was speaking to them, and they went nuts. When Patton called out for enemy blood, they yelled with pleasure. When Patton hailed the fighting prowess of the American man, this meant them. When Patton declared that America had never lost a war and never would, they screamed and shook their fists in the air. I knew this was a long movie and now it looked even longer, so I started looking for a seat to retreat to, but now Patton was denouncing cowards who retreat and the cadets were screaming against cowards who retreat, so I thought better of making myself a conspicuous target.

Then the opening credits rolled and announced that the historical advisor for the movie was Omar Bradley, and the cadets cheered, for Bradley was the local war hero.

The movie started with Bradley looking over a North African battle disaster scene and declaring: this is a job for Patton. Patton rode in heroically, and the cadets cheered. But what's this? Bradley seemed to think Patton was a jerk. A big jerk. The cadets mumbled. Patton and Bradley went out to a Roman battlefield and Patton said he fought here 2,000 years ago, and Bradley looked at him like he's a nutcase. More confused mumbling from the cadets. Patton was also sure he had been a knight in the crusades. He read the Bible "every goddamned day" and was sure God had a special purpose for him. Patton's divine protection seemed proved when he stood fearlessly in a street shooting a pistol at a German plane and then won a great tank battle. But now Bradley stormed into Patton's Sicily headquarters and scolded Patton for endangering Bradley's troops just so Patton could win glory. The cadets were very quiet. Now Patton was in a hospital tent raging at a shell-shocked solider, calling him a coward, threatening to shoot him. The cadets didn't know what to make of this, but Eisenhower did: he promoted Bradley over Patton.

For another two hours the cadets' loyalties were torn back and forth between Patton and Bradley, between a maniacal certitude of glory and a humble concern for the average guy, between America's messianic mission and America's democratic values.

After D-Day Bradley told Patton flat-out how his messianic ego was idiotic and self-destructive. The cadets sat sullenly: wasn't Patton supposed to be the hero of this movie? Bradley reluctantly placed Patton in command of the Third Army. Patton raced heroically across France, and now the cadets got back into the spirit of it. No more of this self-doubt crap. Patton raced heroically to the rescue at the Battle of the Bulge as the heroic music soared again. Patton called upon God to part the blizzard, and God answered him with clear skies and victory at Christmas. American destiny ruled again. The war over, Patton raged that we ought to keep going and fight the Russian bastards now since we would have to sooner or later, and the cadets went nuts.

Reportedly, when President Nixon saw *Patton* he was inspired to invade Cambodia. Some liberal film critics saw the whole movie as a satire, with George C. Scott playing another demented general just like he did in *Dr. Strangelove*, where America's messianic ego, given a paranoid twist, led to nuclear war.

If I had continued driving south and towards the heartland of Pentecostalism, I would have passed through the spread-out site of one of America's largest concentrations of intercontinental ballistic missile silos. The nuclear warheads in this field alone could turn Europe into a wasteland. The high democratic hopes of the Second World War were left disillusioned again by the Cold War and the reality that now all of human progress could be wiped out in a moment by one madman. Intermingled among these missile silos were Pentecostal churches where people were speaking in tongues, screaming and waving their arms maniacally, and eagerly praying for the end of the world. The only thing separating the wish for the end of the world and the means for the end of the world was a few politicians and generals, and now some of them were also eagerly praying for the end of the world. The Assemblies of God has more military chaplains than any other denomination.

Also during the Vietnam War I sat in a meeting room in the Pentagon, listening to an Air Force general. A friend from St. Louis started needling the general about American policy in Vietnam, comments not particularly original or unkind, but then generals aren't accustomed to teenagers strolling into the Pentagon and demanding answers to uncomfortable questions. The general started raising his voice, and then he was yelling, yelling and waving his arms at teenagers, almost screaming about his son risking his life in Vietnam for us unworthy ingrates. We unworthy ingrates looked at one another with amusement over having gotten a general to flip his lid. A few years later this general was appointed the commander of NORAD, the command post buried in a Colorado mountain. In the event of a nuclear attack he would have major responsibilities for directing the response. It was not amusing to know that the means for the end of the world was in the hands of generals who flipped their lids at a few questions from teenagers.

So why did a denomination that consists of less that one percent of America supply the two most controversial cabinet members in decades? John Ashcroft and James Watt even followed similar trajectories, Ashcroft getting kicked out of the senate and Watt getting kicked out of the cabinet. The Pentecostal puzzle becomes even more intriguing when you realize that the Assemblies of God also gave America its two most spectacular moral crack-ups and empire collapses in the history of TV evangelism, the cases of Jimmy Swaggart and Jim and Tammy Faye Bakker. And the other most-famous Pentecostal preacher, Oral Roberts, though not a member of the Assemblies of God, very nearly destroyed his ministry empire when he had a vision of a skyscraper Jesus promising that if Oral built a skyscraper medical center it would discover the cure for cancer; Oral built the skyscraper and went very broke. This much spectacular disaster in one small sect seems more than coincidence. The Pentecostal talent for self-destruction was active from their start, for their first nationally prominent preacher, Aimee McPherson, who was the model for the charismatic woman preacher in *Elmer Gantry* and *The Day of the Locust*, was plagued by scandal. But what could be the common theme in John Ashcroft winning a 60% majority only to overreach and be rejected, and in Jim and Tammy Faye Bakker overreaching in finances, sex, and mascara? Perhaps it's a clue that the word "overreach" fits all six of these cases. What's going on here, and what might it say about the cultural dynamics behind the rise of the religious right?

My curiosity about the Pentecostals arose largely through a very unlikely coincidence. I was traveling through Louisiana in the late 1980s and stopped for the night in Baton Rouge, the home base of Jimmy Swaggart. The big story on the news that night included a picture of a motel in New Orleans. I stared at it in amazement: wasn't that where I had stayed a couple of nights ago? It stuck in my mind because I had driven past a lot of sleazy motels until I found one that looked safe and respectable. Now the news was informing me that this was the very motel where for years Jimmy Swaggart had been taking prostitutes. Swaggart now had my complete attention. In the morning, after following the media coverage of the exploding scandal, my curiosity tugged me out to the campus of Swaggart's Bible college and broadcasting studio.

I immediately felt like a trespasser, for this had to be the last college in America that still had a dress code. I was the only person in sight wearing blue jeans. The female students seemed to be competing in a Tammy Faye beauty contest, with heavy makeup, hairdos on the glamour end of country, and colorful long dresses. I expected that at any moment someone would approach me and say: "Excuse me, do you belong here?" But today everyone was completely preoccupied with the crisis. I overheard snatches of conversation about the lies against brother Swaggart, the devil's work, and this being a sure sign of the end times. I could overhear these conversations because the entire student body was out on the sidewalks heading for an emergency meeting in a big assembly hall. I slipped in and sat in the back row and tried to look inconspicuous.

The leaders of the college and ministry came out and acknowledged the student's concerns and assured them that they were still on the path to glory. Jimmy was the most righteous man God had ever raised up to preach the true gospel and thus the devil was out to destroy him. This was a test of faith and those who remained faithful would be rewarded while those who doubted would lose out. The students were restless and murmuring, and at one point one of them stood up and raised his hands—a Bible in one—and started yelling, quoting verse and yelling about prophecy and wrath and the end times, and the church leader tried to cut him off with something like "Thank you, brother, thank you for your testimony," but the guy just went on yelling, on and on with so much intensity that I was waiting for him to start speaking in tongues, and the church leader tried again to shut him up but he just wouldn't shut up, he was so sure that God was speaking through him that he was obliviously or happily trespassing upon the leader of his own church and a huge hall of people.

And this, perhaps, was a good clue about the disaster syndrome of the Pentecostals, and about the whole career of the religious right.

Jimmy Swaggart and Jim Bakker were bitter rivals who assisted in each other's downfall by digging up dirt on each other. The Pentecostals had a long history of bitter feuds and dirt digging. Swaggart and Bakker had personal jealousies but they also had theological differences. Swaggart was much more of a traditional revival-tent Pentecostal thundering about the end times and against Catholics and everything modern, including Christian rock music. To Swaggart, the Bakker's hugely successful PTL Club was a perversion, a modernistic watering down of Pentecostalism, dressing it up in the happy guises of pop culture. Yet Pentecostals were thrilled with the success of both Swaggart and Bakker and poured in money. Pentecostalism strongly emphasized missionary work, which explains why a small sect jumped at the new power of TV and founded three of the leading TV ministries. Pentecostals had long been socially marginal, both economically and religiously, so it was heady to find that they now had some of the biggest stars in the evangelical world. Apparently it was also heady for Swaggart and Bakker, who now faced all the temptations of success, including women and money.

Despite their rivalries, the Pentecostals shared an emphasis on the ability and need of individuals to be direct conduits of God's power. Thus Pentecostal morality was less filtered by theology or human bureaucracy than that of other Protestants. At the start of their history the Pentecostals didn't bother building systematic theologies, Bible schools, or even church buildings, since the end of the world was imminent and a revival tent would suffice. Only recently has a school of theology building appeared on the Evangel University campus. This lack of structure actually caused rivalries, for when Pentecostals did have different views on questions of theology or morality, everyone was sure they were speaking for God and they went at each other with ferocious self-righteousness. With the end of the world at hand there was no room for compromise. Duke University religious scholar Grant Wacker describes the Pentecostals as especially prone to absolutism: "If piety fostered certitude, certitude fostered absolutism—a propensity to see life in moral extremes. Differently stated, Pentecostals' world often lacked ambiguities or shadings of gray. Disagreements that most folk, even most evangelical folk, interpreted as honest differences of opinion, Pentecostals saw as vast differences of judgment, shadowed with eternal consequences."[47] Thus the Pentecostals crusaded against one another's sins, such as dancing. *From Ballroom to Brothel*, a popular Pentecostal tract, made clear that all exits from the ballroom led straight to the Lake of Fire. That it might be possible to dance with one's spouse in a ballroom and not automatically end up in a brothel eluded the Pentecostal mind. When someone smirked at evangelist Elizabeth Sisson for dancing up and down the aisles "under the spirit," she retorted, in classic Holy Ghost fashion, "It's amusing to you now, but it won't be so funny when you drop into hell."[48] John Ashcroft, by the way, believes that dancing is sinful.

If the Pentecostals could be so self-righteous among themselves, they got worse against outsiders, which is, according to Wacker, "why Pentecostals experienced so much difficulty with their flesh-and-blood neighbors. In their own minds they represented God's chosen people. As such, they bore a lifesaving message for these final days of history. To oppose them was to oppose God himself."[49] Thus, a "form of mundane trouble stemmed from Pentecostals' real or perceived interference in other person's family lives."[50] But "infringing on other people's civil rights constituted the...far most frequent form of trouble that Holy Ghost folk got themselves into."[51]

Does this ring any bells? The examples Dr. Wacker lists are mostly small-town melodramas, such as a Missouri preacher putting a small-town circus out of business in 1909. At that time the Pentecostals were so socially marginal that they had little power to impose their views on American society. Yet in 2001 a dance-is-sin Pentecostal was the chief law enforcement officer of the land.

We arrive back at the question of whether something important has changed in America to allow a once-vilified sect to take national power. The success of Jim Bakker was certainly owed to the Pentecostals adjusting themselves to a more modern, pop-culture America. Yet the disasters of Bakker, Swaggart, Oral Roberts, Senator Ashcroft, and James Watt suggest that the old self-righteousness is not just alive but often so self-absorbed that it collides disastrously with the other realities of American society. In spite of such collisions, it's easy to conclude that Pentecostal-style self-righteousness has simply become more acceptable.

Why should this be the case? This question could consume an enormous amount of historical discussion, so I'm going to try to short-cut the whole discussion by going straight to some basic human psychology. Why do psychologists say people develop self-righteous personalities? First, they are spoiled, self-centered, and arrogant. Or quite the opposite, they are very insecure and self-doubting and need to prove something. The worst self-righteousness comes when you combine these two personalities into someone who is at once spoiled and self-centered and very insecure and needs to prove something. Do any of these personality traits fit America in the twentieth century?

America was certainly spoiled by the twentieth century. At the outbreak of World War One our sense of national destiny was mostly belief and hope, perhaps powerfully backed up by a century of territorial and economic expansion, but never tested directly against the other world powers. After America had vanquished the Kaiser, fascism, communism, and Iraq and built the world's dominant economy and military, could there be any doubt that America was some sort of chosen nation?

On the other hand, all our power was paralyzed for two generations in the Cold War, with a disaster in Vietnam, and just when we thought the world was safe we were attacked bizarrely on September 11. At home average American workers often couldn't see our national economic prowess translating into the American Dream for themselves.

The core appeal of the religious right was the longstanding conviction that America was God's chosen nation, that our national success, especially our economic success, was a direct payment from God for our having faith and doing his will. But this meant that God was ready to withdraw his blessing if Americans didn't live up to their contract. This meant that moral failures like abortion, pornography, and homosexuality took on much greater danger and anxiety, for they threatened to revoke God's blessing upon America. The promise that God rewarded faith economically, not just to America as a whole but to individuals, further raised the stakes and anxiety of those who were not succeeding, implying that their failure was a punishment for lack of faith, impelling them to prove their faith by being more fervent. If they were also being punished for America's sins, then their anxiety and fervor could best be directed against those who were endangering America's contract with God.

And then there was the sheer confusion of everyday life, and it was here that the religious right connected with people who might not worry about God's role in history. The good ol' days might be tainted with nostalgia but they were grounded in a few basic realities: a lifetime of farming the land where you were born; several generations of family sharing the same town or house; a make-your-own-clothes-and-butter self-sufficiency; a church that covered all the rules; and a pop culture so remote that it intruded only once a year in the form of a Sears catalog in the mailbox or a traveling circus in town. But now Americans lived in a dizzying maze of cross-country moves and daily commutes, of college degrees and corporate politics, of relentless bombardment by pop culture, of science and medicine changing the rules of the cosmos and personal choice, of families fractured by divorce and single parenthood, of crime and drugs and sex and rock and roll. It was easy for the religious right to blame it all on modernity, and when liberals felt obligated to defend modernity, and baby boomers tried to defend the countercultural ethos of personal liberation, it left the religious right alone in acknowledging and addressing the honest daily concerns of millions. It addressed them by blaming it all on political liberalism, and then it went further and said that the moral weakness of liberals allowed not just crime and drugs and divorce at home but also left us too weak to fend off the Viet Cong or September 11. This combination of old-time confidence and present-day doubt was more than ample to breed the worst kind of self-righteousness. The only answer to both weaknesses and to evil was a crusade.

I arrived in St. Louis, which was named for the king of France who was canonized for leading two crusades to the Middle East. Both crusades were disasters.

The crusades had already suffered 150 years of disaster when Louis IX organized his crusades. Shortly after the crusaders lost Jerusalem again in 1244, Louis took Christian vows and vowed to retake Jerusalem. He was going to outdo his dad, who had died on a crusade. Louis spent years raising an army of 15,000 knights, which he financed without deficit spending by raising taxes on the rich. But he couldn't build much of an international coalition, so most of the knights were French. Louis' first crusade may have been the best organized ever, but it wasn't the best led, and after French foolishness led to disaster, Louis was captured and the French had to pay a fortune to get him back. On his next crusade Louis could muster only 10,000 knights, and when they stopped in Tunis to baptize its Muslim ruler, disease swept through their ranks and Louis died muttering "Jerusalem, Jerusalem."

The French didn't seem to learn from the disasters of the crusades because a few centuries later they were back in North Africa as imperial crusaders and fighting Algerian terrorists. Could it be that nearly a thousand years of European disaster in the Middle East had something to do with the French reluctance to endorse the Bush crusade? A national memory of a thousand years of failure is inconceivable to Americans.

The city of St. Louis was given its name by Pierre Laclede, and the little town named for Laclede was the birthplace of John J. Pershing, who arrived in France and declared confidently, "Lafayette, we are here." He could have added, "Saint Louis, we are here."

As I was heading into St. Louis it occurred to me that I might not be done with the theme that had sprung up when I had gone through the birth towns of General Pershing and General Bradley. By making one more stop I could complete the theme.

When William Greenleaf Eliot, planning another fiery sermon against slavery and for America being God's instrument for perfecting human reason and justice, drove his carriage through downtown St. Louis in 1857, he probably didn't notice a shabby-looking man standing on a street corner beside a rickety cart loaded with firewood. The man's beard was scruffy, his hat worn and tattered, his blue overcoat frayed and dirty. "Firewood for sale!" he'd call out. Nor was he noticed by other well-dressed men hurrying by—lawyers, clergymen, and other abolitionists—who were talking strategy as the Dred Scott case stood before the U.S. Supreme Court, where at long last reason and justice would prevail and slavery would be declared un-American.

Late in 1857 someone did notice the shabby man selling firewood on the street corner. This man too was doing poorly, his banking career wiped out by that summer's financial panic. Now he was back in St. Louis, the headquarters of the bank he'd worked for, and he settled for managing a horse-drawn streetcar line. The two men had not seen each other for sixteen years, since West Point. The abolitionist lawyers on the street paid no attention as the two men spoke. Now, in the wake of the Dred Scott decision, the abolitionist lawyers had lost their faith that American law would serve cosmic justice.

Over thirty years later a huge funeral procession, the largest ever in St. Louis, would move down this very street, including thousands of Civil War veterans, some in faded blue, many of whom had marched behind this failed banker for a thousand miles through the South, and many of whom had marched behind this shabby wood salesman to Shiloh and Vicksburg and Appomattox. In the funeral procession many of the beating drums were the same drums that had beat on the roads into the South.

Ulysses S. Grant and William T. Sherman first came to St. Louis to serve at Jefferson Barracks, the largest post for the protection of the western frontier. Grant too would have ended up buried in St. Louis if the presidency hadn't snagged him. Grant had married a local girl and when he got tired of being stationed as far away from his wife and children as California, he resigned from the army and returned to St. Louis to try farming. He cleared some land adjacent to his wife's parents' home and built a log cabin. He called the place "Hardscrabble," and the name proved too true. After several years of misfortune Grant was reduced to cutting wood.

I pulled up at the Grant home, actually the home of his wife's parents, to which the Grants had moved after a few months in the log cabin. It was a very nice house for the 1840s frontier. It was a plantation house. Grant's father-in-law had moved out from Maryland and was loudly pro-Southern. The house was called White Haven. In the middle of Grant's financial distress his father-in-law gave Grant a slave, who on the slave market could have fetched $1,000. But Grant had been standing on the street corner long enough—promising how much explosively hot fire was hidden inside a rustic little log from an old plantation called White Haven—to have heard all the despairing and angry talk when the Dred Scott decision was announced. Grant went to the courthouse and filed papers to set his slave free. Already he heard the beating of the drums, the drums, the drums.

It was nearly time for the debate.

The field house at Washington University was named for David R. Francis, who as president of the 1904 world's fair helped raise money to build a gym and stadium for Olympic events. Francis had been a Democratic mayor of St. Louis and governor of Missouri, and as governor he faced a situation very similar to that of a century later, in which a St. Louis liberal tried to hold back the zealotry of Missouri's religious crusaders. Francis forced out of office a president of the University of Missouri who was hiring faculty and staff only if they fit his own conservative religious views and imposing his moral standards on the private lives of students. Francis became nationally famous for suppressing one of America's most infamous outbursts of vigilante justice, the Bald Knobbers. This story is worth pausing over because the Bald Knobbers were led by an ardent Christian preacher from Springfield, and memories and passions of the Bald Knobbers still ran strong half a century later when John Ashcroft was growing up in Springfield.

To this day if you ask people in the Ozarks about the Bald Knobbers you'll get contradictory answers about who were the good guys and who were the bad guys. But Bald Knobber legends live on. The center of Bald Knobber action was Taney County, its courthouse burned and a sheriff named Branson murdered. Bald Knobbers were still alive in 1959 when Branson's first music show called itself the Bald Knobbers, which is still going strong today. At the Branson Imax theater you can watch masked Bald Knobbers galloping through the night with rifles and torches and lynch ropes, terrorizing the countryside. Or was it, as the Bald Knobbers Theater website insists, just a case of bringing justice to the scum of society? At their peak the Bald Knobbers had a thousand members, and for years they rode and shot and burned and lynched and whipped and looted, and riding against them were anti-Bald Knobbers in a virtual civil war.

It was, in fact, the same continuation of the Civil War that produced Jesse James. The Civil War went on even longer in the Ozarks, with its isolation and clannishness and the same do-it-yourself tradition in justice that it had in hunting, faith healing, and Pentecostal religion. The Bald Knobbers were mainly Republican Union men and many of their targets were ex-Confederates who chafed at the new world order, but several other elements got mixed into the conflict. Bald Knobber leader Nathaniel Kinney said he was waging a Christian crusade against godless immoral hillbillies, a large portion of whom lived together unmarried. Many of the anti-Bald Knobbers were solid citizens who objected to the mere idea of vigilantism and thought that the Bald Knobbers were just ruffians entirely out of control. Various political and family rivalries got mixed in, and then the whole thing took on a mindless Hatfields-McCoy feud-and-revenge momentum.

When David Francis became governor in 1889 Missouri had just received a huge international dose of bad press over Kinney being murdered and avenged. Newspapers in Europe were tisking at the barbaric Americans, and even Westerners with their own ongoing vigilante traditions were looking down on the crazy Missouri hillbillies. Francis dreamed of making St. Louis a world-class city worthy of hosting an Olympics, a world's fair, a national political convention (in 1888 the Democrats met in St. Louis and read all about the anarchy in the Ozarks), or for that matter a presidential debate. Francis was embarrassed by the Ozarks violence and moved to put a stop to it. The previous governor had passed the buck on four Bald Knobbers waiting on death row for murdering a man who called Bald Knobbers "sheep killin' dogs." Now appeals for clemency poured in upon Francis, including from a majority of state legislators. But Francis declared that the death sentences were justified and let them go through, and the Ozarks realized it couldn't go on living in its own little world of religious self-righteousness and vigilante justice.

Or could it? I refuse to take the too-facile bait of comparing the Bald Knobbers with Ashcroft-style justice, but at least it's legitimate to point out that whereas in the 1880s a religious crusader from Springfield, Missouri, had only some hillbilly hollows as his field of action, in 2001 a religious crusader from Springfield was readily given the whole country as his field of action.

David Francis' experience with the Bald Knobbers may have served him poorly later on. In 1916 the Democrats met again in St. Louis and sent Woodrow Wilson off to World War One, and Wilson sent Francis off to Moscow as ambassador, just in time for the Russian Revolution. When the czar was overthrown Francis envisioned Russia as a great new force for liberal democracy, and he saw the Bolsheviks as just street rabble, Russian Bald Knobbers, who would soon be defeated by liberalism. Most historians portray Francis as being seriously over his head as ambassador, uncomprehending the magnitude of events unfolding around him. A legend sprang up about Francis standing with a revolver in the door of the American embassy and Lenin leading a mob to storm the embassy, but Francis declared that he would shoot the first man to cross the doorway and then he engaged Lenin in a debate about the virtues of American democracy and Lenin, outmatched, withdrew. The part about Francis standing with a gun in the door was true, but Lenin never showed up for a debate; he was in too big a hurry to the wasteland.

The moderator started the debate with "Good evening from the field house at Washington University in St. Louis," and President Bush and Senator Kerry smiled for the camera. Bush was being especially careful to smile since in the first debate the camera constantly caught him scowling as Kerry spoke, as if no one had any right to question him.

In the town-hall format one voter asked Bush about his criteria for filling the next vacancy on the Supreme Court. Bush's answer was a source of nationwide puzzlement. The leading theory about his answer was that during Bush's debate preparation an aide had tried to throw in a St. Louis history connection, but Bush garbled it. In answering that he would appoint a strict constructionist who "would not allow their personal opinion to get in the way of the law," Bush said: "Another example would be the Dred Scott case, which is where judges, years ago, said that the constitution allowed slavery because of personal property rights. That's a personal opinion. That's not what the constitution says. The constitution of the United States says we're all—you know, it doesn't say that. It doesn't speak to the equality of America."

Bush seemed proud of himself for knowing about this important history stuff, even stuff that happened—you know, years ago. But every single Washington University law school freshman, Republicans included, was thinking *What the hell?* and every African-American faculty member and student and janitor was thinking *What the hell?* and maybe even Chancellor William H. Danforth was thinking *What the hell?* Bush had not only mangled one of the most crucial Supreme Court cases in American history, he had done so right here in a field house named for the David Francis who had suppressed one of the most crucial cases of vigilantism in American history which was centered in the only county in America proudly named for Chief Justice Roger B. Taney whose Dred Scott decision condemned Taney County itself into a long anarchy; he had done so right here in a university founded by the very abolitionists who had pushed the Dred Scott case to the Supreme Court; he had done so right here a few miles from where Dred Scott lay buried and where the skull of William T. Sherman still bore the shadows cast by the fires of Atlanta; he had done so right here in the city where Ulysses S. Grant might have lived out his years peddling firewood to the lawyers and clergy who had emerged victorious in the Dred Scott case and had their faith in American democracy proudly reaffirmed. Was President Bush speaking in tongues?

Now, innocence can be a wonderful thing. Take, for instance, the innocence of children's poetry. The lawyer who defended Dred Scott, Roswell Field, had a son named Eugene Field who wrote famous charming children's poetry, such as "Wynken, Blynken, and Nod." William Greenleaf Eliot's grandson wrote famous charming children's poetry about cats. Maybe T. S. Eliot even had a sense of humor as he was writing *The Waste Land*: there's a St. Louis-born African-American poet Quincy Troupe who swears that even in *The Waste Land* he can hear the whimsical rhythms of the local ragtime music Eliot enjoyed as a youth. But maybe it's not quite so charming if your fathers and grandfathers led the charge for American democracy and all you are doing is writing children's poetry as you sit in an elite British club and speak in a phony British accent. And maybe it's even less charming if while you are writing children's poetry a humorless sect is emerging from the hillbilly hollows of the only county in America proudly named for Roger B. Taney and taking over America's airwaves and setting tongues-sanctified members at the cabinet table and helping to elect a president who lives inside a whole universe of children's poetry, of national innocence.

So we're going to pause the debate right here and conduct a little tutorial on the Dred Scott case, George. You see, the whole problem was that the constitution *didn't* say nearly enough about "the equality of America" and nothing at all about the equality of blacks. Southerners just like Roger B. Taney had made sure of that when the constitution was written. They didn't want dreamers like Thomas Jefferson, who had replaced the British "life, liberty, and property" with "life, liberty, and the pursuit of happiness," trying to take away their property so their property could go pursue happiness. That's why the constitution had to be amended to outlaw slavery and say that blacks were now considered to be humans and not just property. That's why it took a terrible Civil War to get to the point where people like William Greenleaf Eliot could change the constitution. It wasn't just Roger B. Taney's personal opinion that slaves were property, it was the law of the land, or at least half the land. We are explaining all this, George, because we'd find it more reassuring if the man who controlled the powerful apparatus of world democracy and the American military had some comprehension of why democracy succeeds or fails and why terrible wars happen.

But it's so charming to live inside a universe of children's poetry. Both David Francis and Mark Twain showed up to dedicate a plaque on the home of lawyer Roswell Field who defended Dred Scott, but not for his sake, for the sake of his son Eugene's charming children's poetry. After the ceremony Eugene's brother told Mark Twain that the plaque was actually wrong; Eugene wasn't born here but a few blocks away. Twain replied that it didn't matter what the historical facts were, from now on Eugene Field was born in this house. This is the way national myths work too. The facts are less important than what people want to believe, and often what they want to believe is charming children's poetry.

Another voter said to Bush that her mother had just returned from overseas and was "shocked...at the intensity of aggravation that other countries had with how we handled the Iraq situation."

"People love America," Bush answered from the land of children's poetry. "We've got a great country. I love our values. And I recognize I've made some decisions that have caused people to not understand the great values of our country...I remember when Ronald Reagan was the president; he stood on principle. Somebody called that stubborn. He stood on principle standing up to the Soviet Union, and we won that conflict." We're still in Dred Scott historyland: the Soviets didn't just fail, we won because we were great in our righteousness. Later on Bush gave several summaries of the pure longtime faith in America's destiny to save the world. The long-term way to defeat the terrorists "is to spread freedom. Liberty can change habits." In almost his last words in the debate he appealed to "our deep faith in liberty. And we'll continue to promote freedom around the world. Freedom is on the march."

Bush's words were much like the words of the New England abolitionists in their pure simple faith in God-guaranteed and America-implemented human destiny. Perhaps William Greenleaf Eliot had shared this faith when he came out to St. Louis, but then he measured it against the realities of Tara and saw this moral confidence leading to a terrible war and a long tragedy of white persecution and black destitution. After all the traumas that had befallen this faith—the Civil War, American apartheid, the Gilded Age, Wounded Knee, American imperialism in Latin America and beyond, World War One, the Great Depression, the Cold War, McCarthyism, Vietnam, a new Gilded Age without factory jobs, and now Iraq—wasteland liberals had abandoned this faith and its poetry, but still it moved onward, driven by all the momentum of national success. Bush now commanded all the power and poetry of this faith. It really didn't matter that Bush was a lightweight both as a historian and spokesman, for the heavy weight of American myth was on his side. Bush didn't need to have "the vision thing" because centuries of history had supplied it for him. All he needed to do was to pay homage to it and to portray John Kerry as weak on it, a lightweight on American righteousness and destiny. The genius of the Bush attack on Kerry as a flip-flopper was that most people "got it" as meaning Kerry had no deep unquestioning faith in American righteousness and destiny. This was what the election was ultimately all about: do you stand with centuries of American myth and poetry, success and righteousness, or do you doubt it and deny it?

And what's a John Kerry supposed to say? A John Kerry is trapped, because when he points out all the shortcomings of American policy, all the world's doubts and disappointments in America, he is only proving Bush's case that he is a doubter and denier of American myth and success and righteousness. But Kerry spent most of the debate simply being negative about Bush policies. Kerry also didn't "get it" and tried to rebut the flip-flopper attack by addressing the minutia of the specific charges, rather than addressing the larger implication that he was a doubter and denier of American myth. Instead of addressing the basic reality that Bush was living in a universe of children's poetry, it was as if Kerry was saying "Mr. Field, you sent Wynken, Blynken and Nod sailing off in a wooden shoe without any exit strategy for bringing them home," or "Mr. Eliot, the budget projections of Mr. Mistoffelees the conjuring cat are unrealistically optimistic." It didn't address the deeper unrealities of American national poetry. Indeed it was a concession to unrealities being real. At one point, after Bush listed his environmental progress, Kerry was so exasperated that he did directly challenge Bush reality/unreality: "Boy, to listen to that—the president, I don't think, is living in a world of reality with respect to the environment. Now, if you're a Red Sox fan, that's okay. But if you're a president, it's not." But then Kerry had to attack the myth of the ever-more and declare his faith in science. Even the Red Sox would win this year, but attacking American myth and Noah's Ark creationism in one bite was still a losing proposition.

How could anyone address the basic unrealities and realities of American myth? Perhaps by offering an alternative affirmation of American purpose, a liberal version of American myth, which wasn't necessarily anything new. You could start by reminding Mr. Field and Mr. Eliot that their father and grandfather had once dreamed of greater things than cute cats sailing off in wooden shoes. But Kerry offered almost nothing of mythic vision in the debate. In his closing statement he offered "I believe America's best days are ahead of us," and that was about all. For someone who had been inspired by the ringing phrases and confidence of John F. Kennedy, this was thin soup. The best lack all conviction, while the worst…The political commentators would say that Kerry won the debate, but they were counting the intellectual points scored, while much of the American public was keeping score in mythological points.

Much of the public noticed that while Kerry's final words were "Thank you," Bush's final words were "God Bless." This was almost a summary of their entire worldviews. Kerry was living in a world whose goal was for humans to treat each other kindly. This was also the world of William Greenleaf Eliot, though he was more confident that the goal of a kind society had God's mandate. Like W. G. Eliot, G. W. Bush believed that God intended America to redeem the world, but this was an altogether different kind of redemption, one that fully welcomed the ending of the world. That Sunday in the only county in America proudly named for Roger B. Taney and all over America, preachers would be telling their flocks to vote for a man who believed in more than human things and human choice, a man blessed by God to bring God's blessings upon America. The preachers couldn't name names, but everyone knew who they meant.

11

Downward the Course of Empire Takes its Way

Not just places, but moments of history can offer an expansive view.

We had a great view from here high up on Capitol Hill in Des Moines, Iowa. It was a few days before the election, which looked very close, and Iowa was one of the closest states, so John Kerry was holding a rally on the Capitol grounds. The podium faced west, looking out towards the downtown and the prairie and the archetypal direction of American destiny.

The stairwell inside the Iowa Capitol building is dominated by a massive mural, fourteen feet high and forty feet wide, called *Westward*. It features a covered wagon and a band of pioneers heading west, with angel-like spirits in the sky leading them onward, giving their blessing to America's heroic story and purpose. *Westward* is Iowa's version of a great mural in the U. S. Capitol building, *Westward the Course of Empire Takes its Way*.

The painter of *Westward the Course of Empire Takes its Way*, Emanuel Leutze, is best known for *Washington Crossing the Delaware*, one of the most iconic scenes of American history. Yet Leutze was a German and painted *Washington Crossing the Delaware* in Germany as a commentary on German politics. Leutze painted it in 1849, the year after the German democratic revolutions had failed and as German monarchs were retaliating against democratic reformers. Leutze was a passionate liberal. Among the most repressive German monarchs were the Hessians. During the American Revolution the Hessians had dispatched mercenaries to aid the British; it was to attack the Hessian army that Washington crossed the Delaware. In *Washington Crossing the Delaware* Leutze showed German monarchy its coming fate before the inevitable world tide of democracy. The bold and proud George Washington wasn't just an American hero but a symbol of the nobility of democratic ideals. Like most European liberals, Leutze looked to America as the leader of human redemption and progress. In 1859 Leutze gave up on Germany and emigrated to America. Ironically, one of his versions of *Washington Crossing the Delaware* remained in Germany and was destroyed in World War Two as American and Nazi armies fought over German despotism.

Leutze arrived in America at a dark moment for liberal faith in America, for America was on the verge of civil war. Ironically, one of Leutze's first portrait commissions was to paint Chief Justice Roger B. Taney, whose decision in the Dred Scott case had plunged liberals into despair and pushed America toward war. Leutze's portrait of Taney makes quite a contrast with the heroism of his George Washington and of the Union generals he would soon he painting. Leutze's disdain for Taney is almost palpable. He gives Taney cadaverous cheeks, a beady vacuous stare, skeletal hands, deep wrinkles, and he wraps Taney in shadows.

The popularity of *Washington Crossing the Delaware* soon won Leutze a commission for a mural in the stairwell of the still-rising U. S. Capitol. Leutze started work on it in 1861, with Confederate armies not far away and the nation's future in severe doubt. Leutze wanted to offer an image of America triumphantly fulfilling its democratic destiny, and he selected an image of a wagon train struggling to the top of a Rocky Mountain ridge, with a coonskin-capped scout on the crest hailing the abundant lands waiting beyond. Significantly, one of the pioneers is a black man, apparently a freed slave. He is leading a donkey on which rides an Irish-looking woman holding a child, an emigrant Madonna, suggesting that America was a Biblical promised land for the poor and oppressed. For a title Leutze took a line from a 1752 poem by George Berkeley which hailed a great future for a still-British America. Yet for Leutze the "Empire" wasn't just a conquest of the land for the sake of wealth and power, but a god-given mission of redeeming the world.

Westward the Course of Empire Takes its Way inspired many imitations, but they didn't necessarily share Leutze's liberal values. A few years later Andrew Melrose painted *Westward the Star of Empire Takes its Way—Near Council Bluffs, Iowa*. Council Bluffs was the start of the intercontinental railroad, and the Star of Empire was just the headlight of a locomotive. In 1868 Currier and Ives produced *Across the Continent: Westward the Course of Empire Takes its Way*, and here too the main actor was a train.

The *Westward* in the Iowa Capitol was painted forty years after Leutze's mural, but its sense of American destiny was as strong as ever. Fittingly for Iowa, its pioneers are marching across a flat terrain with tall corn. The color scheme and shadows are meant to show the pioneers heading into the sunset. The female spirits floating in front of the pioneers represent Enlightenment and Civilization, and one scatters seeds to symbolize the coming of agriculture to the wilderness. Two floating female spirits follow the covered wagon and hold a steam engine and an electric dynamo to symbolize the coming of American technology. After a century the mural is faded, just like American myths.

From the Iowa Capitol a stairway leads down the hill to another *Westward*, a bronze statue of two scouts in buckskin, one looking like Buffalo Bill and holding his hand to shield his eyes as he stares westward. One scout holds an ax, the other a rifle.

Today as the scouts contemplated the West and American destiny they were also seeing the Kerry rally, part of the democratic ritual by which America regularly reconsiders its identity and destiny. The largest question being considered in this election, usually unspoken but implicit in even small policy matters, was whether the sense of national mission and greatness represented in *Westward* and *Westward the Course of Empire Takes its Way* was still valid. George W. Bush insisted that it was, that American horizons were still unlimited, that the old pioneering spirit would always find new natural resources and technologies and prosperity, that the American Dream was still fully real, and that the rest of the world still looked to America as the beacon of hope for the world. John Kerry was paying nervous homage to the iconography of *Westward*, especially by emphasizing his military heroism, yet his basic message was that something had gone wrong with this iconography, that America's sense of itself was out of touch with reality, that American society was going the wrong way, and that the rest of the democratic world was very disappointed in our leadership of it.

This was the same message I'd heard John Kerry giving a third of a century before, yet then it was more of a warning and now it included regret for decades misdirected and lost; back then Kerry spoke with more urgency and moral earnestness, expecting Americans to recognize obvious truths and to make changes, and now he spoke more warily, fully aware of the power and inertia of national myth and of the punishment aimed at those who challenged it.

Yet I felt reason for hope. I liked being back here in Iowa for the finish of the campaign because I'd been here when the campaign began, when Kerry's victory in the Iowa caucus in January propelled him toward the Democratic nomination. In a few days we'd be gathering in the same hotel ballroom where we'd celebrated Kerry's caucus victory, where Ted Kennedy had been our cheerleader and where Kerry had invited the national TV audience to "stand with me" in a long list of hopeful goals for America. Being back here seemed like the completion of a circle, a circle of hope.

I'd spent many weeks working in the Iowa caucus campaign and ended up feeling good about the workings of American democracy. Iowa is one of the last places in America where Jeffersonian town-hall democracy is still quite alive. Iowa voters take very seriously their responsibility for selecting a president and they do their homework diligently, going out to cafes and senior centers to hear and question the candidates. I had numerous long conversations with Iowans and was impressed by the conscientiousness of their thinking about the historical moment, their sense that some basic matters of America's identity and role in the world had been thrown open to question, and their thinking about which candidate best fit the historical moment.

By all historical standards, John Kerry shouldn't have had a chance of winning the Iowa caucus. Measuring from 1976, when Jimmy Carter turned the Iowa caucus from a peripheral warm-up into a major event, no Northeastern candidate of either party had won the Iowa caucus. This suggests some sort of cultural boundary between the prairie and the Northeast, and a century of presidential elections confirms this boundary. Eight times the Democrats ran prairie populists for president—Bryan, Stevenson, Humphrey, McGovern, and Mondale—and eight times they lost, often disastrously. By contrast the Democrats were usually successful running Northeastern sophisticates (Wilson, FDR, Kennedy) or Southern down-home moderates: Truman, Johnson, Carter, Clinton, Gore. This cultural boundary between the prairie and the rest of America is partly due to liberalism taking different forms according to different historical experiences. On the prairie liberalism was a larger form of Jeffersonian neighborliness in which the natural order of society was friendly and cooperative, leaving a William Jennings Bryan flying into righteous outrage over corporate violations of neighborliness. But in the industrial Northeast no one was shocked by an unfair social order, and the purpose of liberalism there was to intervene in an inherently unfair jungle and redistribute the opportunities and wealth. Even Northeastern liberals found prairie liberalism to be soft and impractical. Yet in 2004 this boundary fell away because of September 11 and Iraq, which rendered the differences between the Northeast and the prairie unimportant and defined Iowans as Americans first, Americans facing a problematic national identity. Iowans decided that Kerry, as a war hero and a Euro-sophisticate with a long, conscious concern for America's misplaced role in the world, was the best fit for the historical moment. I was encouraged at seeing the national unconscious at work, groping for an answer.

Yet I'd also seen abundant signs of the national unconscious failing, especially in the intense hostility of Vietnam vets against Kerry after a third of a century, still refusing to consider that he might have been right. This hostility was echoed by hostility against anyone who doubted American destiny in Iraq. The tone and the very phrases of the campaign repeatedly gave me déjà vu, throwing me back to 1972, leaving me wondering if I would soon be completing a different circle, a circle leading me back to another election-night ballroom in which we'd hoped for a Kerry victory but ended up with a crushing defeat. It would be a circle of failure in which America had been trapped for decades now.

Which circling of history would be completed on November 2? I started watching for signs.

If you wanted to find a symbol of the unhealed wounds of Vietnam, it didn't take much imagination to see it in Max Cleland. A few hours after John Kerry addressed the crowd on the Iowa Capitol grounds, Max Cleland wheeled himself into Kerry headquarters to give the workers a pep talk. The wheels of his wheelchair went round and round like a nation stuck in a vicious circle. Cleland had lost both legs and one arm in Vietnam and come home in despair, but then he'd heard John Kerry articulating his own regrets about the war and felt more hopeful. Cleland became the director of the Veterans Administration and then a U. S. senator, but he was defeated for re-election in 2002 when his opponent smeared him as unpatriotic and weak on defense. Cleland's defeat sent him into new despair about how stupidly America was managing its fate, but Kerry's presidential campaign had given him fresh hope and he'd become an enthusiastic campaigner.

A minute after Cleland came in, a volunteer came in the door and I explained that Max Cleland had "just walked in." I quickly caught my inexact phrasing and was about to correct myself, but I let it stand. I let Cleland stand tall.

Cleland was probably thinking of his own experience when he started talking about the tens of millions of dollars of attack ads against John Kerry, implying his disloyalty to America.

In one respect the attack ads against Cleland and Kerry and other liberals were correct: they were indeed being disloyal to America, or at least to an old sense of American destiny that was now well on its way to becoming little more than a crude nationalism, a self-righteousness increasingly detached from the democratic hopes that first gave rise to it.

For Emanuel Leutze and other frustrated European democrats, America had every right to the heroic and righteous imagery of *Washington Crossing the Delaware* and *Westward the Course of Empire Takes its Way*. America was unquestionably the only hope for the world. If many Europeans found American self-righteousness to be obnoxious, wasn't this just because they were monarchists? By 1914 France and Britain were democracies and willing to put up with America's sense of superiority in exchange for help in the world wars, victories that only strengthened America's sense of destiny. In the Cold War, when the alternative to America was a Stalinist nightmare, Europeans didn't hold America to the highest standards, overlooking matters like racism. But the end of the Cold War allowed a fresh perspective. Compared with European social democracies, America was now among the most retarded of democracies. America retained little moral authority for leading the world. Yet the outcome of the Cold War left American self-righteousness stronger than ever. There was now a severe discrepancy between America's self-image and its image for the rest of the world and hard realities like Iraq. When American liberals tried to point out this discrepancy, even meekly and while waving American flags, they aroused the power and wrath of the old self-righteousness. How many disasters and how much global disrespect would it take before Americans realized that their self-image was now floating in limbo? Or would this self-righteousness prove so powerful that it overrode everything else and defined America mainly by an arrogant nationalism? Could America break out of its vicious circle?

Max Cleland seemed to think so. He talked about how it was here in Iowa that Kerry's campaign had taken off and it would be Iowa that brought it to a final success.

When Cleland was finished talking I went up to thank him, and to my surprise he said he remembered me from the Iowa caucus victory celebration. Cleland had been up on the ballroom stage that night, a stage that didn't have a handicap ramp. Some firefighters had lifted him onto the stage, and now as people filed out of the ballroom it wasn't clear who was going to lift him back down. I had thanked Cleland for his efforts, and Cleland insisted on giving me a hug. Since he didn't have two arms to hug with, he tried to make up for it by hugging me much more vigorously with one arm. I felt the vicious circle and the wound of a nation reaching for healing and completion.

Now Cleland said that since he wouldn't be here on election night he was going to give me a victory hug right now, and he did. I said I wasn't so sure about victory. It was scary that after a third of a century Kerry had stirred up such deep resentments over Vietnam. Cleland agreed: it went so deep. We agreed that if Kerry won it would represent a national healing.

I enjoyed talking with voters but I'd done far too much of it over the phone and not in person, so I was eager to get out on the street and meet voices that actually had faces and clothes and houses that explained their whole lives and gave context to their political viewpoints. The next day, a classic crisp autumn day with rainbow leaves raining down and swirling, I was going door-to-door in

Marshalltown. I was accompanied by Carol, a lawyer from Washington D. C. who'd never been to the Midwest and was delighted with many of the Mayberry realities of Marshalltown, such as the home-cooking cafes. But now she was puzzled by one thing. She'd always heard that in small-town Iowa people left their doors unlocked, but we were finding that nearly every screen/storm door was locked. I told her that this was quite a contrast with the usually unlocked doors of Des Moines. Carol surmised why the doors of Marshalltown were locked, and the answer offered a symbol of the increasingly locked doors to the American Dream.

Until recently the largest employer in Marshalltown was an automotive parts factory, with 2,500 good-paying UAW jobs. But most of these jobs had been shipped overseas. Now the largest employer was a pork processing plant, which paid much less than UAW jobs and couldn't support old mortgages. Many UAW workers had left town. But the Iowa pork industry was thriving, largely because of gigantic corporate hog lots that put family farms out of business and caused massive sewage runoff pollution problems. The Marshalltown pork plant tried hiring local workers but the wages and benefits were so poor and the work so dangerous and disgusting that Americans didn't consider it a rung on the ladder of the American Dream and preferred clerking at Wal-Mart. The worker void drew in Mexicans, and the Mexican population of Marshalltown rose between 1990 and 2000 from 292 to 3,523, to 13% of the population. Many of these Mexicans were illegals, but even after the authorities raided the factory and expelled the illegals, whites refused to take their jobs, viewing them as lifetime poverty traps.

The neighborhood with the locked doors was a pleasant suburban all-white neighborhood.

We also went door-to-door in the Mexican neighborhood, where many of the houses and apartments were tiny and badly run-down and packed with large families. Repeatedly we approached residences where our year-old voter list gave white names, only to find Mexicans, Mexicans often very reluctant to talk with us, not because of any language barrier but because they were illegals and fearful of white people bearing lists. This fear also meant that the illegals would never rock the boat at work by complaining about conditions. Carol had worked as a poverty lawyer on the Texas border and said that by Mexican standards these were good jobs and houses. Didn't this mean, as conservatives insisted, that America was still the land of opportunity, just as it had been for our ancestors who started out with nothing and worked their way up the ladder of the American Dream? Didn't this mean that America was still the envy of the world? But in the nineteenth century the world's poor had to immigrate here for American jobs; now the jobs were immigrating to the poor. Many rungs were being chopped off the ladder of the American Dream, leaving large gaps, gaps crossable only by money. For decades America had been becoming more economically polarized, with the richest top controlling more and more wealth and thus power, including the power to cut wages and benefits and government programs and to send jobs abroad, even as the rich proclaimed the undiminished reality and *Westward* glory of the American Dream.

I was having another flashback; a circle was trying to complete itself. I'd spent the final days of the 1972 campaign going door-to-door in the tenements of Lowell, talking with voters whom our lists said were Democrats, but over and over they were giving me cold stares if not outright hostility. I couldn't even get through by talking about health insurance to poor elderly invalids. It wasn't just the rich who didn't want to hear that the American Dream could become unreal. The Lowell slums hadn't been moving *Westward* for decades but still the iconography of *Westward* remained powerful. One evening when I got back to our headquarters the campaign manager called me into his office and asked me what was going on out there. I was puzzled: the campaign had spent a fortune on sophisticated polling, so why on earth did he need a report from me? I told him about all the cold stares and hostile comments from blue-collar Democrats, and he quietly nodded, for I was giving a hard reality to abstract poll numbers. Now in 2004 I was still seeing too many of those cold stares.

At long last Election Day was here. All over the country people were waking up with relief or disbelief that the endless campaign was finally ending. To the polls each person carried in his or her head a little image of America, of what America was and what it was supposed to be, of heroes and events, triumphs and failures, rules and violations, needs and grievances. This was all America really was, an agreed-upon set of images in millions of heads, images renegotiated every four years. Presidential campaigns tried to fit candidates into those images in ways that made people feel good. Usually candidates became so absorbed in imagery that they ceased being entirely real people, and it always remained an art and a mystery how the realities/unrealities of candidates would mix with the realities/unrealities of people's images of America and turn into the realities/unrealities of feeling good and voting one way or another. This mystery was further complicated by the great diversity of Americans and their images of America. Heading to the polls this morning were Gloucester fishermen and Hopi farmers, Ozark Pentecostals and Santa Fe Catholics, Orthodox rabbis and Malibu surfer girls, Montana cowboys and San Francisco artists, Houston oil executives and

Boulder mountain lovers, Mississippi plantation heirs and Detroit survivors of slavery, veterans of D-Day heroism and of September 11 horror. By tonight all of this would add up into some big numbers and a freshly sanctioned official image of America.

I had expected to spend the day in the madhouse headquarters, but a *USA Today* reporter was looking for a story and I encouraged her to go door-to-door with one of our precinct captains, Elizabeth Hendrix. Back in the caucus campaign Elizabeth had been featured in a Kerry TV ad about health care. Elizabeth was a cancer patient whose husband had died and whose job was outsourced and who had to choose between losing her health insurance and losing her house, and who had three young sons to care for. Still fearful of dying, she wanted to make some difference in the world, so she'd started coming into Kerry headquarters to phone voters about health-care issues, and she found that she so enjoyed talking with people about their problems that she decided to pursue a new career as a hospital chaplain. But this morning the Iowa Kerry media staffers were hesitant about sending a national reporter out alone with Elizabeth; since Elizabeth had been in a campaign ad there was a risk of her showing up in *USA Today* as "a Kerry campaign spokesperson," probably blasting Bush over health care. By now the Iowa media staffers had seen me chaperoning the national press at three Iowa events, so they decided that if I'd chaperone the *USA Today* reporter it would be safe.

Most of the screen doors we tried were unlocked. Elizabeth's hair had grown back after her chemotherapy but she was still low in energy, and today she was struggling to breathe and tiring visibly as the hours passed. I stuck with her even after the reporter left. I was fascinated by the faces and words of America deciding what America was.

We rang one doorbell and had nearly left when a man stumbled up to the door. His stance was awkward, his head rolling and rotating out of control, his smile exaggerated, his speech full of hesitations. He had Parkinson's disease. Elizabeth soon got him talking about health care in America. He was paying $500 a month for health insurance, and a lot more for other medical expenses. He fully supported John Kerry's stand on stem cell research, which offered hope for Parkinson's disease but which Bush had bottled up to please the religious right. Yet he couldn't stand John Kerry. He had spent thirty years in the military and served all over the world, including Korea and Berlin. He'd seen lots of stupidity in the military, including having a good friend die of friendly fire in Vietnam. But he had a big problem with how Kerry had come home from Vietnam and dishonored his fellow soldiers and thrown away his medals.

Elizabeth and I looked at one another in silent recognition. Here in one person was the whole impasse of America, so absorbed in its pride that it couldn't face its failures or its human needs. "America" was so wrapped up in his heroic military identity that he would vote to cripple himself. Elizabeth and I felt a symbolic challenge that went well beyond the value of winning one vote. Since "America" said he was still undecided, we spent nearly an hour trying to coax him to recognition.

Elizabeth had spent years working for big insurance companies, one of Des Moines' biggest industries, so she offered an insider's perspectives on the flaws of the American insurance and health care system, and a victim's perspective on the social toll it was taking. Yet Elizabeth triggered another patriotic pride, for "America" started insisting that free enterprise was the ultimate social value, that insurance companies had to make a profit and had every right to raise rates and cut off clients and cut benefits and lay off employees. Elizabeth had been laid off by an insurance company while she had cancer. She and I looked at one another in silent dismay. "America" was so lonely that he loved talking with us and didn't want us to leave, yet his words were defending mass loneliness and vulnerability. When we finally left, "America" still said he was undecided, and Elizabeth and I agreed we'd come back later, but we ran out of time.

At another house we tried to persuade a guy with a scruffy beard and a beat-up pickup, who was in a rage over Des Moines not having a NASCAR track. He was on our voter list but said he didn't vote because money ruled the world, and then he pointed to heaven and said that God ruled the world. He had served in Vietnam, fueling jet fighters, and dismissed the war as a foolish waste of time. I tried to pursue this lead by asking him about Iraq, but he declared—his eyes wide and arms wide—that those people weren't human, they beheaded people and blew themselves up and didn't care about human life, so we ought to take the bomb—THE BOMB—and wipe them all off the face of the earth. We gave up and moved on.

If I had been flirting with time warps in this campaign, then at sunset, at a house only a block from Elizabeth's house, I arrived at the Twilight Zone itself. I found some friends from my hometown in Missouri, whom I hadn't seen in thirty years. We had worked together in the 1970 congressional campaign of an antiwar candidate, challenging the chairman of the House un-American Activities Committee. Mary and Dale looked eerily like their old selves, if with more gray hair. As I introduced Elizabeth to them, it turned out that Mary had taught Greek at the same Iowa college where Elizabeth had studied Greek. Dale taught theology and Elizabeth had a theology degree. We talked, rather theologically, about American politics, in 1970 and today.

This Twilight Zone sent me back to why I had first taken an interest in John Kerry. I had put my heart into that 1970 Missouri campaign, and on the night we lost, the candidate told me that he'd never really expected to win. I was dismayed by this revelation and vowed that in the future I'd work only for candidates who might achieve something. It would be even better to help start off the career of someone who would make a difference for a long time to come. It would be best of all, it would be great fun, to help start off the career of a future president of the United States. I fully realized the opaqueness of the crystal ball for predicting future presidents. Yet in 1972 when I was considering where to find the most future for my efforts, I looked at John Kerry and decided: he's got what it takes. I got on a Greyhound bus in Missouri and rode two days to Massachusetts and spent the next five months there.

More important than having a future, Kerry had the right spirit. Like many of my generation I was inspired by the Kennedys, by their eloquence and their summoning of youthful idealism to change the world. By 1972 there were quite a few Kennedy impersonators around, politicians who could do the Camelot style but who didn't have much substance to offer. It was clear that John Kerry too had been inspired by the Kennedys, but he seemed like the real deal. During the 1972 campaign I always paid special attention when John Kerry started quoting Robert Kennedy about ripples of hope adding up to change the world, for Kerry quoted this with a special conviction, with real passion. During the Iowa caucus campaign in the fall of 2003 Kerry was floundering, partly because he'd gotten a bad case of front runner's syndrome and was trying to be bland so as not to offend anyone, and thus he wasn't inspiring anyone either. But occasionally I saw the old John Kerry come out of hiding and connect deeply with an audience. Three times I saw Kerry make stops at colleges sandwiched between other stops. In his antiwar years Kerry often spoke to college audiences, and now in 2003 the youthful faces prompted him to talk about his youthful political inspirations, about the Kennedys and Martin Luther King and the first Earth Day, about opposing a war and committing civil disobedience, and he talked with a passion that riveted the audience. Then Kerry went on to a café full of senior citizens and reverted to caution and blandness. Fortunately when Kerry's prospects got bad enough that he had nothing to lose, he started opening up more and telling Iowans who he was and where he was coming from.

Talking with Mary and Dale about our youthful inspirations opened up in me old memories and hopes, and compressed into one place and moment a third of a century of history. But was this compression good or bad? Did it mean that my youthful idealism was still alive and about to triumph? Or did it mean that for a third of a century America had been stuck in the same vicious circle, that we had gone nowhere at all, had actually lost irredeemable time and ground?

As the day wore on, Elizabeth entirely wore out, yet she forced herself onward into the night.

Finally the polls closed, and there was nothing to do but wait. Hundreds gathered in the ballroom of the Hotel Fort Des Moines, one of those grand old downtown hotels where presidents stayed and where a city gathered for special events. We watched the returns coming in from the east coast, spottily and then solidly, fairly close, fairly close to expectations, turning one state blue, another red. With every state awarded blue for Kerry there was a big cheer. But as the returns moved westward there was less to cheer about. Kerry was trailing in crucial Ohio. In the national totals he was behind and slowly losing ground. Still, the ballroom was charged with expectation, with a refusal to believe that so much good will could turn out badly. But the South was solid red. The Pentecostals in Missouri were in rapture. Right from the start Iowa was too close to call, and for awhile it seemed that Iowa could decide the whole thing, but the help that Iowa needed to make that difference wasn't materializing from anywhere obvious, and two days later Iowa would still be too close to call. The high plains and the Rockies were solid red. When California went for Kerry there was a huge cheer, but now even if everything else went right it wasn't going to be enough. The Bush supporters on TV were gloating. Our ballroom got quieter and quieter, and people started melting away. The press packed up and left. At midnight the remaining crowd was going into mourning, and at 1:30 in the mourning a Kerry staffer made the rounds and said we'd only rented the ballroom until 1:00 AM so now we had to leave. Wait a minute, I thought, I'd talked with the hotel owner months ago and he'd told me he was secretly giving John Kerry free use of the presidential suite; he wasn't going to kick us out now. But soon everyone had left. The TVs were dark. I was left alone in the huge ballroom.

I was about to leave, but then I looked back at the stage and the podium waiting for a victory cheer that was never going to happen. It was a safe assumption that this was the same podium from which John Kerry had given his victory speech last January. Now the podium looked terribly lonely and sad. For some reason I wandered towards it. I reached the edge of the stage and stepped onto it. Some sad gravity drew me to take my place behind the podium. I put my hands on its rails and stood looking out over the dim deserted ballroom.

I could see them then, and hear them and feel them, a ballroom full of ghosts. I saw a ballroom full of confetti and jubilant faces. I saw Ted Kennedy standing here and cheerleading, and Max Cleland sitting next to me. I saw Teresa waving greetings to old friends in the crowd. But then I looked again and the ballroom was empty. Then I saw the other ghosts, from a third of a century before, a ballroom full of mourning faces, with a fourteen-year-old Caroline Kennedy wandering about, with Julia Kerry waving greetings to old friends in the crowd.

I looked blankly at the blankness, and then I looked beyond it and looked eastward, eastward up the hill to where *Westward* was looking westward down at me, and further to where *Westward the Course of Empire Takes its Way* was looking westward, westward across the Appalachians and the Ohio valley and the Mississippi River and the prairies and the Rockies and the deserts and the Sierras to the sea, always westward. I saw my own circle through a third of a century and how it had turned out to lead nowhere, only right back to where it began. The next morning I'd wake up with a nightmare Groundhog's Day déjà vu, unbelieving that I had relived the same experience again; this time it was worse, for this time America itself had lost. But for now I only stood there with a numb impulse to make some concluding remark. Closure to the circle. Not out loud, of course; I didn't need to get hauled off by a security guard.

I looked wrong-way-ward at *Westward* and conceded, well, it looks like you've won. You had just too much momentum to pause and change your course. Centuries of momentum. Now you'll just keep going straight onward, always westward, mindlessly onward, self-destructively onward. We weren't even trying to stop you. There's so much good in you: the freed slave, the emigrant Madonna, the promised land for the oppressed and poor. You've come so far and done so much good. But this is the way that nations fail, when visions are too compelling to let you see yourself and the world anew. Once you were the hope of the world, but not any more, and maybe it's already too late to be the hope of the world ever again. It's terribly late.

It was terribly late. It was two in the morning. I stepped off the stage and out the door and into the night and tried to leave all the ghosts behind. *Come my friends, tis not too late to seek a newer world.*

Endnotes

1. Quoted in Ronald L. Davis, *Duke: The Life and Image of John Wayne* (Norman, Oklahoma: University of Oklahoma Press, 1998), p. 289.

2. Ralph Waldo Emerson, *The Fortune of the Republic and other American Addresses* (New York: Houghton Mifflin, 1889), p. 18–19.

3. Ibid, p 42.

4. John Steinbeck, *The Grapes of Wrath* (New York: Viking, 1939, 1967), p. 208.

5. This and following quotes from Charles Dickens, *American Notes*, edited by John S Whitley and Arthur Goldman (Baltimore: Penguin, 1972) chapter 4.

6. Jack Kerouac, *Vanity of Duluoz* (New York: Putnam's Sons, 1979), p. 109.

7. Jack Kerouac, *Visions of Gerard* (New York: Farrar, Straus, Giroux, 1963), p. 5

8. Ernest Hemingway, *Selected Letters of Ernest Hemingway,* EH to Mrs. Paul Pfeiffer, August 2, 1937 (New York: Scribner's, 1981), p. 460.

9. quoted, without further reference, in Mason Wiley and Damien Bond, *Inside Oscar: The Unofficial History of the Academy Awards* (New York: Ballentine Books, 1986), p. 93

10. Daniel J. Boorstin, *The Image: A Guide to Pseudo-Events in America* (New York: Atheneum, 25th anniversary edition, 1987), p. 67.

11. Quoted, without further reference, in Mason Wiley and Damien Bond, op cit, p. 93.

12. Quoted, without further reference, in Ronald Kessler, *The Sins of the Father: Joseph P. Kennedy and the Dynasty He Founded* (New York: Warner Books, 1996), p. 204.

13. Joseph P. Kennedy, letter to Harry Cohn, Columbia Pictures, Nov. 12, 1939, in Arthur Krock papers, Princeton University Seely Mudd Library.

14. quoted in Anthony Holden, *Behind the Oscar: The Secret History of the Academy Awards* (New York: Simon and Schuster, 1993), p. 145.

15. quoted, without further reference, in Wiley and Bond, op cit.

16. Jack Newfield, *Robert Kennedy: A Memoir* (New York: E. P. Dutton & co., 1969), p. 300.

17. quoted in Thomas G. Alexander, *Utah: The Right Place, The Official Centennial History* (Salt Lake City: Gibbs Smith, 1995), p. 233.

18. quoted in *The New York Sun*, May 7, 1903.

19. quoted in *Sierra* July/August 1981, p. 7.

20. Grant Wacker, *Heaven Below: Early Pentecostals and American Culture* (Cambridge: Harvard University Press, 2001), p. 20–21.

21. Theodore Roosevelt, *The Rough Riders* (New York, 1923), p. 124.

22. William J. Bennett, *The Book of Virtues*, (New York: Simon and Schuster, 1993), p. 21.

23. Ibid, p. 47.

24. Herbert Hoover, *The Challenge of Liberty*, speech delivered in Denver, Co., Oct. 30, 1936, on website of Herbert Hoover Presidential Library Association.

25. Roger Morris and Sally Denton, *The Money and the Power* (New York: Random House, 2001), p. 176.

26. Felix Eugene Snider and Earl Augustus Collins, *Cape Girardeau: Biography of a City* (Cape Girardeau, Mo: Ramfre Press, 1956).

27. Mark Twain, *The Tragedy of Pudd'nhead Wilson and the Comedy Those Extraordinary Twins* (New York: Oxford University Press, 1996), p. 20

28. Ibid, p. 22

29. Margaret Mitchell, *Gone with the Wind* (New York: Macmillan, 1936), p. 491.

30. Mark Twain, *Life on the Mississippi* (New York: Harper and Brothers, 1902), p. 184.

31. Ibid, p. 290.

32. Ibid, p. 327–328.

33. Mark Twain, op cit, p. 221–223.

34. Snider and Collins, op cit, p. 319.

35. Mark Twain, "The Private History of a Campaign That Failed" in *Merry Tales* (New York: Oxford University Press, 1996), p. 10.

36. Mark Twain, *The Adventures of Huckleberry Finn* (New York: Oxford University Press, 1996), p. 49.

37. Ibid, p. 50.

38. quoted in Ronald L. Davis, *Duke: The Life and Image of John Wayne* (Norman, Oklahoma: The University of Oklahoma Press, 1998), p. 83.

39. Donald Curtis, quoted in ibid, p. 117.

40. Ibid, p. 142.

41. Davis, op cit, p. 291.

42. Ralph Waldo Emerson, "Letter to Martin Van Buren, President of the United States." in *The Portable Emerson*, edited by Mark Van Doren (New York: Viking Press, 1946), p. 654–655.

43. Ibid, p. 654.

44. Shirley Jackson Chase, *The Millennial Hope: A Phase of Wartime Thinking* (Chicago: 1918), p. v.

45. this and following quotes from Shirley Jackson Chase, "Premillennialial Menace", *Biblical World*, July 1918, p. 16.

46. Omar Bradley, *A General's Life: An Autobiography by General of the Army Omar Bradley* (New York: Simon and Schuster, 1983), p. 98–99.

47. Grant Wacker, *Heaven Below: Early Pentecostals and American Culture* (Cambridge: Harvard University Press, 2001), p. 23.

48. Ibid, p. 25.

49. Ibid, p. 190.

50. Ibid, p. 185.

51. Ibid, p. 186.

978-0-595-40181-9
0-595-40181-3

www.ingramcontent.com/pod-product-compliance
Lightning Source LLC
Chambersburg PA
CBHW030256290526
45785CB00001B/111